TOGETHER *with* GOD

TOGETHER *with* GOD
THE
GOSPELS

DAVE BRANON
EDITOR

Discovery House.
from Our Daily Bread Ministries

TOGETHER *with* GOD

Author and New Testament scholar Joel B. Green told about a person who was investigating Christianity. A friend suggested that she read the Gospels—Matthew, Mark, Luke, and John. After she read them, she returned to her friend and asked, "Why did Jesus have to die four times?"

Indeed, the Gospels could be confusing to the uninitiated. In the pages of these four key Bible books are many stories that are told over and over—all from the perspective of four different writers. The Gospels give us four accounts of the life of one man, Jesus Christ, not to confuse us but to give us a more complete picture of this remarkable God-man. The Gospel accounts differ in some details, because any four witnesses or historians will see things from his or her own unique perspective.

What ties the gospels together are at least two vital truths: The Holy Spirit superintended the words as Matthew, Mark, Luke, and John wrote them, and the accounts are an accurate portrayal of the life and the times of Jesus Christ. This collection of books is vital to our understanding of Jesus's perfection, His interaction with others, His undeniable deity, His immense love for people, and His mission to provide salvation through His death, burial, and resurrection. Knowing that the words we read in this historical account were inspired by the Spirit comforts us with the authenticity of what we read.

In the pages of this book, we are presenting insights and truths gleaned from the Gospels and presented in the devotional style for which *Our Daily Bread* has been known for more than sixty years. You will read how the gospel challenges us to love God wholeheartedly and instructs us in daily Christlikeness.

It is our prayer that you'll gain a new appreciation for the four accounts of our Savior's life and that you'll find yourself increasingly devoted to the abundant life He promised to all who trust Him (John 10:10).

Dave Branon, editor and *Our Daily Bread* writer

Name upon Name

MATTHEW 1:1–17

This is the genealogy of Jesus the Messiah the son of David, the son of Abraham.
MATTHEW 1:1

Dalton Conley, a sociologist at New York University, and his wife, Natalie Jeremijenko, have two children. Several years ago, they sought permission from the city to change their five-year-old son's name to Yo Xing Heyno Augustus Eisner Alexander Weiser Knuckles Jeremijenko-Conley. Actually, much of that name was already his, but his parents added three of the middle names. They had specific reasons for each one.

Names are important, even to God. I believe He had specific reasons for the names He included in the genealogy at the beginning of Matthew's gospel. It may seem like a long, boring list of meaningless names, but those names served at least two purposes. First, they provided the framework by which true Hebrews could establish their family roots and maintain religious purity against outside influences. Second, the names reflected the sovereign work of God. They revealed God's dealings in the past, which resulted in the birth of the Messiah. The Lord used all kinds of people in Jesus's lineage—farmers, kings, a prostitute, adulterers, liars. When we read this list, we are reminded of God's faithfulness.

As you think about being a part of God's family through faith in Jesus Christ, remember His faithfulness to you—no matter what your background—and His desire to use you to bring about His purposes.

MARVIN WILLIAMS

Life's purpose is found in a person—Jesus Christ.

Another Hero

MATTHEW 1:18–25

Because Joseph her husband was faithful to the law, and yet did not want to expose her to public disgrace, he had in mind to divorce her quietly.
MATTHEW 1:19

For most of my life, I missed the importance of Joseph in the story of Jesus's birth. But after I became a husband and father myself, I had a greater appreciation for Joseph's tender character. Even before he knew how Mary had become pregnant, he decided that he wasn't going to embarrass or punish her for what seemed to be infidelity (Matthew 1:19).

I marvel at his obedience and humility, as he not only did what the angel told him (v. 24) but he also refrained from physical intimacy with Mary until after Jesus was born (v. 25). Later we learn that Joseph was willing to flee his home and travel to a foreign land with his little family so he could protect Jesus (2:13–23).

Imagine the pressure Joseph and Mary must have felt when they learned that Jesus would be theirs to raise and nurture! Imagine the complexity and pressure of having the Son of God living with you every moment of every day—a constant call to holiness by His very presence. What a man Joseph must have been to be trusted by God for this task! What a wonderful example for us to follow, whether we're raising our own children or those born to others who are now entrusted to us! He was truly another hero of this remarkable true story.

May God grant us the strength to be faithful like Joseph—even if we don't fully understand God's plan.

RANDY KILGORE

**The secret of true service is absolute faithfulness
wherever God places you.**

A Given Name

MATTHEW 1:18–25

"She will give birth to a son, and you are to give him the name Jesus,
because he will save his people from their sins."

MATTHEW 1:21

Most families have their own family stories. One in our family has to do with how I got my name. Apparently, when my parents were in the early days of their marriage, they disagreed about what to name their first son. Mom wanted a son named after Dad, but Dad wasn't interested in naming a son "Junior." After much discussion, they reached a compromise, agreeing that only if a son were to be born on Dad's birthday would he be given Dad's name. Amazingly, I was born on my dad's birthday. So I was given his name with "Junior" attached to it.

The naming of children is as old as time. As Joseph wrestled with the news that his fiancée, Mary, was pregnant, the angel brought him insight from the Father about naming the Baby: "She will give birth to a son, and you are to give him the name Jesus, because he will save his people from their sins" (Matthew 1:21). Not only would Jesus be His name but it would also explain the reason for His coming into the world: To take on himself the punishment we deserve for our sin. The redemptive purpose behind the babe in the manger is wrapped up in the perfectly given Name above all names.

May our heart's desire be to live in a way that honors Jesus's wonderful name!

BILL CROWDER

Jesus: His name and His mission are one and the same.

Someone to Celebrate

MATTHEW 2:1–12

Come, let us bow down in worship, let us kneel before the LORD our Maker.
PSALM 95:6

Many manger scenes depict the wise men, or magi, visiting Jesus in Bethlehem at the same time as the shepherds. But according to the gospel of Matthew (the only place in Scripture where their story is found), the magi showed up later. Jesus was no longer in the manger in a stable at the inn when they arrived. By then, He was in a house. Matthew 2:11 tells us, "On coming to the house, they saw the child with his mother Mary, and they bowed down and worshiped him. Then they opened their treasures and presented him with gifts of gold, frankincense and myrrh."

Realizing that the magi's visit happened later than we may think provides a helpful reminder: Jesus is always worthy of worship. As the season of remembering Jesus's birth is over and we head back to life's everyday routines, we still have Someone to celebrate.

Jesus Christ is Immanuel, "God with us" (Matthew 1:23), in every season. He has promised to be with us "always" (28:20). Because He is always with us, we can worship Him in our hearts every day and trust that He will show himself faithful in the years to come. Just as the magi sought Him, may we seek Him too and worship Him wherever we are.

JAMES BANKS

When we find Christ, we offer our worship.

Be a Star

MATTHEW 2:1–12

Those who lead many to righteousness [will shine] like the stars for ever and ever.
DANIEL 12:3

Many today seek stardom by trying to get into the media spotlight. But a young Jewish captive achieved "stardom" in a better way.

When Daniel and his friends were taken captive by a ruthless invading nation, it was unlikely that they would be heard from again. But the godly young men soon distinguished themselves as intelligent and trustworthy.

When the king had a dream that his wise men could not repeat nor interpret, he condemned them to death. After a night of prayer with his friends, Daniel received from God the content of the dream and its interpretation. As a result, the king promoted Daniel to be his chief advisor (see Daniel 2).

If the story ended there, it would be remarkable enough. But some scholars believe that Daniel's influence in Babylon made people aware of messianic prophecies about a Savior who would be born in Bethlehem. Daniel's teaching may have been the reason that five hundred years later wise men from the East followed a star to a remote and unfamiliar part of the world to find an infant King, worship Him, and return to their country with the good news of God's incredible journey to earth (Matthew 2:1–12).

By leading others to righteousness, we, like Daniel, can become a star that will shine forever.

JULIE ACKERMAN LINK

You can attract people to Jesus when you have His light in your life.

Out of Egypt

MATTHEW 2:13-21

"Take the child and his mother and escape to Egypt."
MATTHEW 2:13

One year when our family was traveling through Ohio on the way to Grandma's house, we arrived in Columbus just as a tornado warning was issued. Suddenly everything changed as we feared that our children might be in danger.

I mention that story to help us imagine what it was like for Joseph's family as he, Mary, and their young child traveled to Egypt. Herod, not a tornado, threatened them as he sought to kill their little boy. Imagine how frightening it was for them, knowing that "Herod [sought] the child to kill him" (Matthew 2:13).

We usually take a more idyllic view of Christmastime—lowing cattle and kneeling shepherds in a peaceful scene. But there was no peace for Jesus's family as they sought to escape Herod's horror. Only when an angel told them it was safe did the family leave Egypt and go back home to Nazareth (vv. 20–23).

Consider the awe we should feel for the incarnation. Jesus, who enjoyed the majesty of heaven in partnership with the Father, set it all aside to be born in poverty, to face many dangers, and to be crucified for us. Coming out of Egypt is one thing, but leaving heaven for us—that's the grand and amazing part of this story!

DAVE BRANON

Jesus came to earth for us so we could go to heaven with Him.

Unlikely Giants

MATTHEW 3

*"Among those born of women
there is not a greater prophet than John the Baptist."*
LUKE 7:28 (NKJV)

The famous evangelist Dwight L. Moody (1837–1899) was greatly moved by a lay preacher's statement that the world has yet to see what God could do through a person fully yielded to Him. Because an attitude of submission is far more important than outward appearance, some unlikely people have become spiritual giants.

The first time I met Pete, he had a two-day growth of stubble, a missing front tooth, and a suit that looked as if he had slept in it. But I discovered that God was using him in an unusual way to reach disadvantaged people.

Philip Yancey described the late Bill Leslie as "disheveled," "disorganized," and one who "laughed uproariously at his own [bad] jokes." But he points out that as pastor of the LaSalle Street Church in Chicago, this man had led many people to Christ and brought great social and economic changes to that part of the city. This unlikely spiritual giant died at age sixty after three decades of work in the inner city.

Pete and Bill remind me of John the Baptist. Although he lived as a recluse and wore a rough, camel's-hair garment, he had a ministry to thousands. Jesus called him the greatest of the prophets (Luke 7:28).

God uses ordinary people, and He wants to use you and me. Let's serve Him humbly, zealously, and expectantly.

HERB VANDER LUGT

God uses those who are small in their own eyes.

Change

MATTHEW 3:1–12

*"Repent, for the kingdom of heaven has come near.
Produce fruit in keeping with repentance."*
MATTHEW 3:2, 8

Medical studies have shown that even though people who have had heart-bypass surgery are told that they must change their lifestyle or die, about ninety percent do not change. Typically, two years after surgery the patients haven't altered their lifestyle. It seems that most would rather die than change.

Just as doctors preach a physical message of change to prevent death, John the Baptist came preaching a spiritual message of change. "Repent, for the kingdom of heaven has come near" (Matthew 3:2). He was preparing the way for the ultimate manifestation of God's reign—the Messiah, Jesus.

Repentance means, "to change one's mind and attitude about God," which ultimately changes a person's actions and decisions. Everyone who repents and accepts Christ's provision of forgiveness from sin through His death on the cross will escape spiritual death (John 3:16). Repentance involves confessing sin with godly sorrow and then forsaking sin. John the Baptist was calling people to turn from one way of living to ways that honor God.

Today, the Lord is still calling us to repent and then to respond with the "fruit in keeping with repentance" (Matthew 3:8). We demonstrate our love for God when we make that change.

MARVIN WILLIAMS

Repentance means hating sin enough to turn from it.

The Obedience Factor

MATTHEW 3:13–17

Jesus replied, "Let it be so now;
it is proper for us to do this to fulfill all righteousness."
MATTHEW 3:15

Dewey VanderVelde refused to be baptized. He steadfastly resisted, even when his wife and daughters were baptized one Sunday afternoon.

Years later, his pastor preached on the baptism of Jesus. He pointed out that John the Baptist initially refused to baptize Jesus, but Jesus said, "It is proper for us to do this to fulfill all righteousness" (Matthew 3:15). The pastor then added this comment: "If Jesus obeyed the will of the Father, so should we."

After the message, Dewey asked to be baptized. He said that he should have obeyed the Lord's command much sooner, and he regretted having been so stubborn.

The issue, of course, was more than just baptism; it was obedience. The same may be true for us. We may be stubbornly disobeying the Lord in a certain area of our life—and only we know what that disobedience looks like.

Jesus obeyed the Father in everything. His submission took Him from the height of popularity to abandonment. It took Him from public adoration to solitary suffering. It took Him to Pilate's judgment hall, the terrible road to Calvary, the cross, and the tomb.

Our Lord wants us to "fulfill all righteousness."

DAVID EGNER

True faith will obey without delay.

Changed Landscape

MATTHEW 4:1–11

Jesus was led by the Spirit into the wilderness to be tempted by the devil.
MATTHEW 4:1

I love my garden. But the Midwestern US winter we endure each year reduces my beautiful garden to a frozen, snow-covered, barren landscape.

It wasn't like that in the garden of Eden. Eden was a breathtakingly beautiful garden year-round. And it was in this garden that Adam and Eve basked in the stunning creation of God and the joy of perfect harmony with Him and with each other. Until, that is, Satan arrived on the scene, bringing weeds, thorns, destruction, and death.

You can't help but notice the contrast between the landscape of Genesis 1 and the wilderness of Matthew 4. The same tempter who once entered God's garden now welcomes God to his turf—the dangerous, barren wilderness.

The wilderness can be a picture of what the world—and life—becomes when Satan has his way. With one decisive blow, the joy of Eden was replaced with the barrenness of shame (Genesis 3). But Jesus was victorious on Satan's turf! (Matthew 4). In that victory He gives us hope that we too can have victory—a victory that shows us the enemy no longer holds sway. This victory also assures us the day is coming when we will no longer toil in Satan's wilderness but will be ushered into heaven, where the joy of Eden will be ours—forever.

Now, that's something to look forward to!

JOE STOWELL

**As you journey through the wilderness of temptation,
Christ's victory can be yours.**

Dangerous Shortcuts

MATTHEW 4:1–10

*Jesus answered, "It is written: 'Man shall not live on bread alone,
but on every word that comes from the mouth of God.'"*

MATTHEW 4:4

During recent elections in my country, one struggling mom I know exchanged her vote for a bag of diapers. We had discussed the benefits of each candidate, so her choice disappointed me. "But what about your convictions?" I asked. She remained silent. Six months after her candidate won, taxes went even higher. Everything is now more expensive than before . . . even diapers!

In countries around the world, political corruption is not new. Spiritual corruption is not new either. Satan tried to lure Jesus into "selling" His convictions (Matthew 4:1–10). The tempter came to Him when He was tired and hungry. He offered Him immediate satisfaction, instant fresh bread, a miraculous delivery, the kingdoms of the world and their glory.

But Jesus knew better. He knew that shortcuts were dangerous enemies. They may offer a road free from suffering, but in the end the pain they carry is much worse than anything we can imagine. "It is written," Jesus said three times during His temptation (vv. 4, 7, 10). He held firm to what He knew was true from God and His Word.

When we are tempted, God can help us too. We can depend on Him and the truth of His Word to help us avoid dangerous shortcuts.

KEILA OCHOA

God's road is not easy, but it leads to eternal satisfaction.

The Devil's Soup Bowl

MATTHEW 4:1–11

"When [the devil] lies, he speaks his native language,
for he is a liar and the father of lies."

JOHN 8:44

While my sons-in-law and I were hiking in a state park one summer, we noticed a trail marker that pointed toward something called The Devil's Soup Bowl. Intrigued, we took off to find this geologic formation. As we went, we joked about the kind of soup we might find in the bowl.

When we arrived, we discovered it to be a large sunken area of land—something like a deep lake without any water in it. We were rather disappointed to discover that The Devil's Soup Bowl was filled with nothing but trees and weeds.

The Devil's Soup Bowl is the perfect name for a formation that offers something of interest but ends up providing nothing, because the devil is a deceiver. His menu is a bowl of tricks that delivers only empty promises and broken dreams.

Satan began his deceitful work of substituting nothing for something when he tricked the residents of the garden of Eden, and he has not changed his plan since. He tried his deceit on Jesus, but the Lord resisted and "the devil left him" (Matthew 4:11).

So how do you know if you are being offered one of Satan's lies? Test ideas with Scripture. Consult with people you trust to be godly and wise. And pray.

DAVE BRANON

Don't partake of the devil's bowl of empty lies.

Hearing the Sermon Again

MATTHEW 4:12–17

From that time on Jesus began to preach,
"Repent, for the kingdom of heaven has come near."
MATTHEW 4:17

A story is told about a man who preached an impressive sermon, seeking to be the pastor of a new church. Everybody loved it and voted for him to become their new pastor. They were a bit surprised, however, when he preached the same sermon his first Sunday there—and even more surprised when he preached it again the next week. After he preached the same sermon the third week in a row, the leaders met with him to find out what was going on. The pastor assured them, "I know what I'm doing. When we all start living out this sermon, I'll go on to my next one."

Jesus's sermons had a notably recurring theme. Not surprisingly, the King of kings wanted to be sure that the people understood what was required of them to be part of His kingdom. He came to announce a whole new world order that was totally out of step with life as it was usually lived. Themes such as forgiveness, servanthood, and unconditional mercy and grace were repeatedly on His lips.

Two thousand years later we need the same message. How exciting to repent and live under the authority, reign, and rule of Jesus our King! That's when we experience benefit to our lives, glory to His name, and blessing to others.

JOE STOWELL

A sermon isn't complete until it's put into practice.

Tight Lines

MATTHEW 4:18–20

*Always be prepared to give an answer to everyone
who asks you to give the reason for the hope that you have.
But do this with gentleness and respect.*

1 PETER 3:15

Those of us who like to fish sometimes bestow this blessing on one another: "May you keep a tight line," by which we mean, "May you always have a trout on your line."

As I've gotten older, however, I must confess that a tight line means less to me now than it once did. I get as much enjoyment from fishing as I do from catching.

When I'm fishing, I have more time to walk streamside and enjoy the solitude and silence, and to look for places where fish might be lurking. When I try too hard to catch, I lose too many fish and the enjoyment of the day.

Jesus calls us to be fishers of men, not catchers (Matthew 4:19). My job is to go where the fish are, walk among them, study their habitat, and learn their ways. And then to toss out a line and see if one rises to the surface. There's more enjoyment in that easy effort, and I have better results.

So I want to fish for people, looking for opportunities to speak a word about Jesus, casting here and there, and leaving the results with God. It's more calming for me and for the "fish"—the folks who might get spooked by my clumsiness.

Thus I now bless my fellow fishers with: "May you keep your line in the water." Or, as another fisherman once put it, "Always be prepared" (1 Peter 3:15).

DAVID ROPER

**When you fish for souls, cast your nets in faith
and draw them in with love.**

The Honor of Following

MATTHEW 4:18–22

"Come, follow me," Jesus said.
MATTHEW 4:19

While visiting Jerusalem, a friend of mine saw an old rabbi walking past the Wailing Wall. The interesting thing about the aged rabbi was the five young men walking behind him. They too were walking bent over, limping—just like their rabbi. An Orthodox Jew watching them would know exactly why they were imitating their teacher. They were "followers."

Throughout the history of Judaism, one of the most honored positions for a Jewish man was the privilege of becoming a "follower" of the local rabbi. Followers sat at the rabbi's feet as he taught. They would study his words and watch how he acted and reacted to life and others. A follower would count it the highest honor to serve his rabbi in even the most menial tasks. And, because they admired their rabbi, they were determined to become like him.

When Jesus called His disciples to follow Him (Matthew 4:19), it was an invitation to be changed by Him, to become like Him, and to share His passion for those who need a Savior. The high honor of being His follower should show in our lives as well. We too have been called to catch the attention of the watching world as we talk, think, and act just like Jesus—the teacher of our souls.

JOE STOWELL

Follow Jesus and let the world know He is your rabbi.

A Companion on the Road

MATTHEW 4:18–22

As Jesus was walking beside the Sea of Galilee,
he saw two brothers, Simon called Peter and his brother Andrew. . . .
"Come, follow me," Jesus said.

MATTHEW 4:18–19

I love to walk Idaho's paths and trails and enjoy its grandeur and picturesque beauty. I'm often reminded that these treks are symbolic of our spiritual journey, for the Christian life is simply walking—with Jesus alongside as our companion and guide. He walked through the land of Israel from one end to the other, gathering disciples, saying to them, "Follow me" (Matthew 4:19).

The journey is not always easy. Sometimes giving up seems easier than going on, but when things get difficult, we can rest a while and renew our strength. In *Pilgrim's Progress*, John Bunyan describes the arbor on Hill Difficulty where Christian caught his breath before continuing the climb. His scroll provided comfort, reminding him of the Lord's continual presence and sustaining power. He got a second wind so he could walk a few more miles.

Only God knows where the path will take us, but we have our Lord's assurance, "I am with you always" (Matthew 28:20). This is not a metaphor or other figure of speech. He is real company. There is not one hour without His presence, not one mile without His companionship. Knowing He's with us makes the journey lighter.

DAVID ROPER

As you travel life's weary road, let Jesus lift your heavy load.

The Art of Common People

MATTHEW 4:18–25

"I have not come to call the righteous, but sinners to repentance."
LUKE 5:32

The Italian painter Caravaggio (1571–1610) received scathing criticism in his day for depicting people of the Bible as common. His critics reflected a time when only members of royalty and aristocracy were considered appropriate subjects for the "immortality" of art. His commissioned canvas *Saint Matthew and the Angel* so offended church leaders that it had to be redone. They could not accept seeing Matthew with the physical features of an everyday laborer.

According to one biographer, what the church fathers did not understand was that "Caravaggio, in elevating this humble figure, was copying Christ, who had himself raised Matthew from the street."

Caravaggio was right about the people of the Bible. Jesus himself grew up in the home of a laborer. When His time came to go public, He was announced by a weatherworn man of the wilderness known as John the Baptist. His disciples were fishermen and common people.

Jesus also lived, loved, and died for wealthy people. But by befriending those who had been demon-possessed, lepers, fishermen, and even despised tax collectors, the teacher from Nazareth showed that no one is too poor, too sinful, or too insignificant to be His friend.

MART DEHAAN

Jesus wants you for a friend.

Blessed Are the Meek

MATTHEW 5:1–10

"Blessed are the meek, for they will inherit the earth."
MATTHEW 5:5

One problem with the English word *meek* is that it rhymes with weak, and people have linked the two words together for years. A popular dictionary offers a secondary definition of *meek* as "too submissive; easily imposed on; spineless; spiritless." This causes some people to question why Jesus would say, "Blessed are the *meek*, for they will inherit the earth" (Matthew 5:5).

Greek scholar W. E. Vine says that *meekness* in the Bible is an attitude toward God "in which we accept His dealings with us as good, and therefore without disputing or resisting." We see this in Jesus, who found His delight in doing the will of His Father.

Vine goes on to say that "the meekness manifested by the Lord and commended to the believer is the fruit of power. . . . The Lord was 'meek' because He had the infinite resources of God at His command." He could have called angels from heaven to prevent His crucifixion, for instance.

Jesus told His weary, burdened followers, "Take my yoke upon you, and learn of me; for I am meek and lowly in heart: and ye shall find rest unto your souls" (Matthew 11:29 KJV). He was the perfect model of meekness.

When we are tired and troubled, Jesus invites us to discover the peace of meekly trusting Him.

DAVID MCCASLAND

God has two dwellings:
one in heaven and the other in a meek and thankful heart.
—Izaak Walton

God's Lighthouse

MATTHEW 5:1–14

"You are the light of the world. A city that is set on a hill cannot be hidden."
MATTHEW 5:14 (NKJV)

The Mission Point Lighthouse was built in 1870 on a peninsula in Northern Michigan to warn ships of sandbars and rocky shores along Lake Michigan. That lighthouse got its name from another kind of lighthouse, a mission church, which was built thirty-one years earlier.

In 1839, Rev. Peter Dougherty answered the call to become pastor of a church in Old Mission that was made up of Native Americans who lived farther south on the same peninsula. Under his leadership, a thriving community of farmers, teachers, and craftsmen worked side by side to build a better life for the community.

When believers in Christ work together in unity, their fellowship of faith provides spiritual light in the world's darkness (Philippians 2:15–16). Jesus said, "You are the light of the world. A city that is set on a hill cannot be hidden. . . . Let your light so shine before men, that they may see your good works and glorify your Father in heaven" (Matthew 5:14–16 NKJV).

The Mission Point Lighthouse warned ships of danger, but the original Old Mission Church provided spiritual direction to all who would listen. Believers do the same individually and through our churches. We are God's lighthouse because Jesus, the Light of the World, lives in us.

DENNIS FISHER

**Believers help the lost to find their way home
when their life shines brightly.**

Shine Through

MATTHEW 5:13–16

"Let your light shine before others."
MATTHEW 5:16

A little girl wondered what a saint might be. One day her mother took her to a great cathedral to see the gorgeous stained-glass windows with scenes from the Bible. When she saw the beauty of it all, she cried out loud, "Now I know what saints are. They are people who let the light shine through!"

Some of us might think that saints are people of the past who lived perfect lives and did Jesus-like miracles. But when a translation of Scripture uses the word *saint*, it is actually referring to anyone who belongs to God through faith in Christ. In other words, saints are people like us who have the high calling of serving God while reflecting our relationship with Him wherever we are and in whatever we do. That is why the apostle Paul prayed that the eyes and understanding of his readers would be opened to think of themselves as the treasured inheritance of Christ and saints of God (Ephesians 1:18).

What then do we see in the mirror? No halos or stained glass, that's for sure. But if we are fulfilling our calling, we will look like people who, maybe even without realizing it, are letting the rich colors of the love, joy, peace, patience, kindness, gentleness, faithfulness, and self-control of God shine through.

KEILA OCHOA

Saints are people through whom God's light shines.

A Lasting Imprint

MATTHEW 5:13–20

"Let your light shine before others, that they may see your good deeds and glorify your Father in heaven."

MATTHEW 5:16

Caerleon is a Welsh village with deep historical roots. It was one of three sites in the United Kingdom where Roman legions were posted during Rome's occupation of Britain. While the military presence ended some 1,500 years ago, the imprint of that occupation can still be seen today. People come from all over the world to visit the military fort, the barracks, and the amphitheater that are reminders of the days when Rome ruled the world and occupied Wales.

It amazes me that fifteen centuries later, the evidence of Rome's presence can still so clearly be seen in that small community.

I wonder, though, about another kind of imprint—the imprint of Christ on our lives. Do we allow His presence to be clearly seen by others? Is it possible for people who interact with us to know that Jesus occupies our lives?

Jesus calls us to make known His presence in our lives to the glory of God the Father. He says, "Let your light shine before others, that they may see your good deeds and glorify your Father in heaven" (Matthew 5:16). Through the light of our testimony and the impact of our deeds of service, people should be able to see evidence of the presence of God in our lives. Is it true? Can they see His imprint?

BILL CROWDER

Let your testimony be written in large enough letters so the world can always read it.

Reflecting the Son

MATTHEW 5:14–16

The light shines in the darkness, and the darkness has not overcome it.
JOHN 1:5

Because of its location among sheer mountains and its northern latitude, Rjukan, Norway, does not see natural sunlight from October to March. To lighten up the town, the citizens installed large mirrors on the mountainside to reflect the sun's rays and beam sunlight into the town square. The continuous glow during the day is made possible because the giant mirrors rotate with the rising and setting sun.

I like to think of the Christian life as a similar scenario. Jesus said His followers are "the light of the world" (Matthew 5:14). John the disciple wrote that Christ the true light "shines in the darkness" (John 1:5). So too, Jesus invites us to reflect our light into the darkness around us: "Let your light shine before others, that they may see your good deeds and glorify your Father in heaven" (Matthew 5:16). That is a call for us to show love in the face of hatred, patience in response to trouble, and peace in moments of conflict. As the apostle Paul reminds us, "For you were once darkness, but now you are light in the Lord. Live as children of light" (Ephesians 5:8).

Jesus also said, "I am the light of the world. Whoever follows me will never walk in darkness, but will have the light of life" (John 8:12). Our light is a reflection of Jesus the Son. Just as without the sun the large mirrors of Rjukan would have no light to reflect, so too we can do nothing without Jesus.

LAWRENCE DARMANI

Reflect the Son and shine for Him.

I'm Sorry, Man

MATTHEW 5:21–26

"Be reconciled to your brother."
MATTHEW 5:24 (NKJV)

When my son-in-law Ewing and I attended a major league baseball game at Marlins Park in Miami, we enjoyed watching both the game and the people around us.

One of those people showed both the bad and good side of humanity. This man had apparently lost track of his seat. As he was looking for it, he stood squarely between the field and us. A man sitting in front of us had his view blocked, so he asked the guy, "Could you move? We can't see."

The lost man responded sarcastically, "Too bad." A second request got a similar but more heated response. Finally the man moved on. Later came a surprise. He returned and told the man he had blocked, "Hey, I'm sorry, man. I was upset that I couldn't find my seat." They shook hands and the incident ended well.

That interaction made me think. As we go through life striving to find our way, situations may frustrate us and cause us to respond to others in an un-Christlike way. If so, we must ask God to give us the courage to apologize to those we have offended. Our worship, according to Jesus, depends on it (Matthew 5:23–24).

We honor God when we make reconciliation with others a priority. After we have been reconciled, we can then fully enjoy communion with our heavenly Father.

DAVE BRANON

Confession of sin is the soil in which forgiveness flourishes.

Be True to Your Word

MATTHEW 5:33–37

"All you need to say is simply 'Yes' or 'No.'"
MATTHEW 5:37

Shortly before his death, the Duke of Burgundy was presiding over the Cabinet Council of France. The ministers made a proposal that would violate a treaty but would secure important advantages for the country. Many reasons were offered to justify the deed. The Duke listened in silence, and when all had spoken he closed the conference without giving approval. Placing his hand on a copy of the original agreement, he said with firmness in his voice, "Gentlemen, we have a treaty!"

It's important that Christians act and speak so that the Savior is glorified. When we give our word, we should keep it. If we make a commitment, we must honor it. If we take on an obligation, we will want to fulfill it. As Jesus said in Matthew 5:37, "All you need to say is simply 'Yes' or 'No.'"

Our honesty and reliability should be so evident that we can be trusted for any contract we make. What better testimony could be said of a believer than this: "He gave his word; that's good enough for me." And if non-Christians can trust us in business matters, they are more likely to believe us when we speak about the gospel.

If you are tempted to go back on a promise, think again of the words of the Duke of Burgundy: "Gentlemen, we have a treaty!"

RICHARD DEHAAN

Never give your word unless you intend to keep it.

Quote Misquote

MATTHEW 5:27–42

"You have heard that it was said, 'Eye for eye, and tooth for tooth.'"
MATTHEW 5:38

In the opening chapters of *The Adventures of Huckleberry Finn*, Mark Twain presents an interesting conversation that reflects human nature. Tom Sawyer tries to persuade his friend Huckleberry Finn to join him in his plans to form a band of robbers and to take captives much like pirates used to do. Huck asks Tom what pirates do with the captives they take, and Tom answers, "Ransom them." "Ransom? What's that?" asks Huck. "I don't know. But that's what they do. I've seen it in books; and so of course that's what we got to do," explains Tom. "Do you want to go to doing different from what's in the books, and get things all muddled up?"

This dialog represents a way of thinking that's not much different from what Jesus encountered. The people were also quoting and repeating things they had found in a book—the Old Testament. But they were merely mouthing words. The ideas had been separated from the spirit of the original revelation. By misapplying Mosaic principles of conduct, the people were justifying their sinful attitudes and actions (Matthew 5:27–42).

This should be a reminder to us. When we quote the Bible, let's be sure we understand its meaning and context. Then we won't get things "all muddled up."

MART DEHAAN

A text taken out of context can be a dangerous pretext.

Changing Enemies into Friends

MATTHEW 5:43–48

"But I say to you, love your enemies . . . do good to those who hate you."
MATTHEW 5:44 (NKJV)

During the US Civil War, hatred became entrenched between the North and South. In one instance, President Abraham Lincoln was criticized for speaking of benevolent treatment for the Southern rebels. The critic reminded Lincoln that there was a war going on, the Confederates were the enemy, and they should be destroyed. But Lincoln wisely responded, "I destroy my enemies when I make them my friends."

Lincoln's comment is insightful. In many ways it reflects Jesus's teaching in the Sermon on the Mount: "I say to you, love your enemies, bless those who curse you, do good to those who hate you, and pray for those who spitefully use you and persecute you, that you may be sons of your Father in heaven" (Matthew 5:44–45 NKJV).

We will encounter difficult people in our lives—some on whom we will need to set limits. But to give in to the temptation to undermine or hurt them in any way is not God's way. Instead, we should pray for them, show consideration, look out for their best interests, and emphasize the positive. This may result in changing an enemy into a friend—and perhaps an unbeliever into a fellow Christian.

Not everyone will respond positively to us, but we can pray and plan for a more harmonious relationship. What difficult person can you start befriending for God's glory?

DENNIS FISHER

**It's hard to hate someone
when you're doing something good for that person.**

Thoughts on Rain

MATTHEW 5:38–48

*"[Your Father in heaven] causes his sun to rise on the evil and the good,
and sends rain on the righteous and the unrighteous."*

MATTHEW 5:45

When torrential downpours beat on the heads of my newly planted petunias, I felt bad for them. I wanted to bring them inside to shelter them from the storm. By the time the rain stopped, their little faces were bowed to the ground from the weight of the water. They looked sad and weak. Within a few hours, however, they perked up and turned their heads skyward. By the next day, they were standing straight and strong.

What a transformation! After pounding them on the head, the rain dripped from their leaves, soaked into the soil, and came up through their stalks, giving them the strength to stand straight.

Because I prefer sunshine, I get annoyed when rain spoils my outdoor plans. I sometimes wrongly think of rain as something negative. But anyone who has experienced drought knows that rain is a blessing. It nourishes the earth for the benefit of both the just and the unjust (Matthew 5:45).

Even when the storms of life hit so hard that we nearly break from the force, the "rain" is not an enemy. Our loving God has allowed it to make us stronger. He uses the water that batters us on the outside to build us up on the inside, so we may stand straight and strong.

JULIE ACKERMAN LINK

The storms that threaten to destroy us God will use to strengthen us.

Let Honor Meet Honor

MATTHEW 6:1–6

"Be careful not to practice your righteousness in front of others to be seen by them. If you do, you will have no reward from your Father in heaven."
MATTHEW 6:1

I've always been impressed by the solemn, magnificent simplicity of the Changing of the Guard at the Tomb of the Unknown Soldier at Arlington National Cemetery in Virginia. The carefully choreographed event is a moving tribute to soldiers whose names—and sacrifice—are "known but to God." Equally moving are the private moments of steady pacing when the crowds are gone: back and forth, hour after hour, day by day, in even the worst weather.

In September 2003, Hurricane Isabel was bearing down on Washington, DC, and the guards were told they could seek shelter during the worst of the storm. Surprising almost no one, the guards refused! They unselfishly stood their post to honor their fallen comrades even in the face of a hurricane.

Underlying Jesus's teaching in Matthew 6:1–6, I believe, is His desire for us to live with an unrelenting, selfless devotion to Him. The Bible calls us to good deeds and holy living, but these are to be acts of worship and obedience (vv. 4–6), not orchestrated acts for self-glorification (v. 2). The apostle Paul endorses this whole-life faithfulness when he pleads with us to make our bodies "a living sacrifice" (Romans 12:1).

May our private and public moments speak of our devotion and wholehearted commitment to you, Lord.

RANDY KILGORE

The more we serve Christ, the less we will serve self.

Supernatural Surveillance

MATTHEW 6:1–6, 16–18

"Your Father, who sees what is done in secret, will reward you."
MATTHEW 6:18

Not far from my house, authorities have rigged a camera to snap pictures of drivers who race through red lights. The offenders later receive in the mail a ticket along with a "red-light photo," which is visual proof of their traffic violation.

Sometimes I think of God in the same way I think of that camera—He's up there, just waiting to catch me doing the wrong thing. While God does see our sin (Hebrews 4:13), He sees and takes interest in our good deeds as well. Due to His supernatural surveillance, God sees the size of our sacrifice when we give money to the church or to those in need (Mark 12:41–44). He hears our private prayers (Matthew 6:6). And when we fast, we can carry on as usual being assured that our "Father . . . sees what is done in secret" (v. 18).

Knowing that God sees everything frees us from thinking about the watchful eyes of others. When we do what is right, we need no applause from onlookers; when we sin, we do not need to worry about our reputation once we settle the issue with God and anyone we've harmed. We can rest knowing that "the eyes of the LORD range throughout the earth to strengthen those whose hearts are fully committed to him" (2 Chronicles 16:9).

JENNIFER BENSON SCHULDT

Others see what we do, but God sees why we do it.

The Night No One Came

MATTHEW 6:1–7

*"Be careful not to practice your righteousness
in front of others to be seen by them."*
MATTHEW 6:1

As the story goes, one winter night composer Johann Sebastian Bach was scheduled to debut a new composition. He arrived at the church expecting it to be full. Instead, he learned that no one had come. Without missing a beat, Bach told his musicians they would still perform as planned. They took their places, Bach raised his baton, and soon the empty church was filled with magnificent music.

This story made me do some soul-searching. Would I write if God were my only audience? How would my writing be different?

New writers are often advised to visualize one person they are writing to as a way of staying focused. I do this when I write devotionals; I try to keep readers in mind because I want to say something they will want to read and that will help them on their spiritual journey.

I doubt that the "devotional writer" David, whose psalms we turn to for comfort and encouragement, had "readers" in mind. The only audience he had in mind was God.

Whether our "deeds," mentioned in Matthew 6, are works of art or acts of service, we should keep in mind that they're really between us and God. Whether or not anyone else sees does not matter. He is our audience.

JULIE ACKERMAN LINK

Serve for an audience of one.

Jehovah-Jireh

MATTHEW 6:5–15

"Your Father knows what you need before you ask him."
MATTHEW 6:8

In my early years as a pastor, I served in small churches where finances were often tight. Sometimes our family finances felt the weight of that pressure. On one occasion, we were down to the last of our food and payday was still several days away. While my wife and I fretted about how we would feed our kids in the next few days, our doorbell rang. When we opened the door, we discovered two bags of groceries. We had not told anyone of our plight, yet our provider God had led someone to meet that need.

This reminds me of the Old Testament account of Abraham when he was asked to sacrifice his son Isaac. At just the right moment, God provided a ram instead. Abraham called this place Jehovah-Jireh, "The Lord Will Provide" (Genesis 22:14). He is the One who still cares deeply for His children.

Jesus said, "Your Father knows what you need before you ask him" (Matthew 6:8). He is constantly caring for and seeking the best for us—a reminder that in times of hardship, need, and fear, we have Someone who cares. Peter wrote that we can cast all our cares upon Jesus, because He cares for us (1 Peter 5:7). We can turn to Him in our time of need.

BILL CROWDER

What God promises, God will provide.

Our Source of Provision

MATTHEW 6:9–15

The LORD is near to all who call on him.
PSALM 145:18

In August 2010, the attention of the world was focused on a mineshaft near Copiapó, Chile. Thirty-three miners huddled in the dark, trapped 2,300 feet underground. They had no idea if help would ever arrive. After seventeen days of waiting, they heard drilling. Rescuers produced a small hole in the mineshaft ceiling, and that hole was followed by three more—establishing a delivery path for water, food, and medicine. The miners depended on those conduits to the surface above ground, where rescuers had the provisions they would need to survive. On day sixty-nine, rescuers pulled the last miner to safety.

None of us can survive in this world apart from provisions that are outside of ourselves. God, the Creator of the universe, is the one who provides us with everything we need. Like the drill holes for those miners, prayer connects us to the God of all supply.

Jesus encouraged us to pray, "Give us today our daily bread" (Matthew 6:11). In Jesus's day, bread was the basic staple of life and contained all the daily needs of the people. Jesus was teaching us to pray not only for our physical needs but also for everything we need—comfort, healing, courage, wisdom.

Through prayer we have access to Him at any moment, and He knows what we need before we even ask (v. 8). What might you be struggling with today? "The Lord is near to all who call on him" (Psalm 145:18).

BILL CROWDER

Prayer is the voice of faith, revealing that we trust God.

Bread for the Coming Day

MATTHEW 6:9–13

"Give us today our daily bread."
MATTHEW 6:11

Not long ago, I traveled to the Democratic Republic of Congo to lead a Bible conference. I took in the beauty of the Nyungwe Forest and the Ruzizi River, which separates Congo from Rwanda. I experienced the amazing hospitality of the Congolese people, and I was moved by their sincere faith in God's provision.

Because unemployment, poverty, and malnutrition are serious problems there, the people often don't know where their next meal will come from. So each time they sit down to eat, they thank God and ask Him to provide the next meal.

Their prayer sounds a lot like Jesus's prayer in Matthew 6:11, "Give us today our daily bread." The word *bread* refers to any food. The phrase "this day" indicates provisions that came to them one day at a time.

Many first-century workers were paid one day at a time, so a few days' illness could spell tragedy. The word *daily* could be translated "for the coming day." The prayer would read: "Give us today our bread for the coming day." It was an urgent prayer to those who lived from hand to mouth.

This prayer calls Jesus's followers everywhere to recognize that our ability to work and earn our food comes from God's hand.

MARVIN WILLIAMS

Our needs are never a strain on God's provision.

For the God I Love

MATTHEW 6:16–18

"When you fast, do not look somber as the hypocrites do."
MATTHEW 6:16

A couple of years ago in our church we did a sermon series on the Old Testament tabernacle. Leading up to the message on the table of showbread, I did something I had never done before—I fasted from food for several days. I fasted because I wanted to experience the truth that "man does not live by bread alone but on every word that comes from the mouth of the LORD" (Deuteronomy 8:3). I wanted to deny myself something I love, food, for the God I love more. As I fasted, I followed Jesus's teaching about fasting in Matthew 6:16–18.

Jesus gave a negative command: "When you fast, do not look somber as the hypocrites do" (v. 16). Then He gave a positive command about putting oil on your head and washing your face (v. 17). The two commands taken together meant that they should not draw attention to themselves. Jesus was teaching that this was a private act of sacrificial worship that should not provide any room for religious pride. Finally, He gave a promise: "Your Father, who sees what is done in secret, will reward you" (v. 18).

Although fasting isn't required, in giving up something we love, we may have a deeper experience of the God we love. He rewards us with himself.

MARVIN WILLIAMS

Moving away from the table can bring us closer to the Father.

Treasures in Heaven

MATTHEW 6:19–24

"Lay up for yourselves treasures in heaven,
where neither moth nor rust destroys
and where thieves do not break in and steal."

MATTHEW 6:20 (NKJV)

Poorly installed electric wiring caused a fire that burned down our newly built home. The flames leveled our house within an hour, leaving nothing but rubble. Another time, we returned home from church one Sunday to find our house had been broken into and some of our possessions were stolen.

In our imperfect world, loss of material wealth is all too common—vehicles are stolen or crashed, ships sink, buildings crumble, homes are flooded, and personal belongings are stolen. This makes Jesus's admonition not to put our trust in earthly wealth very meaningful (Matthew 6:19).

Jesus told a story of a man who accumulated abundant treasures and decided to store up everything for himself (Luke 12:16–21). "Take life easy," the man told himself; "eat, drink and be merry" (v. 19). But that night he lost everything, including his life. In conclusion, Jesus said, "This is how it will be with whoever stores up things for themselves but is not rich toward God" (v. 21).

Material wealth is temporary. Nothing lasts forever—except what our God enables us to do for others. Giving of our time and resources to spread the good news, visiting those who are lonely, and helping those in need are just some of the many ways to store up treasure in heaven (Matthew 6:20).

LAWRENCE DARMANI

Our real wealth is what we invest for eternity.

The Money

MATTHEW 6:24–34

"You cannot serve both God and money."
MATTHEW 6:24

Early in my career, while doing work that I saw as more of a mission than a job, another company offered me a position that would give a significant increase in pay. Our family could surely have benefited financially from such a move. There was one problem. I hadn't been looking for another job because I loved my current role, which was growing into a calling.

But the money . . .

I called my father, then in his seventies, and explained the situation. Although his once-sharp mind had been slowed by strokes and the strain of years, his answer was crisp and clear: "Don't even think about the money. What would you do?"

In an instant, my mind was made up. The money would have been my only reason for leaving the job I loved! Thanks, Dad.

Jesus devoted a substantial section of His Sermon on the Mount to money and our fondness for it. He taught us to pray not for an accumulation of riches but for "our daily bread" (Matthew 6:11). He warned against storing up treasures on earth, and He pointed to the birds and flowers as evidence that God cares deeply about His creation (vv. 19–31). "Seek first his kingdom and his righteousness," Jesus said, "and all these things will be given to you as well" (v. 33).

Money does matter! But money shouldn't rule our decision-making process. Tough times and big decisions are opportunities to grow our faith in new ways. Our heavenly Father cares for us.

TIM GUSTAFSON

Never confuse temptation with opportunity.

Your Father Knows

MATTHEW 6:25–34

"Your Father knows what you need before you ask him."
MATTHEW 6:8

I was only four years old as I lay by my father on a floor mat on a hot summer night. (My mother, with a baby, had her own room at the time.) This was in northern Ghana where the climate is mostly dry. Sweat covered my body, and the heat parched my throat. I felt so thirsty I shook my father awake. In the middle of that dry night, he rose up and poured water from a jar for me to quench my thirst. Throughout my life, as he did that night, he exemplified the image of a caring father. He provided what I needed.

Some people may not have a good father figure in their lives. But we all have a Father who is strong and ever-present and who does not disappoint us. Jesus taught us to pray to "our Father in heaven" (Matthew 6:9). He told us that when our daily needs confront us—food, clothing, shelter, protection (v. 31)—"your Father knows what you need before you ask him" (v. 8).

We have a Father who is always there. Night or day, whenever the going gets tough, we can trust that He will never abandon us. He has promised to care for us, and He knows better than we do what we need.

LAWRENCE DARMANI

Your loving heavenly Father never takes His eyes off you.

Food in the Cupboard

MATTHEW 6:25–34

*"Do not worry about your life, what you will eat or drink;
or about . . . what you will wear."*
MATTHEW 6:25

My friend Marcia, the director of the Jamaica Christian School for the Deaf, recently illustrated an important way to look at things. In a newsletter article she titled "A Blessed Start," she pointed out that for the first time in seven years the boarding school began the new year with a surplus. And what was that surplus? A thousand dollars in the bank? No. Enough school supplies for the year? No. It was simply this: A month's supply of food in the cupboard.

When you're in charge of feeding thirty hungry kids on a shoestring budget, that's big! She accompanied her note with this verse from 1 Chronicles 16:34, "Give thanks to the LORD, for he is good; his love endures forever."

Year after year Marcia trusts God to provide for the children and staff at her school. She never has much—whether it's water or food or school supplies. Yet she is always grateful for what God sends, and she is faithful to believe that He will continue to provide.

As we look at our future—whether we are just starting a year or halfway through it—do we have faith in God's provision? To do so is to take our Savior at His word when He said, "Do not worry about your life, . . . Do not worry about tomorrow" (Matthew 6:25, 34).

DAVE BRANON

**Worry does not empty tomorrow of its sorrow;
it empties today of its strength.**
—Corrie ten Boom

Can't Die but Once

MATTHEW 6:26–32

"Do not be afraid of those who kill the body but cannot kill the soul."
MATTHEW 10:28

Born into slavery and badly treated as a young girl, Harriet Tubman (c. 1820–1913) found a shining ray of hope in the Bible stories her mother told her. The account of Israel's escape from slavery under Pharaoh, for example, showed her a God who desired freedom for His people.

Harriet found freedom at age twenty-nine when she slipped over the Maryland state line and out of slavery. She couldn't remain content, however, knowing so many were still trapped in captivity. So she led more than a dozen rescue missions to free those still in slavery, dismissing the personal danger. "I can't die but once," she said.

Harriet knew the truth of the statement: "Do not be afraid of those who kill the body but cannot kill the soul" (Matthew 10:28). Jesus spoke those words as He sent His disciples on their first mission. He knew they would face danger and that not everyone would receive them warmly. So why expose the disciples to the risk? The answer is found in the previous chapter. "When he saw the crowds, [Jesus] had compassion on them, because they were harassed and helpless, like sheep without a shepherd" (9:36).

When Harriet Tubman couldn't forget the people still trapped in slavery, she showed us a picture of Christ, who did not forget us when we were trapped in our sins. Her courageous example inspires us to remember those who remain without hope in the world.

TIM GUSTAFSON

True freedom is found in knowing and serving Christ.

The Speck

MATTHEW 7:1–6

*"Why do you look at the speck of sawdust in your brother's eye
and pay no attention to the plank in your own eye?"*

LUKE 6:41

It was just a speck, a tiny foreign object flying through the air on a windy day while I was cutting the grass. Somehow that speck made its way into my left eye.

For the next few hours that little speck caused quite a bit of irritation. I tried washing it out. My wife, Sue, a nurse, tried everything she could think of. Finally, we went to a Med Center, where the medical personnel on duty couldn't get it out either. Only after applying some ointment and waiting several more annoying hours did I get relief from the speck.

This tiny, nagging irritant made me think anew about Jesus's teaching in Matthew 7 about criticizing others. My first thought was to be impressed with the practicality of Jesus's illustration. Using the effective literary tool of hyperbole, or exaggeration, He explained for His listeners how foolish it is for a person to criticize someone without seeing that he or she is also guilty of error. If you can find someone else's little speck while ignoring the hunk of wood in your own eye, something's wrong. It should be unthinkable to ignore our own faults while pointing out someone else's.

An attitude of self-righteousness has no place in the Christian life. That should be plain to see.

DAVE BRANON

**Inspect your own life before you look for
little problems in the lives of others.**

Jesus and the Golden Rule

MATTHEW 7:7–12

"Therefore, whatever you want men to do to you, do also to them."
MATTHEW 7:12 (NKJV)

The concept of the Golden Rule—treat others as you would like to be treated—appears in many religions. So what makes Jesus's version of the saying so exceptional?

Its uniqueness lies in a single word, "therefore," which signals the generosity of our heavenly Father. Here is what Jesus said: "If you, then, being evil, know how to give good gifts to your children, how much more will your Father who is in heaven give good things to those who ask Him! Therefore, whatever you want men to do to you, do also to them" (Matthew 7:11–12 NKJV).

All of us fall short of what we know to be true: We do not love others the way God loves us. Jesus lived out that admirable ethic with perfect love by living and dying for all our sins.

We have a loving, giving Father who set aside His own self-interest to reveal the full measure of His love through His Son Jesus. God's generosity is the dynamic by which we treat others as we would like to be treated. We love and give to others because He first loved us (1 John 4:19).

Our heavenly Father asks us to live up to His commands, but He also gives us His power and love to carry it out. We need only ask Him for it.

DAVID ROPER

We have committed the Golden Rule to memory;
now let us commit it to life.
—Edwin Markham

Our Chief Task

MATTHEW 7:12–23

"I am the way and the truth and the life.
No one comes to the Father except through me."

JOHN 14:6

When a British scholar called on the world's religions to work together for worldwide unity, people everywhere applauded. Pointing out that the major religions share a belief in the Golden Rule, she suggested, "The chief task of our time is to build a global society where people of all persuasions can live together in peace and harmony."

Jesus cited the Golden Rule in His Sermon on the Mount: "Do to others what you would have them do to you" (Matthew 7:12). In the same sermon, He said, "Love your enemies and pray for those who persecute you" (5:44). Putting those radical commands into practice would indeed go a long way toward peace and harmony. But immediately following the Golden Rule, Jesus called for discernment. "Watch out for false prophets," He warned. "They come to you in sheep's clothing, but inwardly they are ferocious wolves" (7:15).

Respect for others and discernment of the truth go hand in hand. If we have the truth, we have a message worth telling. But God extends to everyone the freedom to choose Him or reject Him. Our responsibility is to lovingly present the truth and respect the personal choice of others just as God does.

Our respect for others is vital to winning their respect. It's an important step in gaining an opportunity to convey the message of Jesus, who said, "I am the way and the truth and the life" (John 14:6).

TIM GUSTAFSON

Love people; love the truth.

Ignoring Grace

MATTHEW 7:13-23

*"Small is the gate and narrow the road that leads to life,
and only a few find it."*
MATTHEW 7:14

In the hectic downtown of one of Asia's great cities, I marveled at the busy sidewalks filled with people. There seemed to be no room to move in the crush of humanity, yet it also seemed that everyone was moving at top speed.

My attention was drawn to the soft, almost mournful sound of a single trumpeter playing "Amazing Grace." The crowds appeared oblivious to both the musician and the music. Still, he played—sending out a musical message of the love of God to whoever knew the song and would think about the words as he played.

I thought of this experience as a parable. The music seemed to be an invitation to the masses to follow Christ. As with the gospel message, some believe in God's amazing grace and choose the narrow way. Others ignore His grace, which is the broad way that leads to everlasting destruction. Jesus said, "Enter through the narrow gate. For wide is the gate and broad is the road that leads to destruction, and many enter through it. But small is the gate and narrow the road that leads to life, and only a few find it" (Matthew 7:13–14).

Jesus died so that "everyone who calls" on His name (Romans 10:13) can find forgiveness in His grace.

BILL CROWDER

Christ believed is salvation received.

A Donkey in Lion's Clothing

MATTHEW 7:15–23

"Watch out for false prophets . . . in sheep's clothing,
but inwardly they are ferocious wolves."
MATTHEW 7:15

In the final book of C. S. Lewis's Chronicles of Narnia, *The Last Battle*, a devious ape named Shift finds an old lion's skin and persuades a simpleminded donkey to put it on. Shift then claims that the disguised donkey is Aslan (the Lion who is the rightful king of Narnia) and forms an alliance with Narnia's enemies. Together they set out to control and enslave the subjects of Narnia. Young King Tirian, however, can't believe that Aslan would actually be involved with such brutal practices. So, with the help of the real Aslan, he defeats Shift and his counterfeit lion.

The Bible tells us that the devil is in the business of imitating God. His goal is to be "like the Most High" (Isaiah 14:12–15). Through deception, Satan tries to replace Christ with a substitute. Jesus himself warned us of false prophets and false christs: "Watch out that no one deceives you. For many will come in my name, claiming, 'I am the Messiah,' and will deceive many" (Matthew 24:4–5).

How can we tell the real Christ from the counterfeit? The only authentic Christ is the one described in Scripture. Anyone or anything that portrays a different Jesus than the One represented in the Bible is promoting "a donkey in lion's clothing."

DENNIS FISHER

God's Word gives wisdom to discern what is false.

Firm Foundation

MATTHEW 7:21–27

"Everyone who hears these words of mine and puts them into practice is like a wise man who built his house on the rock."

MATTHEW 7:24

Earthquakes are prevalent in the Pacific Rim region known as the "Ring of Fire." Ninety percent of the world's total earthquakes and eighty-one percent of the world's largest earthquakes occur there. I learned that many buildings in the city of Hong Kong have been built on granite, which could help minimize damage in the event of an earthquake. The foundation of buildings is especially important in earthquake-prone regions of the world.

Jesus Christ told His followers that a stable foundation is critical in building lives. He said, "Therefore everyone who hears these words of mine and puts them into practice is like a wise man who built his house on the rock. The rain came down, the streams rose, and the winds blew and beat against that house; yet it did not fall, because it had its foundation on the rock" (Matthew 7:24–25). The foundation of Jesus Christ is what will give us the stability our hearts and lives need now and into the future.

By allowing the Lord's wisdom to guide us in our relationships, decisions, and priorities, we find that He provides the most trustworthy foundation any life could be built upon.

BILL CROWDER

Jesus is the best foundation upon which to build a solid life.

Just a Touch

MATTHEW 8:1–4

Jesus reached out his hand and touched the man.
MATTHEW 8:3

Kiley leaped at the chance to go to a remote area of East Africa to assist a medical mission, yet she felt uneasy. She didn't have any medical experience. Still, she could provide basic care.

While there, she met a woman with a horrible but treatable disease. The woman's distorted leg repulsed her, but Kiley knew she had to do something. As she cleaned and bandaged the leg, her patient began crying. Concerned, Kiley asked if she was hurting her. "No," she replied. "It's the first time anyone has touched me in nine years."

Leprosy is another disease that can render its victims repulsive to others, and ancient Jewish culture had strict guidelines to prevent its spread: "They must live alone," the law declared. "They must live outside the camp" (Leviticus 13:46).

That's why it's so remarkable that a leper approached Jesus to say, "Lord, if you are willing, you can make me clean" (Matthew 8:2). "Jesus reached out his hand and touched the man. 'I am willing,' he said. 'Be clean!' " (v. 3).

In touching a lonely woman's diseased leg, Kiley began to show the fearless, bridge-building love of Jesus. A single touch made a difference.

TIM GUSTAFSON

No one is too troubled or unclean to be touched by Jesus.

Childlike Faith

MATTHEW 8:5–10

Jesus replied, "What is impossible with man is possible with God."
LUKE 18:27

On the way home from a family camping trip, six-year-old Tanya and her dad were the only ones still awake in the car. As Tanya looked at the full moon through the car window, she asked, "Daddy, do you think I can touch the moon if I stand on my tiptoes?"

"No, I don't think so," he smiled.

"Can you reach it?"

"No, I don't think I can either."

She was quiet for a moment—then she said confidently, "Daddy, maybe if you hold me up on your shoulders?"

Faith? Yes—the childlike faith that daddies can do anything. True faith, though, has the written promise of God for its foundation. In Hebrews 11:1, we read, "Faith is confidence in what we hope for and assurance about what we do not see." Jesus talked a lot about faith, and throughout the Gospels we read of His response to those who had great faith.

When a paralyzed man's friends brought him to Jesus, He "saw their faith," forgave the man of his sins, and healed him (Matthew 9:2–6). When the centurion asked Jesus to "say the word, and my servant will be healed" (8:8), Jesus "was amazed" and said, "I have not found anyone in Israel with such great faith" (8:10).

The possibilities are endless when we have faith in God (Luke 18:27).

CINDY HESS KASPER

A childlike faith unlocks the door to the kingdom of heaven.

Under Authority

MATTHEW 8:5–13

We are therefore Christ's ambassadors,
as though God were making his appeal through us.
We implore you on Christ's behalf:
Be reconciled to God.

2 CORINTHIANS 5:20

In answer to a Roman centurion's earnest plea to heal his desperately ill slave, Jesus started to go to the man's house. The man, however, said that he was unworthy of such attention. He said, "Just say the word, and my servant will be healed. For I myself am a man under authority, with soldiers under me" (Matthew 8:8–9). If he, an officer in the Roman army, could have things done by a word of command, surely Jesus, the great prophet of God, could do likewise.

A centurion had one hundred men under his command. Above him was the senior centurion, and above the senior centurion, the sixty centurions of the Roman legion. Above the sixty centurions were the six tribunes, and above the six tribunes the two consuls. Above the two consuls was the emperor himself. It was because the Roman centurion stood in this long line of delegated authority that he was able to give orders and have them obeyed. He had authority because he himself was under authority.

Today, those of us who submit to Christ are men and women "under authority." Because of our relationship to Him, we have the authority to speak on His behalf, declaring forgiveness of sins to all who believe in Him.

What a great responsibility to live and speak as people under God's authority!

HADDON ROBINSON

We can speak for Christ only when we listen to Christ.

Storms on the Horizon

MATTHEW 8:23-28

"What kind of man is this? Even the winds and the waves obey him!"
MATTHEW 8:27

For a time, our son Josh was a commercial salmon fisherman in Kodiak, Alaska. While there, he sent me a photograph he took of a tiny vessel a few hundred yards ahead of his boat moving through a narrow pass. Ominous storm clouds loom on the horizon. But a rainbow, the sign of God's providence and loving care, stretches from one side of the pass to the other, encircling the little boat.

The photograph reflects our earthly voyage: We sail into an uncertain future, but we are surrounded by the faithfulness of God!

Jesus's disciples were surrounded by a storm, and He used the experience to teach them about the power and faithfulness of God (Matthew 8:23–27). We seek answers for the uncertainties of life. We watch the future growing closer and wonder what will happen to us there. Puritan poet John Keble captured this in one of his poems in which he observed the future as it drew near. But as he watched, he was "waiting to see what God will do."

Whether young or old we all face uncertain futures. Heaven answers: God's love and goodness encircle us no matter what awaits us. We wait and see what God will do!

DAVID ROPER

**We sail into the uncertain future
surrounded by the faithfulness of God!**

Actions Speak Louder

MATTHEW 9:1–8

*Dear children, let us not love with words or speech
but with actions and in truth.*

1 JOHN 3:18

Irritated with a young athlete who had accomplished little yet boasted about his ability, a TV commentator said, "Don't tell me what you're going to do—tell me what you've done!" Actions speak louder than words.

This principle is seen in Jesus's life. In Matthew 9, a paralytic was brought to Him. Jesus's response? "Your sins are forgiven." When the religious leaders objected, He raised the question of the hour: "Which is easier: to say, 'Your sins are forgiven,' or to say, 'Get up and walk'?" (v. 5).

The answer is obvious. To say He had forgiven the man's sins was simple, because it couldn't be proven or disproven. But to say, "Get up and walk" was different. It was instantly verifiable. So to prove His authority to forgive sins, Jesus said to the paralytic, "Get up, take your mat and go home" (v. 6). And he did!

Jesus's actions supported His words, and so should ours. John wrote, "Dear children, let us not love with word or speech but with actions and in truth" (1 John 3:18). What we say will influence a watching world only if it's consistent with what we do. As we tell people about Christ's love, those words will communicate powerfully if surrounded by acts of love and kindness. Actions do speak louder!

BILL CROWDER

Our works and words should say the same thing.

Extending Grace

MATTHEW 9:9–13

Jesus said, "It is not the healthy who need a doctor, but the sick."
MATTHEW 9:12

In the mid-1970s, divorce filings and final decrees appeared in the Public Records section of our local newspaper. As Rev. Bill Flanagan, a pastor at our church, noticed those names week after week, he began to picture people, not statistics. So he created a Divorce Recovery Workshop to offer help and healing in Christ to hurting people during a difficult time. When concerned church members suggested to Bill that he was condoning divorce, he softly replied that he was simply extending God's grace to folks in need.

When Jesus invited Matthew the tax collector to follow Him, he accepted. Matthew then invited Jesus to dinner at his house. After the religious leaders criticized Jesus for eating with tax collectors and sinners, He said, "It is not the healthy who need a doctor, but the sick. But go and learn what this means: 'I desire mercy, not sacrifice.' For I have not come to call the righteous, but sinners" (Matthew 9:12–13). Jesus, the Great Physician, wants to meet each of us at our point of need, offering forgiveness, healing, and hope. What we don't deserve, He freely gives.

By reaching out to people in need, we can extend to others this grace of God in Christ—guiding them to His healing touch.

DAVID McCASLAND

When you know God's grace, you'll want to show God's grace.

Making a Difference

MATTHEW 9:27–38

When [Jesus] saw the crowds, he had compassion on them.
MATTHEW 9:36

Elizabeth's story was moving, to say the least. Following a terribly humiliating experience in Massachusetts, she caught a bus to New Jersey to escape her embarrassment. Weeping uncontrollably, she hardly noticed that the bus had made a stop along the way. A passenger sitting behind her, a total stranger, began making his way off the bus when he suddenly stopped, turned, and walked back to Elizabeth. He saw her tears and handed her his Bible, saying that he thought she might need it. He was right. But not only did she need the Bible but she also needed the Christ it speaks of. Elizabeth received Him as a result of this simple act of compassion by a stranger who gave a gift.

Jesus is our example of compassion. In Matthew 9, we read, "When he saw the crowds, he had compassion on them, because they were harassed and helpless, like sheep without a shepherd" (v. 36). Not only did our Lord notice the pain and hurt of broken people but He also responded to it by challenging His followers to pray for the Father to send out workers to respond to the hurts and needs of this dying world (v. 38).

As we follow Christ's example, a heart of compassion for shepherdless people can compel us to make a difference in the lives of others.

BILL CROWDER

A world in despair needs Christians who care.

Any Distance, Any Time

MATTHEW 9:35–38

Jesus went through all the towns and villages, teaching . . .
[and] proclaiming the good news of the kingdom.
MATTHEW 9:35

For several years, I've corresponded with a pastor in Nepal who often travels with his church members to distant communities in the Himalayas to preach God's Word and plant churches. Recently he sent me his itinerary for the following week and asked me to pray.

His busy schedule revealed that over the course of a week he planned to travel by motorcycle about 160 kilometers (100 miles) to several cities to preach and hand out gospel tracts.

I wondered at the great distances my friend would cover over mountainous terrain, and I wrote to ask how he was holding up. He replied, "We had a wonderful time of marching in the mountains with our church members. All do not have motorcycles . . . so we all walked. It was a blessed time. Still more places to go." And then I was reminded of how "Jesus went through all the towns and villages, teaching in their synagogues, proclaiming the good news of the kingdom" (Matthew 9:35).

I thought of my reluctance to drive across town in the snow to visit a lonely widower; to walk across the street to help a neighbor; to answer a knock on the door from a needy friend when I'm busy; to go any time, any place, any distance for the sake of love. And I thought of our Lord, for whom no distance was too great.

DAVID ROPER

What God gave to us, He wants us to share.

Working in the Harvest

MATTHEW 9:35-10:4

"Ask the Lord of the harvest, therefore, to send out workers into his harvest field."
MATTHEW 9:38

While Dwight L. Moody was attending a convention in Indianapolis on mass evangelism, he did more than just talk about it. He asked a friend who was a gifted musician to meet him on a street corner at six o'clock one evening. The man stood on a box and sang a song. When a crowd gathered, Moody spoke briefly and then invited the people to follow him to the nearby convention hall.

Soon the auditorium was filled with spiritually hungry people, and Moody preached to them. When the convention attendees began to arrive, the evangelist stopped preaching and said, "Now we must close, as the brethren of the convention want to discuss the topic, 'How to reach the masses.'"

When Jesus saw the masses, He "had compassion on them" (Matthew 9:36). He said to His disciples, "The harvest is plentiful . . . . Ask the Lord of the harvest, therefore, to send out workers" (vv. 37–38). And He sent them out to preach the good news of His kingdom (10:1).

It is estimated that only ten percent of the world's population of more than seven and a half billion people are believers in Jesus Christ. And more than twenty-five percent have never heard of Jesus's love even once.

More than ever, we can see that indeed "the harvest is plentiful."

ANNE CETAS

The next person you meet may be your mission field.

Taking the Cross

MATTHEW 10:1–7, 24–39

"He who does not take up his cross and follow after Me is not worthy of Me."
MATTHEW 10:38 (NKJV)

The cross. We see it today as the rough, wooden instrument of death for Jesus Christ.

But before His followers had even a faint idea that Jesus would die that way, He spoke of the cross. As He stood near the Sea of Galilee preparing the disciples to reach "the lost sheep of Israel" (Matthew 10:6), Jesus told them, "He who does not take up his cross and follow after Me is not worthy of Me" (v. 38 NKJV).

The men didn't associate the cross with Jesus's approaching death, but they knew what a cross signified. Crucifixions were a common method of execution. The disciples had a vivid picture of the agony, punishment, and misery that a cross represented. Taking a cross meant walking life's toughest road.

So why was Jesus promoting cross-bearing? Because He wanted disciples who were willing to face the difficulties it would take to serve His cause. Soon Jesus would be killed, and His followers would have to carry on His message alone. To stand against the forces that would seek to quiet the gospel would take total commitment.

That's still our challenge today. Are we willing to take the cross and serve Christ in self-denial? The task is great—but it is eternally rewarding.

DAVE BRANON

**After everything that Christ has done for us,
how can we do less than give Him our best?**

He Watches Me

MATTHEW 10:16–31

"Don't be afraid; you are worth more than many sparrows."
MATTHEW 10:31

One Sunday morning at church, we sang "His Eye Is on the Sparrow" as a congregational hymn. It was a rare opportunity to give voice to a song usually performed by a soloist.

During the first chorus, I noticed a friend who was weeping so hard he couldn't sing. Knowing a bit of what he had been through recently, I recognized his tears as ones of joy at realizing that, no matter what our situation, God sees us, knows us, and cares for us.

Jesus said, "Are not two sparrows sold for a penny? Yet not one of them will fall to the ground outside your Father's care. And even the very hairs of your head are all numbered. So don't be afraid; you are worth more than many sparrows" (Matthew 10:29–31). The Lord spoke these words to His twelve disciples as He sent them out to teach, heal, and bear witness of Him to "the lost sheep of Israel" (v. 6). He told them that even though they would face persecution for His sake, they should not be afraid, even of death (vv. 22–26).

When threatening circumstances press us to lose hope, we can find encouragement in the words of this song: "I sing because I'm happy, I sing because I'm free. For His eye is on the sparrow, and I know He watches me." We are under His watchful care.

DAVID MCCASLAND

**When you put your cares in God's hands,
He puts His peace in your heart.**

Waiting . . .

MATTHEW 10:28–33

Precious in the sight of the LORD is the death of his faithful servants.
PSALM 116:15

My mother, so dignified and proper her entire life, lay in a hospice bed, held captive by debilitating age. As she struggled for breath, her declining condition contradicted the gorgeous spring day that danced invitingly on the other side of the windowpane.

All the emotional preparation in the world cannot sufficiently brace us for the stark reality of goodbye. *Death is such an indignity!* I thought.

I diverted my gaze to the birdfeeder outside the window. A grosbeak flitted close to help itself to some seed. Instantly a familiar phrase popped into my mind: "Not a single sparrow can fall to the ground without your Father knowing it" (Matthew 10:29 NLT). Jesus had said that to His disciples as He gave them marching orders for a mission to Judea, but the principle applies to all of us. "You are worth more than many sparrows," He told them (v. 31).

My mom stirred and opened her eyes. Reaching back to her childhood, she used a Dutch term of endearment for her own mother and declared, "Muti's dead!" "Yes," my wife agreed. "She's with Jesus now." Uncertain, Mom continued. "And Joyce and Jim?" she questioned of her sister and brother. "Yes, they're with Jesus too," said my wife. "But we'll be with them soon!" "It's hard to wait," Mom said quietly.

TIM GUSTAFSON

Death is the last shadow before heaven's dawn.

We Can Trust Him

MATTHEW 10:32–38

"Bless those who curse you, do good to those who hate you,
and pray for those who spitefully use you and persecute you."
MATTHEW 5:44 (NKJV)

I know very little about persecution. My physical well-being has never been threatened because of what I believe or what I say. What little I "know" about the subject comes from what I hear and read. But that is not true for many of our brothers and sisters around the world. Some of them live in danger every day simply because they love Jesus and want others to know Him too.

There is another form of persecution that may not be life-threatening, but it is heartbreaking. It's the persecution that comes from non-Christian family members. When loved ones ridicule our faith and mock us for what we believe and how we express our love for God, we feel rejected and unloved.

Paul warned believers that following Jesus would result in persecution: "Everyone who wants to live a godly life in Christ Jesus will be persecuted" (2 Timothy 3:12), and we know that sometimes rejection will come from those we love (Matthew 10:34–36). But when people we love reject the God we love, the rejection feels personal.

Jesus told us to pray for those who persecute us (Matthew 5:44), and that includes more than strangers who hate us. God is able to give us grace to persevere through persecution even when it comes from those we love.

JULIE ACKERMAN LINK

People may mock our message, but they can't stop our prayers.

Losing to Find

MATTHEW 10:37–42

"Whoever loses their life for my sake will find it."
MATTHEW 10:39

When I married my English fiancé and moved to the United Kingdom, I thought it would be a five-year adventure in a foreign land. I never dreamed I'd still be living here nearly twenty years later, or that at times I'd feel like I was losing my life as I said goodbye to family and friends, work, and all that was familiar. But in losing my old way of life, I've found a better one.

The upside-down gift of finding life when we lose it is what Jesus promised to His apostles. When He sent out the twelve disciples to share His good news, He asked them to love Him more than their mothers or fathers, sons or daughters (Matthew 10:37). His words came in a culture where families were the cornerstone of the society and highly valued. But He promised that if they would lose their life for His sake, they would find it (v. 39).

We don't have to move abroad to find ourselves in Christ. Through service and commitment—such as the disciples going out to share the good news of the kingdom of God—we find ourselves receiving more than we give through the lavish love the Lord showers on us. Of course He loves us no matter how much we serve, but we find contentment, meaning, and fulfillment when we pour ourselves out for the well-being of others.

AMY BOUCHER PYE

We are most useful to God when we are most useful to others.

Saying Goodbye

MATTHEW 11:7–19

*"There has not risen anyone greater than John the Baptist;
yet whoever is least in the kingdom of heaven is greater than he."*
MATTHEW 11:11

If you've ever been asked to say a few words at a memorial service, you know how difficult, yet important, it can be. Cyrus M. Copeland, compiler of two books of tributes to famous people, said: "A great eulogy is both art and architecture—a bridge between the living and the dead, memory and eternity."

The Bible contains little that corresponds to our modern eulogy. Yet Jesus paid a great tribute to John the Baptist when he faced the looming threat of execution by Herod. From prison, John sent his disciples to confirm the identity of Jesus the Messiah (Matthew 11:2–6). Jesus talked with them, then told the listening crowd, "Among those born of women there has not risen anyone greater than John the Baptist; yet whoever is least in the kingdom of heaven is greater than he" (v. 11).

Jesus's tribute captured the essence of the desert-dwelling, straight-preaching John, who was maligned and misunderstood as he prepared the way for the Son of God. John's greatness was more than personal; it was wrapped up in the kingdom of God. He wrote his own eulogy by his actions.

As we ponder what we might say about others at their passing, it's also good to ask, "What will people say about me when it's time to say goodbye?"

DAVID MCCASLAND

Living for the Lord today leaves a lasting legacy when we're gone.

Rocks of Unbelief

MATTHEW 11:20-34

The law of the LORD is perfect, refreshing the soul.
PSALM 19:7

Rocks. That's all that's left of the city of Chorazin. Just the rubble of a few buildings made of volcanic rock—yet this was once a thriving city on the Sea of Galilee.

Not far from Chorazin is another pile of rocks—the former city of Capernaum.

Same with Bethsaida. Once a bustling city where children played, men did business, and mothers ran households. Rocks. Nothing but rocks.

When Jesus walked the streets of those towns, He knew this would happen. In Matthew 11:21–23, He said, "Woe to you, Chorazin! Woe to you, Bethsaida! . . . And you, Capernaum, will you be lifted to the heavens? No, you will go down to Hades."

In those cities, Jesus clearly showed himself to be the Son of God—the One who had almighty power and could perform miracles. But the people refused to listen to His message. As a result, Chorazin, Capernaum, and Bethsaida were cursed by God and reduced to heaps of rocks—monuments to unbelief.

The lesson for us today is clear. When Jesus speaks, we must take His words to heart. In fact, all of Scripture needs to be taken seriously. To disregard God's Word shows a heart of unbelief and will leave our lives in ruins. But to heed its life-giving instruction brings reward and blessing.

DAVE BRANON

To ignore the Bible is to invite disaster.

Put Down Your Burdens

MATTHEW 11:25–30

"Come to me, all you who are weary and burdened, and I will give you rest."
MATTHEW 11:28

A man driving his pickup truck on a country road saw a woman carrying a heavy load, so he stopped and offered her a lift. The woman expressed her gratitude and climbed into the back of the truck.

A moment later, the man noticed a strange thing: the woman was still holding onto her heavy load despite sitting in the vehicle! Astonished, he pleaded, "Please, Madam, put down your load and take your rest. My truck can carry you and your stuff. Just relax."

What do we do with the load of fear, worry, and anxiety we often carry as we go through life's many challenges? Instead of relaxing in the Lord, I sometimes behave like that woman. Jesus said, "Come to me, all you who are weary and burdened, and I will give you rest" (Matthew 11:28), yet I've caught myself carrying burdens I should offload onto Jesus.

We put down our burdens when we bring them to the Lord in prayer. The apostle Peter says, "Cast all your anxiety on [Jesus] because he cares for you" (1 Peter 5:7). Because He cares for us, we can rest and relax as we learn to trust Him. Instead of carrying the burdens that weigh us down and weary us, we can give them to the Lord and let Him carry them.

LAWRENCE DARMANI

Prayer is the place where burdens change shoulders.

Dead Giveaway

MATTHEW 12:33-37

"By your words you will be acquitted,
and by your words you will be condemned."
MATTHEW 12:37

Lucy had never gone fishing, but she wanted to spend time with Willie. So she told him she loved to fish. He was delighted to find a girl who could share his love for fishing.

One day they went out to Willie's favorite fishing spot. The fish weren't biting, but Lucy didn't care. The sun was shining and the water lapped gently at the sides of the boat. Just being with Willie was all that mattered.

After a while, Lucy said, "Willie, you know that red and white thing you put on my line?" "You mean the bobber?" he replied. "Yeah," said Lucy. "How much did it cost?" "About fifty cents." "Then I owe you fifty cents. Mine just sank," said Lucy. She didn't know she had a fish on the line. It was now obvious that Lucy had lied about her love for fishing. Her words betrayed her.

Sooner or later our words will unmask the true condition of our hearts. If our hearts are filled with love for God, our words will be marked by honesty, gratefulness, love, encouragement, wise counsel, and concern for others. But if our hearts are filled with selfishness, our words will be filled with deceit, criticism, complaining, broken confidences, and insults. By our words we will be judged (Matthew 12:37).

Father, may our words today reflect our love for you and clearly show that Christ is living in us.

MART DEHAAN

What we say reveals who we are.

Scattering Seeds

MATTHEW 13:1–9

"The seed falling on good soil . . . produces a crop,
yielding a hundred, sixty or thirty times what was sown."
MATTHEW 13:23

I received a wonderful email from a woman who wrote, "Your mom was my first-grade teacher at Putnam City in 1958. She was a great teacher and very kind, but strict! She made us learn Psalm 23 and say it in front of the class, and I was horrified. But it was the only contact I had with the Bible until 1997 when I became a Christian. And the memories of Mrs. McCasland came flooding back as I re-read it."

Jesus told a large crowd a parable about the farmer who sowed his seed that fell on different types of ground—a hard path, rocky ground, clumps of thorns, and good soil (Matthew 13:1–9). While some seeds never grew, "the seed falling on good soil refers to someone who hears the word and understands it" and "produces a crop yielding a hundred, sixty or thirty times what was sown" (v. 23).

During the twenty years my mother taught first grade in public schools, along with reading, writing, and arithmetic she scattered seeds of kindness and the message of God's love.

Her former student's email concluded, "I have had other influences in my Christian walk later in life, of course. But my heart always returns to [Psalm 23] and [your mom's] gentle nature."

A seed of God's love sown today may produce a remarkable harvest tomorrow.

DAVID MCCASLAND

We sow the seed—God produces the harvest.

Matters of the Heart

MATTHEW 13:10–15

"This people's heart has become calloused;
they hardly hear with their ears, and they have closed their eyes."
MATTHEW 13:15

At the beginning of a spiritual retreat, our speaker, Matt Heard, asked, "How's your heart?" It stunned me, because I tend to focus on believing with my mind and working with my hands. In the activity of thinking and serving, my heart is pushed to the side. As we were led through the Bible's repeated emphasis on this crucial center of our lives, I began to grasp his premise that belief and service are, more than anything else, matters of the heart.

When Jesus told a story to illustrate how people receive and respond to His teaching (Matthew 13:1–9), His disciples asked, "Why do you speak to the people in parables?" (v. 10). In reply, Jesus quoted the prophet Isaiah: "For this people's heart has become calloused; they hardly hear with their ears, and they have closed their eyes. Otherwise they might see with their eyes, hear with their ears, understand with their hearts and turn, and I would heal them." (v. 15; see Isaiah 6:10).

How dangerously easy it is to neglect our hearts. If we become calloused, we find no joy in living or serving. Life seems hollow. But when our hearts are tender toward God, understanding and gratefulness flow through us to others.

So, how's your heart?

DAVID MCCASLAND

We can become so busy doing good that we lose our heart for God.

Dealing with Distractions

MATTHEW 13:14–22

"The cares of this world . . . choke the word."
MATTHEW 13:22 (NKJV)

A restaurant owner in the village of Abu Ghosh, just west of Jerusalem, offered a fifty-percent discount for patrons who turned off their cell phones. Jawdat Ibrahim believes that smartphones have shifted the focus of meals from companionship and conversation to surfing, texting, and business calls. "Technology is very good," Ibrahim says. "But . . . when you are with your family and your friends, you can just wait for half an hour and enjoy the food and enjoy the company."

How easily we can be distracted by many things, whether in our relationship with others or with the Lord.

Jesus told His followers that spiritual distraction begins with hearts that have grown dull, ears that are hard of hearing, and eyes that are closed (Matthew 13:15). Using the illustration of a farmer scattering seed, Jesus compared the seed that fell among thorns to a person who hears God's Word but whose heart is focused on other things. "The cares of this world and the deceitfulness of riches choke the word, and he becomes unfruitful" (v. 22 NKJV).

There is great value in having times throughout each day when we turn off the distractions of mind and heart and focus on the Lord.

DAVID MCCASLAND

Focusing on Christ puts everything else in perspective.

Unexpected Alligators

MATTHEW 13:18–23

*"But since they have no root, they last only a short time.
When trouble or persecution comes because of the word,
they quickly fall away."*

MATTHEW 13:21

A friend of actress and comedienne Gracie Allen once sent a small, live alligator to her as a gag. Not knowing what to do with it, Gracie put it in the bathtub and then left for an appointment. When she returned home, she found a note from her maid. "Dear Miss Allen: Sorry, but I have quit. I don't work in houses where there is an alligator. I would have told you this when I started, but I never thought it would come up."

Some people who say they'll serve Christ are quick to leave when trouble comes. In Jesus's parable of the soils, He pictured the various responses that people have to the gospel. For example, a person may seem to accept God's truth, but he stumbles in his faith when difficulties arise (Matthew 13:20–21). Such troubles test the sincerity of one's faith and expose the weakness of one's commitment to Christ.

But someone may say, "Shouldn't our Lord tell us up front what is involved in following Him?" He does. He appeals to us with one invitation: "Trust Me." If we let trouble or disillusionment shake our faith, we are breaking the spirit of the trust that brought us to Christ in the first place.

Father, when life brings us the unexpected and we feel like quitting, help us to be faithful to you.

MART DeHaan

Tough times can teach us to trust.

Eureka Stone

MATTHEW 13:44–50

*"The kingdom of heaven is like treasure hidden in a field.
When a man found it, he hid it again,
and then in his joy went and sold all he had and bought that field."*
MATTHEW 13:44

In 1867 on a farm in South Africa, fifteen-year-old Erasmus Jacobs saw a stone glistening in the sun. The shining rock was eventually reported to a neighbor, who wanted to buy it from the family. Not knowing its value, Erasmus's mother told the neighbor, "You can keep the stone if you want it."

Eventually, a mineralogist determined the stone to be a 21.25 carat diamond and worth a great sum. It became known as the "Eureka Diamond." (The Greek word *eureka* means, "I found it!") Soon the fields near the Jacobs' farm soared in value. Underneath the land was one of the richest diamond deposits ever discovered.

Jesus said that the value of being part of God's kingdom is like treasure: "The kingdom of heaven is like treasure hidden in a field. When a man found it, he hid it again, and then in his joy went and sold all he had and bought that field" (Matthew 13:44).

When we put our faith in Christ, a spiritual "eureka moment" arrives. God gives us forgiveness in His Son. It is the greatest treasure that could ever be found. Now all of life can begin to center on the value of becoming a joyous member of His eternal kingdom. It's our joy to share that valuable discovery with others.

DENNIS FISHER

God's kingdom is a treasure meant to be shared.

Happy Ending

MATTHEW 13:53–58

When Christ, who is your life, appears,
then you also will appear with him in glory.
COLOSSIANS 3:4

By the end of his life, musician Giuseppe Verdi (1813–1901) was recognized as a master of dramatic composition. But he didn't begin his career with such success. As a youth, he had obvious musical ability, but he was denied entrance to the Milan Conservatory because he lacked the required education and background.

Yet time does strange things. After Verdi's fame had spread worldwide, the school was renamed the Verdi Conservatory of Music.

Verdi's experience reminds me of the experience of our Lord and of all who trust in Him. The Son of God was rejected by His countrymen because they didn't feel He had adequate training or the right family background (Matthew 13:53–58). Even though Jesus spoke the truth in a powerful, irrefutable way, and even though His works spoke for themselves, He did not receive the recognition He deserved. Yet someday everyone will bow before Him and give Him the honor due His name (Philippians 2:9–11).

We who have put our faith in Christ as our personal Savior will have a part in that great day, for He plans to share the honor with us (Ephesians 1:18; 2 Timothy 2:12; Revelation 22:5). Even though our beginnings may seem insignificant, we can look forward to a glorious, happy ending.

MART DEHAAN

All that we long to become will find fulfillment when we see Jesus.

God Cares for You

MATTHEW 14:1–14

When Jesus . . . saw a great crowd, he had compassion on them.
MATTHEW 14:14

John the Baptist had been martyred by King Herod. John was Jesus's cousin and friend, and his death must have touched Jesus deeply. I believe that's why He sought refuge from the crowds. Matthew wrote, "He withdrew by boat privately to a solitary place" (14:13).

Jesus wanted to be alone to grieve, but the crowd pressed Him with their needs and wouldn't let Him get away (v. 13). Seeing the multitudes and their pain, Jesus was moved with compassion for them. Despite His own heartache, He began to heal their sick (v. 14). He didn't let His own grief keep Him from ministering to them.

Perhaps you're a caregiver—a pastor, a teacher, a nurse, or a counselor. Maybe you're a mother with small children or the spouse of an invalid. You have your own struggles, disappointments, heartaches—and no one seems to care about you.

But there is Someone who cares. God does. He knows your sorrow as no one else does, and He understands the depths of your misery. You can give your cares to Him (1 Peter 5:7) and find in His presence His love, consolation, and the strength you need to move from your own grief to the grief of others. You can care for others because God cares for you.

DAVID ROPER

Because God cares for us, we can care for others.

Retreating Forward

MATTHEW 14:13-23

After [Jesus] had dismissed them,
he went up on a mountainside by himself to pray.
Later that night, he was there alone.

MATTHEW 14:23

A friend told me about his church's leadership retreat. For two days, church leaders pulled away for a time of prayer, planning, and worship. My friend was not only refreshed but also energized. He told me, "This retreat is really going to help us move forward as a church ministry."

It sounded funny to me—this notion of retreating in order to move forward. But it is true. Sometimes you have to pull back and regroup before you can make meaningful forward progress. This is particularly true in our relationship with God.

Jesus himself practiced "retreating forward." After a busy day of ministry in the region of the Sea of Galilee, He retreated. Matthew 14:23 tells us that "after he had dismissed them, he went up on a mountainside by himself to pray. Later that night, He was there alone." Alone in the presence of the Father.

In this fast-paced, get-ahead world, it's easy to wear ourselves down—pressing ahead and moving forward at all costs. But even in our desire to be effective Christians, we must consistently be willing to retreat into God's presence. Only in the refreshing of His strength can we find the resources to move forward in our service for Him. Retreat to Jesus before moving forward.

BILL CROWDER

Alone with the Father is the only place to find the strength to press on.

He Is Enough

MATTHEW 14:22–33

Jesus immediately said to them, "Take courage! It is I. Don't be afraid."
MATTHEW 14:27

Sometimes we are overwhelmed by life. The crushing waves of disappointment, endless debt, debilitating illness, or trouble with people can cause hopelessness, depression, or despair. It happened to Jesus's disciples. And it has happened to me.

Three statements by the Lord beginning with the words "It is . . ." offer us comfort, reassurance, and hope that Jesus is enough. The first is in Matthew 4 and is repeated three times: "It is written" (vv. 4, 7, 10). In responding to the three temptations of Satan, Jesus gave us proof enough that the Word of God is true and overcomes the most powerful forms of temptation and pressure.

The second statement, "It is I" (Matthew 14:27), was spoken when Jesus told His terrified disciples that He himself was presence enough to stop the howling storm and calm the raging seas.

Jesus spoke the third "It is" from the cross: "It is finished!" (John 19:30). He assured us that His death was provision enough to pay the debt for our sins and set us free.

Whatever our circumstances, Jesus is present with His love, compassion, and grace. He is proof, presence, and provision enough to carry us safely through.

DAVID EGNER

God's love does not keep us from trials; it helps us get through them.

Agreeing with God

MATTHEW 15:1–9

"These people honor me with their lips, but their hearts are far from me."
MATTHEW 15:8

The caller to the radio program mentioned religion, so the radio talk show host began to rant about hypocrites. "I can't stand religious hypocrites," he said. "They talk about religion, but they're no better than I am. That's why I don't like all this religious stuff."

This man didn't realize it, but he was agreeing with God. God has made it clear that He can't stand hypocrisy either. It's ironic, though, that something God opposes is used by some people as an excuse not to seek Him.

Jesus said this about hypocrisy: "These people honor me with their lips, but their hearts are far from me. They worship me in vain; their teachings are merely human rules" (Matthew 15:8–9).

Notice what Jesus said to perhaps the biggest hypocrites of His day, the Pharisees. In Matthew 23, He called them hypocrites—not once, not twice, but seven times! They were religious people who were putting on a big show, but God knew their hearts. He knew they were far from Him.

Non-Christians who point out hypocrisy in us when they see it are right in doing so. They are agreeing with God, who also despises it. Our task is to make sure our lives honor the One who deserves our total dedication.

DAVE BRANON

The devil is content to let us profess Christianity as long as we do not practice it.

Both Near and Far

MATTHEW 15:7-20

Turn my eyes away from worthless things;
preserve my life according to your word.

PSALM 119:37

Everything was quiet in our yard. While I worked at the patio table, our dog, Maggie, lay nearby in the grass. A slight rustling of dry leaves changed everything. Maggie made her move, and suddenly she was circling a tree, where a woodchuck clung tightly to the trunk.

Maggie came when I called, but I couldn't get her to look at me. Her neck was in a rigidly fixed position. Although she was near me physically, her thoughts and desires were with that woodchuck.

Maggie and the woodchuck remind me of how quickly I become preoccupied with things that take my eyes off Jesus. Old temptations, new responsibilities, or ongoing desires for possessions or pleasure can quickly divert my attention from the One who knows and wants what is best for me.

A similar spiritual condition afflicted the Pharisees (Matthew 15:8–9). They were serving in the temple and instructing others, but their hearts were far from God.

We too can teach and serve at church but be far from God. Even our religious activity becomes meaningless when our focus is not on Jesus. But if we stop being "stiff-necked" (Acts 7:51), the Lord can turn our eyes away from worthless things and revive our hearts.

JULIE ACKERMAN LINK

When Christ is the center of our life, all else comes into proper focus.

Positive Words

MATTHEW 15:17–20

Those who guard their lips preserve their lives,
but those who speak rashly will come to ruin.

PROVERBS 13:3

Recently I overheard an older woman speaking to a friend about the modern emphasis on dieting. "These days," she mused, "I'm more concerned with what comes out of my mouth than what goes into it." There's a world of wisdom in those words.

Jesus put it this way: "The things that come out of a person's mouth come from the heart, and these defile them. For out of the heart come evil thoughts—murder, adultery, sexual immortality, theft, false testimony, slander. These are what defile a person; but eating with unwashed hands does not defile them" (Matthew 15:18–20).

What we say affects others. "The words of the reckless pierce like swords," says Proverbs 12:18. But what we may overlook is the effect our reckless words have on us. When we gossip or when we malign others, our words begin to ruin us, for we gratify the evil that is in us and strengthen it until it overthrows us.

On the contrary, when we guard our lips, we strike a blow at this negative way of talking. "The tongue of the wise brings healing," continues Proverbs 12:18. We protect our souls, for we weaken the very thing that lies in wait to ruin us.

Ask God to "set a guard" over your mouth and "keep watch over the door" of your lips (Psalm 141:3). Let your words always promote life and wisdom.

DAVID ROPER

A word from your mouth speaks volumes about your heart.

Bold Persistence

MATTHEW 15:21–28

Jesus said to her, "Woman, you have great faith! Your request is granted."
MATTHEW 15:28

In 1953, a fledgling business called Rocket Chemical Company and its staff of three set out to create a line of rust-prevention solvents and degreasers for use in the aerospace industry. It took them forty attempts to perfect their formula. The original secret formula for WD-40—which stands for Water Displacement, fortieth attempt—is still in use today. What a story of persistence!

The gospel of Matthew records another story of bold persistence. A Canaanite woman had a daughter who was possessed by a demon. She had no hope for her daughter—until she heard that Jesus was in the region.

This desperate woman came to Jesus with her need because she believed He could help her. She cried out to Him even though everything and everybody seemed to be against her—race, religious background, gender, the disciples, Satan, and seemingly even Jesus (Matthew 15:22–27). Despite all of these obstacles, she did not give up. With bold persistence, she pushed her way through the dark corridors of difficulty, desperate need, and rejection. The result? Jesus commended her for her faith and healed her daughter (v. 28).

We too are invited to approach Jesus with bold persistence. As we keep asking, seeking, and knocking, we will find grace and mercy in our time of need.

MARVIN WILLIAMS

Persistence in prayer pleases God.

Signs and Feelings

MATTHEW 16:1–4

Your word is a lamp for my feet, a light on my path.
PSALM 119:105

A young man I know has a habit of asking God for signs. That's not necessarily bad, but his prayers tend to seek confirmation of his feelings. For instance, he'll pray, "God, if you want me to do X, then you please do Y, and I'll know it's okay."

This has created a dilemma. Because of the way he prays and the way he thinks God is answering, he feels that he should get back with his ex-girlfriend. Perhaps unsurprisingly, she feels strongly that God doesn't want that.

The religious leaders of Jesus's day demanded a sign from Him to prove the validity of His claims (Matthew 16:1). They weren't seeking God's guidance; they were challenging His divine authority. Jesus replied, "A wicked and adulterous generation looks for a sign" (v. 4). The Lord's strong response wasn't a blanket statement to prevent anyone from seeking God's guidance. Rather, Jesus was accusing them of ignoring the clear prophecies in Scripture that indicated He was the Messiah.

God wants us to seek His guidance in prayer (James 1:5). He also gives us the guidance of the Spirit (John 14:26) and His Word (Psalm 119:105). He provides us with mentors and wise leaders. And He's given us the example of Jesus himself.

TIM GUSTAFSON

The best way to know God's will is to say, "I will" to God.

Are You Ready?

MATTHEW 16:1–4; 24–27

*"The Son of Man is going to come . . . , and then he will reward
each person according to what they have done."*
MATTHEW 16:27

I love to fish. One summer a good friend invited me to go with him to
Canada, where a guide would take us to a special place where there were
supposed to be plenty of "big ones."

After a grueling hike, finally we were drifting quietly in a canoe on a
beautiful lake. Loons screamed their disapproval of our intrusion. A big
black bear ambled out of the brush to the shore. And then an owl broke
the silence with a long, "Whoo, whoo, whooooo." Our guide stopped
paddling and said, "Did you hear that? The owl said, 'Drop everything and
set up camp. Get ready for a storm.' When an owl hoots in the daytime, it
means rain before the next day." Sure enough, that night it rained.

In Matthew 16, Jesus rebuked the religious leaders because they
knew how to predict the weather (vv. 2–3), but they failed to recognize
the obvious signs that revealed Jesus as the promised Messiah. Later, He
warned His hearers about the judgment to come (vv. 24–28). He said it is
foolish to grab the things of this present world and yet lose one's own soul
for eternity (v. 26).

Have you trusted Jesus as your personal Savior? Have you turned to
Him for refuge from the coming storm? If not, drop everything. It's time
to get ready.

M. R. DeHaan

Jesus may come any time, so we must be ready all the time.

The Right Answer

MATTHEW 16:13-17

Simon Peter answered, "You are the Messiah, the Son of the living God."
MATTHEW 16:16

When Jesus asked a question, it was not because He didn't know the answer. You can be sure He was making a point.

Jesus and His disciples were in Caesarea Philippi, away from their own territory. It was a place of idolatry and oppression—a threatening place both politically and spiritually. In this environment, Jesus posed two important questions about the perception of His identity. He wasn't interested in His popularity rating. He wanted His followers to know for sure who they were following.

Today our culture is just as hostile and opposed to Jesus as when He first asked the question: "Who do people say the Son of Man is?" (Matthew 16:13). Just as in Jesus's day, people today offer a long list of inadequate and incorrect ideas about Jesus, ranging from "just a good teacher" all the way to "divisive" and "intolerant."

The real question was and continues to be this one from Jesus's lips: "Who do you say I am?" (16:15). Peter boldly declared, "You are the Messiah, the Son of the living God" (v. 16). Jesus said that Peter's accurate confession was a God-given insight and that he was blessed because of his declaration (v. 17).

Join Peter in confessing that Jesus is your Savior. That's the right answer to Jesus's eternally important question.

JOE STOWELL

Everyone who believes that Jesus is the Christ is born of God.
—1 John 5:1

Living Backward

MATTHEW 16:21–28

"Whoever loses his life for My sake will find it."
MATTHEW 16:25 (NKJV)

The Chicago River is unusual because it flows backward. In 1900, engineers reversed its direction because city-dwellers were using it as a dump. Dishwater, sewage, and industrial waste all funneled into the river, which emptied into Lake Michigan. Since the lake supplied drinking water for the city, thousands grew sick and died before city authorities decided to redirect the river to flow backward, away from the lake.

When we look at the earthly life of Jesus, it may seem backward from what we would expect. As the King of glory, He came to earth as a vulnerable infant. As God in the flesh, He endured accusations of blasphemy. As the only sinless man, He was crucified as a criminal. But Jesus lived on earth according to God's will (John 6:38).

As followers of Christ, to clothe ourselves with Jesus's attitudes and actions may appear "backward." Blessing our enemies (Romans 12:14), valuing godliness over wealth (1 Timothy 6:6–9), and taking joy in hardship (James 1:2) seem to oppose worldly wisdom. Yet Jesus said, "Whoever loses his life for My sake will find it" (Matthew 16:25 NKJV).

Don't worry if living your life sometimes means operating in reverse. God will give you the strength to honor Him, and He will propel you forward.

JENNIFER BENSON SCHULDT

**Clothing ourselves with Jesus's attitudes and actions
reveals His presence in our lives.**

Worth the Cost

MATTHEW 16:24–28

He who wins souls is wise.
PROVERBS 11:30 (NKJV)

According to a *Wall Street Journal* article, Hemant Mehta wanted to find out if he was "missing something" as an atheist. So the DePaul University graduate student went on eBay with this proposition: He would spend one hour of church attendance for each $10 bid by the highest bidder. A former evangelical minister won with an offer of $504.

How much would you pay for the opportunity to present Christ to an unbeliever? The apostle Paul gave a lot more than $504 in his endeavor to bring the gospel to people who had never heard of Jesus Christ. He traveled many long, hard miles across the world. In a gripping account he told of his experiences: shipwreck, imprisonment, floggings, stoning, beatings, exhaustion, hunger, cold, and peril (2 Corinthians 11:23–28).

In the past 2,000 years of missionary effort, valiant men and women have left their homelands to proclaim Christ in remote and dangerous settings. Many have lost their lives; others have suffered persecution. In many parts of the world today, to talk publicly about Jesus is to risk hardship, jail, and even death.

When we consider Jesus's sacrifice for us, any sacrifice we make to bring others to Him is worth the cost.

DAVID EGNER

When we open our heart to the Lord, He opens our eyes to the lost.

Life's Ups and Downs

MATTHEW 17:1–21

*After six days Jesus took Peter, James and John with him and led them
up a high mountain, . . . There he was transfigured before them. . . .
As they were coming down the mountain, Jesus gave them orders
not to tell anyone what they had seen.*

MARK 9:2, 9

My son Kirk loved to climb mountains. For several years he led groups of young people through the White Mountains of New Hampshire and the Rockies of Colorado. Kirk told me that standing on a peak is an unforgettable experience. It's like being on top of the world! The breathtaking vistas lift your spirit heavenward. God seems so near as your soul drinks in the grandeur of His handiwork. Life's true values come into focus, and your faltering faith grows strong.

So it is in the Christian life. God gives us high points where faith almost becomes sight. Spiritual realities seem more vivid than the physical world around us. How we long for these feelings to last so we can draw on their exhilarating power each day! But like a vapor, the mountaintop experience soon fades, leaving only a vivid memory and the stark demands of daily duties. This is both normal and good. An unbroken spiritual high cannot build character. The transfiguration account teaches us that Jesus would not let His disciples stay on the mount. They had to come down into the lowlands of human suffering and need, but He would go with them.

Are you longing to find release from some difficulty by having a mountaintop experience? Remember that even in the valley, you'll gradually learn that Jesus is as real there as He is on the highlands.

DENNIS DEHAAN

Never doubt in the valley what you found to be true on the mountain.

Gentle Jesus

MATTHEW 18:1–10

"Unless you change and become like little children,
you will never enter the kingdom of heaven."

MATTHEW 18:3

Charles Wesley (1707–1788) was a Methodist evangelist who wrote more than 9,000 hymns and sacred poems. Some, like "O for a Thousand Tongues to Sing," are great, soaring hymns of praise. But his poem "Gentle Jesus, Meek and Mild," first published in 1742, is a child's quiet prayer that captures the essence of how all of us should seek the Lord in sincere, simple faith.

Loving Jesus, gentle Lamb,
In Thy gracious hands I am;
Make me, Savior, what Thou art,
Live Thyself within my heart.

When some followers of Jesus were jockeying for position in His kingdom, the Lord "called a little child to him, and placed the child among them. And he said, 'Truly I tell you, unless you change and become like little children, you will never enter the kingdom of heaven'" (Matthew 18:2–3).

Not many children seek position or power. Instead, they want acceptance and security. They cling to the adults who love and care for them. Jesus never turned children away.

The last stanza of Wesley's poem shows a childlike desire to be just like Jesus: "I shall then show forth Thy praise,/ Serve Thee all my happy days; / Then the world shall always see / Christ, the holy Child, in me."

DAVID MCCASLAND

Faith shines brightest in a childlike heart.

Childlike Humility

MATTHEW 18:1–14

*"Whoever takes the lowly position of this child
is the greatest in the kingdom of heaven."*
MATTHEW 18:4

In the mid-1970s, my husband Bill and I befriended a drug addict named Derek on the London subway. Days later we invited him to come and live with our family. He soon received Christ and His forgiveness.

Until then, the world had been shouting to Derek, "Why don't you grow up?" That day Jesus tenderly said to him, "Unless you change and become like little children, you will never enter the kingdom of heaven" (Matthew 18:3). Derek became a child of God! We expected this young man to learn a lot through us about God, but little did we expect to learn about God through him.

For example, one afternoon we discussed the possibility of someday opening a Christian rehabilitation center for addicts. None of us knew when, where, how, or if it would ever happen. I said, "Well, we know God won't let us down." Derek, however, added, "God won't let himself down." His words echoed Psalm 23:3, "He guides me along the right paths for his name's sake."

Not long after that, God brought that rehabilitation center into being "for his name's sake," and I began learning and relearning childlike humility anew.

JOANIE YODER

A person filled with pride won't have room for wisdom.

The Importance of One

MATTHEW 18:7–14

"There will be more rejoicing in heaven over one sinner who repents than over ninety-nine righteous persons who do not need to repent."

LUKE 15:7

When we think of the multitudes of non-Christians we encounter, we can easily be discouraged in the task of telling others about Jesus. And when we consider the number of people around the world who have never heard of Jesus Christ, we are almost overwhelmed at the immensity of the job before us. But when we begin to feel hopelessness, we can be encouraged by the fact that people are saved one at a time.

To underscore this point, Hugh Duncan gave an apt illustration in *Leadership Journal*. He wrote, "I recently read about an old man, walking the beach at dawn, who noticed a young man ahead of him picking up starfish and flinging them into the sea. Catching up with the youth, he asked what he was doing. The answer was that the stranded starfish would die if left in the morning sun. 'But the beach goes on for miles and miles, and there are millions of starfish,' countered the man. 'How can your effort make any difference?' The young man looked at the starfish in his hand and then threw it to safety in the waves. 'It makes a difference to this one,' he said."

Sometimes the task seems so great that we don't even try to witness. But just as a huge wall is built one brick at a time, so the church, the body of Christ, is built one soul at a time. Therefore, if we speak of Jesus to our neighbors and tell them of the good news God has brought into our life, what a difference it could make! That's the importance of one.

DAVID EGNER

Evangelism is one beggar telling another beggar where to find bread.

Let's Talk about It

MATTHEW 18:15–20

*Let love and faithfulness never leave you; bind them around your neck,
write them on the tablet of your heart.*

PROVERBS 3:3

The police in San Diego received complaints from a woman who said she was getting annoying phone calls. In the middle of the night a person would phone her, bark like a dog, and then hang up. Police eventually discovered that the source of the calls was a neighbor. He said that whenever he was awakened during the night by the barking of her dog, he wanted to make sure she was awake too.

The neighbor's approach certainly didn't express the wisdom of God. The Scriptures tell us that it is often necessary to face a problem head-on (Matthew 18:15–20). At the right time and for the sake of all parties involved, an honest discussion is part of the solution.

Such a loving, open approach should be our goal as Christ-followers. We should trust God and walk into a tense situation with a clear conscience and a desire for peace. These situations can best be resolved through a wise combination of mercy and truth (Proverbs 3:3).

Our complaints against others cannot be smoothed with anger. If a problem is not small enough to overlook graciously, then let's talk about it.

MART DEHAAN

The best way to destroy your enemy is to make that person your friend.

Forgive and Forget!

MATTHEW 18:15–22

Be kind and compassionate to one another, forgiving each other,
just as in Christ God forgave you.
EPHESIANS 4:32

Old Joe was dying. Realizing that time was running out, he wanted to make everything right. But something bothered him. He was at odds with Bill, formerly one of his best friends. Joe had often argued with him, and in recent years they hadn't spoken at all. Wanting to resolve the problem, he asked for Bill to visit him. When Bill arrived, Joe told him he was afraid to go into eternity with bad feelings between them. He wanted to make things right. He reached out for Bill's hand and said, "I forgive you; will you forgive me?" Everything seemed fine. Just as Bill was leaving, however, Joe shouted after him, "But remember, if I get better, this doesn't count!"

We smile. Yet what a clear picture this gives of how we sometimes treat one another! The forgiveness we profess is superficial. It's prompted by fear, to gain some selfish advantage, or to clear our conscience—not out of genuine love for God and the one who has wronged us. Yes, we may *say* we forgive, but when the least little friction arises, how quick we are to resurrect past grievances! We like to "bury the hatchet" but leave the handle sticking out. How different is the forgiveness Jesus was talking about in Matthew 18!

And in Ephesians, Paul left no doubt about the nature of genuine forgiveness when he said, "just as in Christ God forgave you" (4:32). That means forgive—and forget.

RICHARD DeHAAN

To forgive and forget is far better than to resent and remember.

Peace and Reconciliation

MATTHEW 18:21–35

"Shouldn't you have had mercy on your fellow servant just as I had on you?"
MATTHEW 18:33

When the US Civil War ended in 1865, more than half a million soldiers lay dead, the economy was shattered, and people remained deeply divided politically. But two women sought peace and reconciliation during this time of anguish—and Mother's Day was born in the USA. In 1870, Julia Ward Howe called for an International Mother's Day on which women would unite in opposing war in all its forms. A few years later, Anna Reeves Jarvis began her annual Mother's Friendship Day in an effort to reunite families and neighbors alienated by the war. There is always great suffering when friends and families are fractured and unwilling to forgive.

The gospel of Jesus Christ also brings the promise of peace and reconciliation. But this is in the all-important aspect of peace with God and with each other. When Peter asked Jesus how often he should forgive a brother who sinned against him (Matthew 18:21), the Lord surprised everyone with His answer of "seventy times seven" (v. 22 NKJV). Then He told an unforgettable story about a servant who had received forgiveness and failed to pass it on (vv. 23–35). As God freely forgives us, so He requires that we extend what we have received to others.

With God's love and power, forgiveness is always possible.

DAVID MCCASLAND

Forgiveness is Christianity in action.

Should I Forgive?

MATTHEW 18:23-35

Forgive as the Lord forgave you.
COLOSSIANS 3:13

I arrived early at my church to help set up for an event. A woman stood crying at the opposite end of the sanctuary. She had been cruel and gossiped about me in the past, so I quickly drowned out her sobs with a vacuum cleaner. Why should I care about someone who didn't like me?

When the Holy Spirit reminded me how much God had forgiven me, I crossed the room. The woman shared that her baby had been in the hospital for months. We cried, embraced, and prayed for her daughter. After working through our differences, we're now good friends.

In Matthew 18, Jesus compares the kingdom of heaven to a king who decided to settle his accounts. A servant who owed a staggering amount of money pleaded for mercy. Soon after the king canceled his debt, that servant tracked down and condemned a man who owed him far less than what he had owed the king. When word got back to the king, the wicked servant was imprisoned because of his unforgiving spirit (vv. 23–34).

Choosing to forgive doesn't condone sin, excuse the wrongs done to us, or minimize our hurts. Offering forgiveness simply frees us to enjoy God's undeserved gift of mercy as we invite Him to accomplish beautiful works of peace-restoring grace in our lives and our relationships.

XOCHITL DIXON

Forgiving others expresses our trust in God's right to judge according to His perfection and goodness.

The Children's Friend

MATTHEW 19:13–15

Jesus said, "Let the little children come to me, and do not hinder them, for the kingdom of heaven belongs to such as these."
MATTHEW 19:14

One of the great storytellers of children's literature is Hans Christian Andersen. The lessons and encouragement contained in his tales of *The Ugly Duckling, The Little Mermaid*, and *The Emperor's New Clothes* are still considered a great gift to children everywhere.

I'm reminded, however, that Jesus Christ is the greatest friend of children the world has ever known. No one has done more for them than Jesus.

When Jesus's disciples reprimanded people for bringing little ones to Him, the Lord said, "Let the little children come to me, and do not hinder them, for the kingdom of heaven belongs to such as these" (Matthew 19:14).

Jesus valued children as persons of worth. After His triumphal entry into Jerusalem, the Lord accepted the praise of children and reminded those who criticized them that God has ordained praise even "from the lips of children and infants" (Matthew 21:16; see Psalm 8:2).

Companionship with the Savior is the privilege of everyone who trusts Him with the simple faith of a child. His loving arms and tender heart are ready to embrace every child who accepts Him. He willingly receives all who open their hearts to Him. He is the children's Friend.

DAVID MCCASLAND

**The Creator hides secrets from sages,
yet He can be known by children.**

I'm Good

MATTHEW 19:16–26

*"Why do you ask me about what is good?" Jesus replied.
"There is only One who is good. If you want to enter life,
keep the commandments."*

MATTHEW 19:17

When someone asks, "How are you?" it has become common for the response to be, "I'm good." When we say this, we are really saying, "I'm well" or "I'm doing fine," speaking of our general well-being and not our character. I have answered with that response more times than I can count, but lately it has begun to bother me. Whether we realize it or not, we are saying something specific when we use the word *good*.

Jesus once encountered a wealthy young man who called Him "Good Teacher" (Matthew 19:16 NKJV). The young man was right, for Jesus is both good (completely perfect) and the Teacher. He is the only One who can truly make that claim.

The Lord, however, challenged the man to think about what he was saying in using that term *good*. "So He said to him, 'Why do you call Me good? No one is good but One, that is, God. But if you want to enter into life, keep the commandments'" (v. 17 NKJV). Jesus wanted the man to understand that the assertion he was making needed to be taken seriously. Jesus can be called "good" because He is God.

Next time someone asks you, "How are you?" it is great to be able to say, "I'm well." But remember, only Jesus is truly good.

BILL CROWDER

God is great and God is good, but without Him we are neither.

Comparison Obsession

MATTHEW 20:1–16

"Don't I have the right to do what I want with my own money?
Or are you envious because I am generous?"

MATTHEW 20:15

Thomas J. DeLong, a professor at Harvard Business School, has noted a disturbing trend among his students and colleagues—a "comparison obsession." He writes: "More so than ever before, . . . business executives, Wall Street analysts, lawyers, doctors, and other professionals are obsessed with comparing their own achievements against those of others. . . . This is bad for individuals and bad for companies. When you define success based on external rather than internal criteria, you diminish your satisfaction and commitment."

Comparison obsession isn't new. The Scriptures warn us of the dangers of comparing ourselves to others. When we do so, we become proud and look down on them (Luke 18:9–14). Or we become jealous and want to be like them or have what they have (James 4:1). We fail to focus on what God has given us to do. Jesus indicated that comparison obsession comes from believing that God is unfair and that He doesn't have a right to be more generous to others than He is to us (Matthew 20:1–16).

By God's grace we can learn to overcome comparison obsession by focusing on the life God has given to us. As we take moments to thank God for everyday blessings, we change our thinking and begin to believe deep down that God is good.

MARVIN WILLIAMS

God expresses His goodness to His children in His own way.

Servants Anonymous

MATTHEW 20:17–28

"Whoever wants to be great must become a servant."
MATTHEW 20:27 (MSG)

A truly humble person will want to do things for others without calling attention to himself or to his deeds.

Jean Frederic Oberlin, a minister in eighteenth-century Germany, was traveling by foot in winter when he was caught in a severe snowstorm. He soon lost his way in the blowing snow and feared he would freeze to death. In despair he sat down, not knowing which way to turn. Just then, a man came along in a wagon and rescued Oberlin. He took him to the next village and made sure he would be cared for.

As the man prepared to journey on, Oberlin said, "Tell me your name so I may at least have you in grateful remembrance before God." The man, who by now had recognized Oberlin, replied, "You are a minister. Please tell me the name of the Good Samaritan." Oberlin said, "I cannot do that, for it is not given in the Scriptures." His benefactor responded, "Until you can tell me his name, please permit me to withhold mine."

Jesus is our example. He did not come to be praised and served, but to serve others unselfishly (Matthew 20:28). That same quality should mark our service as well.

It doesn't matter whether people know our name or not as long as the kindness we show reminds them of Jesus.

PAUL VAN GORDER

When we forget about ourselves, we do things others will remember.

Power That Corrupts

MATTHEW 20:20–28

"The Son of Man did not come to be served, but to serve."
MATTHEW 20:28

What does it take to disrupt the good work of a church? Just one power-hungry person.

One of my college friends, a pastor, wrote to me about a disruption in his church. People had come to faith in Christ, and membership had quadrupled. The members were active in serving the church and community.

But then one man in a leadership position began to envy the pastor's influence. He felt he deserved more power, so he began to tear down the pastor—thinking that would increase his own stature. It didn't matter to him what he was doing to God's work; he wanted power and recognition. He caused such an uproar that my friend finally had to resign.

When it comes to serving Christ, we have no right to seek power. We have no calling for prestige. We have no reason to look for self-aggrandizement and recognition. How much better to serve quietly in the background, keeping in mind that Jesus, our example, "did not come to be served, but to serve" (Matthew 20:28).

Are you a pastor? A teacher? A deacon? A missionary? A church member? If you look for power, you may get it, but it will become power that disrupts the good work of your church ministry.

DAVE BRANON

We lose the approval of God when we seek the applause of people.

Time for Compassion

MATTHEW 20:29-34

Jesus had compassion on them and touched their eyes.
MATTHEW 20:34

You have a full day of activity lined up—washing, shopping, errands—when your neighbor calls and invites you over for coffee. You don't think she's a believer in Christ, and you've been praying for a chance to talk with her. You know she's been having a rough time.

Or a friend asks if you will consider being a big brother to a teenager who desperately needs a father figure. It will take precious hours out of your day.

Jesus often interrupted His schedule to minister to people He met along the way. In Matthew 20:29–34, we read that He stopped and healed two blind men who called for His help, ignoring the crowd that tried to keep the two quiet. On another occasion, Jesus rebuked His disciples for keeping little children away from Him (Luke 18:15–17).

Author Henri Nouwen mirrored this sense of service. For the last ten years of his life he ministered at a home for the seriously disabled, taking two hours every morning to bathe, shave, dress, and feed a profoundly disabled man.

Serving a man incapable of responding is a perfect example of true compassion. But when we look at the example Jesus set, we learn that love and service are just what He has called us to do!

DAVID EGNER

We serve God by serving others.

Who Are You?

MATTHEW 21:1–11

When Jesus entered Jerusalem,
the whole city was stirred and asked,
"Who is this?"

MATTHEW 21:10

From time to time, we read of people who are offended at not being treated with what they consider due respect and deference. "Do you know who I am?" they shout indignantly. And we are reminded of the statement, "If you have to tell people who you are, you probably really aren't who you think you are." The polar opposite of this arrogance and self-importance is seen in Jesus, even as His life on earth was nearing its end.

Jesus entered Jerusalem to shouts of praise from the people (Matthew 21:7–9). When others throughout the city asked, "Who is this?" the crowds answered, "This is Jesus, the prophet from Nazareth in Galilee" (vv. 10–11). He didn't come claiming special privileges, but in humility He came to give His life in obedience to His Father's will.

The words Jesus said and the things He did commanded respect. Unlike insecure rulers, He never demanded that others respect Him. His greatest hours of suffering appeared to be His lowest point of weakness and failure. Yet the strength of His identity and mission carried Jesus through the darkest hours as He died for our sins so we could live in His love.

He is worthy of our lives and our devotion today. Do we recognize who He is?

DAVID MCCASLAND

When once you have seen Jesus, you can never be the same.
—Oswald Chambers

Young Teachers

MATTHEW 21:12–16

*"From the lips of children and infants you,
Lord, have called forth your praise."*

MATTHEW 21:16

Children seem to be more comfortable using computers than their parents are. Because of this, a manufacturer trying to increase sales to adults advertised a certain computer with the slogan: "So easy, even an adult can operate it!" (And if they still have problems, they can ask their children.)

This isn't the first time adults have had something to learn from children. When Jesus came to Jerusalem and performed healings in the temple, it was the children who were quick to recognize who He was and to shout, "Hosanna to the Son of David!" (Matthew 21:15).

The chief priests and scribes, though, weren't willing to listen and learn from the children. They refused to take Jesus seriously. Instead, they took Him to task by asking, "Do you hear what these children are saying?" "Yes!" Jesus replied. Then, quoting from Psalm 8:2, He said, "Have you never read, 'From the lips of children and infants you, Lord, have called forth your praise'?" (Matthew 21:16).

Those of us who have reached adulthood should remind ourselves that we don't know it all. Let's be humble enough to listen and learn something God wants to teach us through the faith of a child.

JOANIE YODER

Big lessons can be learned from little children.

Words and Actions

MATTHEW 21:28–32

"'Let us not love with words or speech but with actions and in truth.'"
1 JOHN 3:18

The email from the student in my college writing class expressed urgency. It was the end of the semester, and he realized he needed a better grade to participate in sports. What could he do? He had missed some assignments, so I gave him two days to complete those papers and improve his grade. His response: "Thank you. I'll do it."

Two days—and the deadline—passed, and no papers appeared. He didn't back up his words with action.

Jesus told about a young man who did something similar. The boy's dad asked him to do some work in the vineyard. The son said, "I will, sir" (Matthew 21:30). But he was all talk and no action.

In commenting on this parable, Matthew Henry concluded: "Buds and blossoms are not fruit." The buds and blossoms of our words, which breed anticipation of what we might do, are empty without the fruit of our follow-through. Jesus's main application was to religious leaders who spoke of obedience yet refused to follow through with repentance. But the words apply to us as well. It is in following God "with actions and in truth" (1 John 3:18)—not in making empty promises—that we honor our Lord and Savior.

Our actions in obeying God show Him more love, honor, and praise than any empty words we might say to try to appear good.

DAVE BRANON

Words are the blossoms; action, the fruit.

Bring Them In!

MATTHEW 22:1–10

"'Compel them to come in, so that my house will be full.'"
LUKE 14:23

If we put up a beautiful building, hang out a sign, and put an ad on social media, will people who don't know Jesus flock to church? Probably not. There is sense in which we must reach out personally to friends and neighbors to introduce them to the gospel.

In Dwight L. Moody's day (late nineteenth century), it was a common practice for people to rent a church pew. One Sunday morning, nineteen-year-old Moody marched down the aisle with a motley crew of Chicago's outcasts trailing behind him. He had rented four pews and was determined to fill them with those who were spiritually needy. Having taken the Savior's "go and make disciples" personally (Matthew 28:19), he literally "went out into the streets and gathered all the people [he] could find" (22:10).

Jesus's words in Matthew 28:19 don't apply only to missionaries in faraway places. All of us as followers of Jesus are to share the good news of salvation. Ask the Lord to place a burden on your heart for a friend or loved one who needs to hear about Jesus.

RICHARD DEHAAN

We must go to sinners if we expect sinners to come to the Savior.

Two Kingdoms

MATTHEW 22:15–22

"Give back to Caesar what is Caesar's, and to God what is God's."
MATTHEW 22:21

In a report in *USA Today*, Rick Hampson wrote: "The young generally don't have the old-time political religion. They look at voting and see a quaint, irrational act." One graduate was quoted as saying, "I don't care enough to care about why I don't care." I wonder if this is how we as Jesus-followers sometimes view our civic responsibility!

The insights of Jesus in Matthew 22 helped His followers think clearly about their civic duty in the world. The Jews were required to pay taxes to the Roman government. They hated this taxation because the money went directly into Caesar's treasury, where some of it supported the pagan temples and decadent lifestyle of the Roman aristocracy. They may have questioned whether they even had a civic responsibility to Caesar. Jesus reminded them, however, that they had dual citizenship. They lived in a world with two kingdoms—Caesar's kingdom (human authority) and God's kingdom (spiritual authority). They had responsibilities to both, but their greater responsibility was to God and His kingdom (Acts 5:28–29).

As followers of Christ, we are commanded to cooperate with our rulers, but we are called to give God our ultimate obedience and commitment.

MARVIN WILLIAMS

Government has authority, but God has ultimate authority.

Heading for a Wedding

MATTHEW 22:23–33

Let us rejoice and be glad and give him glory! For the wedding of the Lamb has come, and his bride has made herself ready.

REVELATION 19:7

After the death of her beloved husband, a certain Christian woman felt saddened by these words of Jesus: "At the resurrection people will neither marry nor be given in marriage" (Matthew 22:30). Intensely missing her husband and the life they had enjoyed together, she thought of heaven without marriage as drab compared to the satisfying life she and her husband cherished on earth.

During the early days of my own widowhood, I fully accepted the reality of heaven without marriage. Yet I felt I was overlooking something vital. And I was! While meditating one day on God's promises about heaven, my earthbound brain woke up to the realization that Jesus didn't say heaven would be without marriage, only without earthly marriage. In Revelation 19:6–9, we're told that everyone heading for heaven is heading for a celestial wedding, banquet and all! It's the long-planned marriage of God's Lamb to His long-prepared bride, God's redeemed people.

As we continue to get ready for it, let's remember this: Although the marriage of the Lamb is wonderfully foreshadowed by Christian marriage on earth (Ephesians 5:23–27), it is an event all redeemed people can look forward to. It's our wedding!

JOANIE YODER

Even so, come, Lord Jesus!
—Revelation 22:20 NKJV

Two Rules to Live By

MATTHEW 22:34–40

"All the Law and the Prophets hang on these two commandments."
MATTHEW 22:40

Have you ever felt overwhelmed by rules and expectations? Think of how the Jewish people must have felt as they tried to keep up with more than six hundred rules from the Old Testament and many more that had been imposed on them by the religious leaders of their day. And imagine their surprise when Jesus simplified the pursuit of righteousness by narrowing the list down to just two—"love the Lord your God" (Matthew 22:37) and "love your neighbor as yourself" (v. 39).

In essence, Jesus is telling us that the way God knows we love Him is by how we treat people. All of them. Let's face it—loving our neighbor can be a challenge. But when we do it to express our love to God, we unleash a powerful motivation that helps us love whether the person deserves it or not. As we love God and our neighbor, everything else falls into place. If I love my neighbor, I won't bear false witness against him, covet his wealth or his wife, or steal from him. Loving others for God's sake even provides the grace and strength to forgive those who have heaped injustices on us.

Who needs to see God's love today through you? The more unlovable the person, the greater the statement about how much you love God!

JOE STOWELL

Loving God is the key to loving others.

Best in Show?

MATTHEW 23:1-12

The LORD said to Samuel, "Do not consider his appearance or his height, for I have rejected him. The LORD does not look at the things people look at. People look at the outward appearance, but the LORD looks at the heart."

1 SAMUEL 16:7

I enjoy watching dog shows on TV. The dog owners are impeccably dressed and trot along with their pedigreed pooches as they show off their unique canine beauty. The dogs have been trained to stand confidently with chins lifted high, their shiny coats carefully brushed and styled. To me, they all look like winners.

But I wonder sometimes, when their audience is gone, what are these dogs really like? Do they ever relax and let their sleek fur get so matted they're mistaken for mutts? Does their doggie breath start smelling foul?

More important, what are we really like when nobody's watching? In Matthew 23:2–7, Jesus rebuked those who were interested in how they looked in public rather than how they were seen by God. He wants us to be obedient, faithful, and committed to Him—even when nobody else sees. The Pharisees focused on the way they were perceived by other people. God's focus is on what we're like inside. His desire is for us to look like His Son.

We're not in a competition with other Christians. God will never ask us to compete for "best in show." He measures us by the perfect standard of His Son (Ephesians 4:13). And in love, He provides the righteousness we need so that we can be blameless before Him (Colossians 1:21–23).

CINDY HESS KASPER

Living for God's approval is better than living for man's applause.

Looking Good

MATTHEW 23:23–31

"First clean the inside."
MATTHEW 23:26

"Your hair is really healthy," said my hairdresser after giving me a haircut. "I hope it's because you use our products." "No. I'm sorry," I said. "I just use whatever product is cheap and smells good." But then I added, "I try to eat well. I think that makes a big difference."

When I think about the things we do to make ourselves look good, I'm reminded of some of the things we do to make ourselves look good spiritually. Jesus addressed this issue with the religious leaders in Jerusalem (Matthew 23). They followed an elaborate set of religious rules that went well beyond the ones God had given them. They worked hard to look good to their peers, to prove that they were better than others. But their hard work didn't impress God. Jesus said to them, "You clean the outside of the cup and dish, but inside [you] are full of greed and self-indulgence" (v. 25). What the Pharisees did to make themselves look good to others actually revealed that they were not good at all.

Every culture values different religious behaviors and traditions, but God's values transcend cultures. And what He values isn't measured by what others see. God values a clean heart and pure motives. Spiritual health is expressed from the inside out.

JULIE ACKERMAN LINK

**We might look good on the outside
without really being good on the inside.**

A Change of Heart

MATTHEW 23:25-28

*"First clean the inside of the cup and dish,
and then the outside also will be clean."*

MATTHEW 23:26

Have you heard about the man who took his old car to a dealer and asked him to sell it for him? When the dealer asked how many miles were on it, the man replied, "It's got 230,000." The salesman replied, "It'll never sell unless you turn back the mileage." So the man left with the car.

When the salesman hadn't heard from the man for several weeks, he called him. "I thought you were going to sell that old car."

"I don't have to anymore," came the reply. "It's only got 77,000 miles on it now. Why should I sell it?"

Is it possible people are doing something similar regarding faith? Could people be fooling themselves into thinking they're pleasing God by just changing their external behavior when what they need is a new heart.

That old car still had a sick engine, bad rings, and a transmission that slipped. Turning back its odometer had not changed anything! In the same way, if we try to please God by living a good life without first trusting in Christ, we are like the Pharisees who were clean on the outside but still filthy on the inside (Matthew 23:25).

Good works can't change your heart. Only personal faith in Christ brings cleansing inside and out. Then your good works and righteous life will be pleasing to God.

DAVID EGNER

We're saved by God's good work, not by our good works.

Barrier-Free Love

MATTHEW 23:37–39

"Jerusalem . . . how often I have longed to gather your children together, as a hen gathers her chicks under her wings, and you were not willing."
MATTHEW 23:37

Not long ago I heard the distressed chirping of a bird coming from the side of my neighbor's house. I discovered that a nest of baby birds was inside a vent covered by a screen, placing a barrier between the mother bird and her hungry chicks. After I told the neighbors, they removed the screen.

Few things are as heartbreaking as a barrier to love. Christ, the long-awaited Messiah of Israel, experienced a barrier to His love when His chosen people rejected Him. He used the word picture of a hen and her baby chicks to describe their unwillingness to receive it: "Jerusalem, Jerusalem . . . how often I have longed to gather your children together, as a hen gathers her chicks under her wings, and you were not willing" (Matthew 23:37).

Our sin is a barrier that separates us from God (Isaiah 59:2). But "God so loved the world that he gave his one and only Son, that whoever believes in him shall not perish but have eternal life" (John 3:16). Jesus took care of the barrier to God's love by His sacrificial death on the cross and His resurrection (Romans 5:8–17; 8:11). Now He longs for us to experience His love and accept this gift.

DENNIS FISHER

Through His cross, Jesus rescues and redeems.

Day Unknown

MATTHEW 24:1–8

"About that day or hour no one knows, not even the angels in heaven, nor the Son, but only the Father."

MATTHEW 24:36

To many Londoners, 1666 looked like the year when Jesus would return. Prophecy enthusiasts had added 1,000 years since Christ's birth to 666, the number of Antichrist, to arrive at the date 1666.

The world did seem to be on the verge of destruction when in 1665 a plague claimed the lives of 100,000 people in London. Then in September 1666, a London fire destroyed tens of thousands of buildings. Some wondered, *Didn't the Bible predict catastrophes at the end of the world?* (see Matthew 24:1–8). Yet the year 1666 passed, and life went on seemingly as it had before.

Even in our own day, there are those who have predicted the end of the world. A date is predicted, the media covers the frenzy, and then that day passes uneventfully.

In God's wisdom, the actual time of Christ's return has been kept from us. Jesus said, "But about that day or hour no one knows, not even the angels in heaven, nor the Son, but only the Father" (Matthew 24:36). This any-moment aspect of Jesus's return helps keep believers motivated in Christian service and spiritual growth all the time—not just near a certain date (25:1–13; 1 John 3:2–3). Be assured, Christ's personal return will take place. And as we await that day, our lives should be marked by "holy conduct and godliness" (2 Peter 3:11 NKJV).

DENNIS FISHER

No doctrine is more closely linked to practical daily living than that of the Lord's return.

The Eleventh Hour

MATTHEW 24:3-14

Nation will not take up sword against nation,
nor will they train for war anymore.

ISAIAH 2:4

World War I has been ranked by many as one of the deadliest conflicts in human history. Millions lost their lives in the first global modern war. On November 11, 1918, a ceasefire was observed on the eleventh hour of the eleventh day of the eleventh month. During that historic moment, millions around the world observed moments of silence while they reflected upon the war's terrible cost—the loss of life and suffering. It was hoped that "the Great War," as it was called, would truly be "the war to end all wars."

Despite the many deadly military conflicts that have followed, the hope for lasting peace has not faded. And the Bible offers a hopeful and realistic promise that someday wars will finally end. When Christ returns, Isaiah's prophecy will come true: "Nation will not take up sword against nation, nor will they train for war anymore" (Isaiah 2:4). Then the eleventh hour will pass and the first hour of lasting peace in a new heaven and new earth will begin.

Until that day comes, those who follow Christ are to be people who represent the Prince of Peace in the way we conduct our lives and in the way we make a difference in our world.

DENNIS FISHER

Only in Christ can true peace be realized.

A Discerning Eye

MATTHEW 24:3–24

"Watch out that no one deceives you."
MATTHEW 24:4

Seeing used to be believing, but not anymore. With today's computer technology, anyone can easily change a photographic image.

Perhaps you've seen the altered photo of Churchill, Roosevelt, and Stalin at the Yalta Conference. Stalin has been replaced by Groucho Marx, and behind the Big Three stands a stone-faced Sylvester Stallone. The scene looks real, but it isn't. Because things are not always what they appear to be, it requires a discerning eye to separate fact from fiction.

In answer to the disciples' question about the sign of His coming and the end of the age, Jesus told them, "Watch out that no one deceives you. . . . False messiahs and false prophets will appear and perform great signs and wonders to deceive, if possible, even the elect" (Matthew 24:4, 24).

Notice that the appeal is visual rather than verbal. There will be amazing sights, but like altered photographs they will not be what they appear to be. These "signs" will be the work of false prophets, not of true representatives of God.

The disciples were warned by Jesus's words, and the same is true for us today. Every event must be seen and evaluated in the light of the Bible. The closer we come to Christ's return, the more we need a discerning eye.

DAVID McCASLAND

To detect error, expose it to the light of God's Truth.

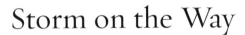

Storm on the Way

MATTHEW 24:15-27

*"For then there will be great distress,
unequaled from the beginning of the world until now—
and never to be equaled again."*

MATTHEW 24:21

In 1895, the president of the Graham and Morton Transportation Company decided to send one of his wooden ships on a daring mid-winter crossing of Lake Michigan. But early on the morning of departure, he panicked when he read the barometer. It was at 28, the lowest he had ever seen. It meant that a terrible storm was coming. Immediately he sent a telegram to the dock in Milwaukee, ordering the ship to stay in port. The message arrived too late—moments after the ship had cleared the harbor.

Later that morning the storm broke in full fury, smashing the ship against massive ice floes, and sending it to an icy grave. A bottle was found on shore with this note: "All is lost . . . . Captain and Clark are swept off and we have a hard time of it—10:15 o'clock. Goodbye."

For the sinful and rebellious of this world, a terrible storm of judgment is coming, but the biblical warnings of the great tribulation seem remote and irrelevant. Many people live in relative peace, and the world's trouble spots of conflict and violence seem far away. Most people are complacent and see no cause for concern. But the wrath of God will fall. He will judge this sinful world. Christians must send the warning before it's too late: A storm is on the way!

DAVID EGNER

**If sinners are to escape God's judgment,
God's people must point the way.**

Once upon a Time

MATTHEW 24:32–44

*Now the LORD provided a huge fish to swallow Jonah,
and Jonah was in the belly of the fish three days and three nights.*
JONAH 1:17

Some people say that the Bible is just a collection of fairy tales. A boy slaying a giant. A man swallowed by a big fish. Noah's boat-building experience. Even some religious people think that these events are just nice stories with a good moral.

Jesus himself, however, spoke of both Noah's flood and Jonah's fish visit as actual events. He said, "As it was in the days of Noah, so it will be at the coming of the Son of Man. For in the days before the flood, people were eating and drinking, marrying and giving in marriage, up to the day Noah entered the ark; and they knew nothing about what would happen until the flood came and took them all away. That is how it will be at the coming of the Son of Man" (Matthew 24:37–39). His return will happen when we're not expecting it.

Jesus compared Jonah's three days inside the big fish to the three days He would experience in the grave before His resurrection (Matthew 12:40). And Peter talked about Noah and the flood when he equated it to a future day when Jesus comes back (2 Peter 2:4–9).

God gave us His Word. It's a book filled with truth—not fairy tales. And one day we will live happily ever after with Him when Jesus comes again and receives His children to himself.

CINDY HESS KASPER

We have reason for optimism if we're looking for Christ's return.

Ready for the Wedding

MATTHEW 25:1–13

"Therefore keep watch, because you do not know the day or the hour."
MATTHEW 25:13

"I'm hungry," said my eight-year-old daughter. "I'm sorry," I said. "I don't have anything for you. Let's play tic-tac-toe." We had been waiting over an hour for the bride to arrive at the church for what was supposed to be a noon wedding. As I wondered how much longer it would be, I hoped I could occupy my daughter until the wedding started.

As we waited, I felt like we were enacting a parable. Although the vicarage where we live is a stone's throw from the church, I knew if I went to fetch some crackers, the bride could come at any moment and I would miss her entrance. As I employed many distraction techniques with my hungry daughter, I also thought about Jesus's parable about the ten virgins (Matthew 25:1–13). Five came prepared with enough oil for their lamps to stay lit as they waited for the bridegroom, but five did not. Just as it was too late for me to dash back to the vicarage, so it was too late for the young women to go and buy more oil for their lamps.

Jesus told this parable to emphasize that we need to be prepared, for when He comes again we will give an account over the state of our hearts. Are we waiting and ready?

AMY BOUCHER PYE

We need to be ready for Christ to come again.

Still Working

MATTHEW 25:14–21

"Well done, good and faithful servant!"
MATTHEW 25:23

Vivian and Don are in their late 90s and have been married for eighty years. Recently Vivian suffered a setback when she broke her hip. That has been additionally difficult because for several years both Don and Vivian were saddened by the realization that they were no longer strong enough to be active in the life and work of their church.

However, Vivian and Don remained hard at work for the Lord as prayer warriors. While they can no longer be present and visible in the life of the church, they are faithful "behind the scenes" in their service for Him.

The parable of the talents in Matthew 25 reminds us that we must use the "talents" God has given us wisely. All of us have God-given skills and abilities at various levels—and we must not bury, unused, what God has given us.

It is not only in years of strength that God will use us but also in years of sickness and weakness. Vivian and Don continue to serve by praying. And like them, we honor our Savior by using our skills—"each according to his ability" (v. 15) to serve Him who is worthy.

DAVE BRANON

God can use you at any age—if you are willing.

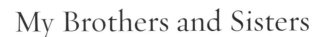

My Brothers and Sisters

MATTHEW 25:31–40

*"Whatever you did for one of the least of these brothers
and sisters of mine, you did for me."*

MATTHEW 25:40

Several years ago when the Southern California economy took a downturn, Pastor Bob Johnson saw not only difficulty but also opportunity. So he scheduled a meeting with the mayor of his city and asked, "What can our church do to help you?" The mayor was astonished. People usually came to him for help. Here was a minister offering him the services of an entire congregation.

Together the mayor and pastor came up with a plan to address several pressing needs. In their county alone, more than 20,000 seniors had gone the previous year without a single visitor. Hundreds of foster children needed families. And many other kids needed tutoring to help them succeed in school. Some of those needs could be addressed without much financial investment, but they all required time and interest. And that's what the church had to give.

Jesus told His disciples about a future day in which He would say to His faithful followers, "Come, you who are blessed by my Father; take your inheritance" (Matthew 25:34). He also said they would express surprise at their reward. Then He would tell them, "Whatever you did for one of the least of these brothers and sisters of mine, you did for me" (v. 40).

God's kingdom work gets done when we give generously of the time, love, and resources He has provided us.

TIM GUSTAFSON

Giving isn't just for the wealthy; it's for all of us.

The Arlington Ladies

MATTHEW 26:6–13

"Truly I tell you, wherever this gospel is preached throughout the world, what she has done will also be told, in memory of her."
MATTHEW 26:13

In 1948, the US Air Force Chief of Staff noticed that no one attended the funeral of an airman at Arlington National Cemetery, and that deeply disturbed him. He talked with his wife about his concern that each soldier be honored at burial, and she began a group called the Arlington Ladies.

Someone from the group honors each deceased soldier by attending his or her funeral. The ladies also write personal notes of sympathy and speak words of gratitude to family members when they are present. If possible, a representative keeps in contact with the family for months afterward.

Margaret Mensch, an Arlington Lady, says, "The important thing is to be there for the families. . . . It's an honor to . . . pay tribute to the everyday heroes that make up the armed forces."

We see clearly in Matthew 26:13 that Jesus showed the importance of paying tribute. After a woman poured a costly, fragrant oil on His head, He said she would be honored for many years to come. The disciples were indignant and thought her act was wasteful, but Jesus called it "a beautiful thing" (v. 10) for which she would be remembered.

We know heroes who have given their lives in service to God and their country. Let's honor them by paying them appropriate tribute.

ANNE CETAS

We honor God when we honor one another.

Praise in the Dark

MATTHEW 26:17–30

God has said, "Never will I leave you; never will I forsake you."
HEBREWS 13:5

Even though my friend Mickey was losing his eyesight, he told me, "I'm going to keep praising God every day because He's done so much for me."

Jesus gave Mickey, and us, the ultimate reason for such never-ending praise. The twenty-sixth chapter of Matthew tells us about how Jesus shared the Passover meal with His disciples the night before He went to the cross. Verse 30 shows us how they concluded the meal: "When they had sung a hymn, they went out to the Mount of Olives."

It wasn't just any hymn they sang that night—it was a hymn of praise. For millennia, Jews have sung a group of Psalms called "The Hallel" at Passover (*hallel* is the Hebrew word for "praise"). The last of these prayers and songs of praise, found in Psalms 113–118, honors God, who has become our salvation (118:21). It refers to a rejected stone that became a cornerstone (v. 22) and one who comes in the name of the Lord (v. 26). They may very well have sung, "This is the day the LORD has made; we will rejoice and be glad in it" (v. 24 NKJV).

As Jesus sang with His disciples on this Passover night, He was giving us the ultimate reason to lift our eyes above our immediate circumstances. He was leading us in praise of the never-ending love and faithfulness of our God.

JAMES BANKS

Praising God helps us recall His goodness that never ends.

World's Longest Table

MATTHEW 26:26–30

"I tell you, I will not drink from this fruit of the vine from now on until that day when I drink it new with you in my Father's kingdom."

MATTHEW 26:29

A few years ago, one of the busiest highways in Europe became what some called "the longest table in the world." Officials closed a sixty-kilometer (thirty-seven-mile) section of the A40 Autobahn in Germany's Ruhr region so people could walk and bicycle or sit at one of 20,000 tables set up on the roadway. An estimated two million people came to enjoy an event the director hoped would connect people from many cultures, generations, and nations.

This event made me think of an even grander table around which believers gather to share the Lord's Supper. During communion, we remember Jesus's death for us as we anticipate the culmination of history at His return.

Just before Jesus was crucified, He shared the Passover meal with His disciples, telling them, "I will not drink from this fruit of the vine from now on until that day when I drink it new with you in my Father's kingdom" (Matthew 26:29).

The Lord's Table unites everyone Christ has redeemed by His blood "from every tribe and language and people and nation" (Revelation 5:9). One day, in a scene of reunion and joy, all who belong to Jesus will sit down together with Him at a table that will dwarf the Autobahn gathering. We joyfully anticipate sharing that table together!

DAVID MCCASLAND

Christ's love creates unity out of diversity.

When Not to Witness

MATTHEW 26:57–64

But Jesus remained silent. The high priest said to him, "I charge you under oath by the living God: Tell us if you are the Messiah, the Son of God."
MATTHEW 26:63

Here in New England where I live, baseball is a near-religious pursuit. Even if it were against the law to talk about the Boston Red Sox while at work, the fans couldn't stop—they love their team that much.

That raises a question in my mind for Christians: Are there times when a Christian shouldn't talk about God? I think so. In the face of insincere challenges to our faith, silence may often be the best response. In the hostile situation of Jesus's exchange with the high priest Caiaphas, He chose silence at first (Matthew 26:63). He understood that Caiaphas wasn't interested in the truth (v. 59). While we don't always know another's heart, we must be sensitive to the leading of the Spirit in every situation so we "may know how to answer everyone" (Colossians 4:6).

Also, if an answer to a question will move the discussion down a rabbit trail and away from Christ, we might want to stop the conversation and pick it up another day.

Are there other times when silence may be best? If talking about faith distracts us or co-workers from performing our job, we should stay focused on our work. Or if someone has shown a continual resistance, we might choose to stop pressing that person. Remember, we can be a witness of God's grace with our conduct as well as with our words (1 Peter 3:1–2).

RANDY KILGORE

Silence can be one tool in evangelism.

All of Me

MATTHEW 27:45–54

*Therefore, I urge you, brothers and sisters, in view of God's mercy,
to offer your bodies as a living sacrifice, holy and pleasing to God—
this is your true and proper worship.*

ROMANS 12:1

Young Isaac Watts found the music in his church sadly lacking, and his father challenged him to create something better. Isaac did. His hymn "When I Survey the Wondrous Cross" has been called by some the greatest in the English language.

Watts's worshipful third verse ushers us into the presence of Christ at the crucifixion.

*See from His head, His hands, His feet,
Sorrow and love flow mingled down.
Did e'er such love and sorrow meet,
Or thorns compose so rich a crown?*

The crucifixion Watts describes so elegantly stands as history's most awful moment. The Son of God strains for breath, held by crude spikes driven through His flesh. After tortured hours, a supernatural darkness descends. Finally, mercifully, the Lord of the universe dismisses His anguished spirit. An earthquake rattles the landscape. Back in the city the thick temple curtain rips in half. Graves open, and dead bodies resurrect, walking about the city (Matthew 27:51–53). These events compel the centurion who crucified Jesus to say, "Surely he was the Son of God!" (v. 54).

Watts's song could only conclude: "Love so amazing, so divine demands my soul, my life, my all."

TIM GUSTAFSON

**It is our privilege to give everything we have
to the One who gave us everything on the cross.**

Is There Hope?

MATTHEW 28:1–10

"He is not here; he has risen, just as he said."
MATTHEW 28:6

I sat quietly at the graveside of my father, waiting for the private family burial of my mother to begin. The funeral director carried the urn that held her ashes. My heart felt numb and my head was in a fog. How can I handle losing them both within just three months? In my grief I felt loss and loneliness and a little hopeless facing a future without them.

Then the pastor read about another graveside. On the first day of the week, early in the morning, women went to Jesus's tomb, carrying spices for His body (Matthew 28:1; Luke 24:1). There they were startled to find an open and empty tomb—and an angel. "Do not be afraid," he said to them (Matthew 28:5). They didn't need to be afraid of the empty tomb or of the angel, because he had good news for them.

Hope stirred when I heard the next words: "He is not here; he has risen, just as he said" (v. 6). Because Jesus had come back to life, death had been conquered! Jesus reminded His followers just a few days before His death: "Because I live, you also will live" (John 14:19).

Even though we grieve at the loss of our loved ones, we find hope through the resurrection of Jesus and His promise that there is life after death.

ANNE CETAS

Because He lives, we live.

A New Purpose

MARK 1:16–22

"Come, follow me," Jesus said, "and I will send you out to fish for people."
MARK 1:17

Jacob Davis was a tailor with a problem. It was the height of the Gold Rush in the 1800s American West, and the gold miners' work pants kept wearing out. His solution? Davis went to a local dry goods company owned by Levi Strauss, purchased tent cloth, and made work pants from that heavy, sturdy material—and blue jeans were born. Today, denim jeans in a variety of forms (including Levi's) are among the most popular clothing items in the world, and all because tent material was given a new purpose.

Simon and his friends were fishermen on the Sea of Galilee. Then Jesus arrived and called them to follow Him. He gave them a new purpose. No longer would they fish for fish. As Jesus told them, "Come, follow me, . . . and I will send you out to fish for people" (Mark 1:17).

With this new purpose set for their lives, these men were taught and trained by Jesus so that, after His ascension, they could be used by God to capture the hearts of people with the message of the cross and resurrection of Christ. Today, we follow in their steps as we share the good news of Christ's love and salvation.

May our lives both declare and exhibit this love that can change the lives, purposes, and eternal destinies of others.

BILL CROWDER

With our new life in Christ we have been given a new purpose.

Obey the Call

MARK 1:16–20

At once they left their nets and followed him.
MARK 1:18

I read a story about Captain Ray Baker, who flew for the Strategic Air Command during the Vietnam War. The Air Force trained him, along with the other pilots, to run out of their barracks to their planes at the sound of a buzzer. Many times during dinner he had to drop his utensils and bolt to his bomber. He had been trained to respond to the call with immediate obedience. He was so well-trained that one day while on furlough, he ran out of a restaurant when he heard a buzzer.

When Jesus called His first followers, they had an immediacy in their response to His call. The call of these fishermen was abrupt: "At once they left their nets and followed him" (Mark 1:18). The author of this account, Mark, may have wanted to impress upon his readers the authority of Jesus. When He extended the call, these men jumped to obey because helping people enter the kingdom of God was a more compelling adventure and a grander vision than catching fish.

When Jesus issues a call to follow Him, He doesn't want us to delay. He expects immediate obedience when it comes to telling others the good news. Bring someone the story of salvation today!

MARVIN WILLIAMS

Wanted: Messengers to deliver the good news.

In Search of Silence

MARK 1:35–45

I have calmed and quieted myself,
I am like a weaned child with its mother;
like a weaned child I am content.

PSALM 131:2

"My next record should be forty-five minutes of silence," said singer Meg Hutchinson, "because that's what we're missing most in society."

Silence is indeed hard to find. Cities are notoriously noisy with their high concentration of traffic and people. There seems to be no escape from loud music, loud machines, and loud voices. But the kind of noise that endangers our spiritual well-being is not the noise we can't escape but the noise we invite into our lives. Some of us use noise as a way of shutting out loneliness: voices of TV and radio personalities give us the illusion of companionship. Some of us use it as a way of shutting out our own thoughts: other voices and opinions keep us from having to think for ourselves. Some of us use noise as a way of shutting out the voice of God: constant chatter, even when we're talking about God, keeps us from hearing what God has to say.

But Jesus, even during His busiest times, made a point of seeking out places of solitude where He could carry on a conversation with God (Mark 1:35). Even if we can't find a place that is perfectly quiet, we need to find a place to quiet our souls (Psalm 131:2), a place where God has our full attention.

JULIE ACKERMAN LINK

Don't let the noise of the world keep you from
hearing the voice of the Lord.

All Rise

MARK 2:1–12

"I tell you, get up, take your mat and go home."
MARK 2:11

When I asked my husband to buy eggs on his way home so I could make cornbread for supper, he said, "I've got something better than cornbread." Coming from Jay, that was a surprising statement. But I learned what he meant when he walked into the house and handed me a fresh loaf of homemade cinnamon bread. A label on the wrapper said, "Thanks for the dough. We kneaded it." The bread was made by Sue Kehr and given as a "thank you" for a donation to a youth organization.

Sue started making bread after she had to quit her job as a nurse because of a head injury. Instead of letting circumstances pull her down when she could no longer help people in her usual ways, Sue rose to the challenge and created a unique expression of gratitude. She now makes and gives away delicious homemade bread to ministries that can then distribute the loaves to others.

Although Sue did not receive complete physical healing like the paralytic Jesus healed (Mark 2), she did rise up and cause many to be amazed at the work of God in her life.

God has something for each of us to do, despite our limitations. Rise up and ask what He might want to do through you.

JULIE ACKERMAN LINK

Step up to the tasks and do what God asks.

Follow Me

MARK 2:13–17

On hearing this, Jesus said to [the teachers of the law],
"It is not the healthy who need a doctor, but the sick.
I have not come to call the righteous, but sinners."
MARK 2:17

Health clubs offer many different programs for those who want to lose weight and stay healthy. One fitness center caters only to those who want to lose at least fifty pounds and develop a healthy lifestyle. One member says she quit her previous fitness club because she felt the slim and fit people were staring at her and judging her out-of-shape body. She now works out five days a week and is achieving healthy weight loss in a positive and welcoming environment.

Two thousand years ago, Jesus came to call the spiritually unfit to follow Him. Levi was one such person. Jesus saw him sitting in his tax collector's booth and said, "Follow me" (Mark 2:14). His words captured Levi's heart, and he followed Jesus. Tax collectors were often greedy and dishonest in their dealings and were considered religiously unclean. When the religious leaders saw Jesus having dinner at Levi's house with other tax collectors, they asked, "Why does he eat with tax collectors and sinners?" (2:16). Jesus replied, "I have not come to call the righteous, but sinners" (2:17).

Jesus came to save sinners, which includes all of us. He loves us, welcomes us into His presence, and calls us to follow Him. As we walk with Him, we grow more and more spiritually fit.

MARVIN WILLIAMS

Jesus's arms of welcome are always open.

Tell It on the Mountain

MARK 3:1–15

*"Jesus went up on a mountainside and called to him
those he wanted, and they came to him."*

MARK 3:13

I was surprised to see a nationally distributed news article commending a group of teenage snowboarders who hold weekly church services on a Colorado ski slope. In the *Summit Daily News*, Kimberly Nicoletti's story captured a wide audience with her account of teens who love to snowboard and to tell how Jesus changed their lives. Undergirding the teenagers is a Christian youth organization equipping them to demonstrate God's love.

It's easier to do things yourself than to train others, yet Jesus poured himself into a dozen disciples through whom His work would reach the world. In the midst of the pressing need of people clamoring to be healed, He climbed a mountain where "He appointed twelve that they might be with him and that he might send them out" (Mark 3:14).

One of those snowboarders in Colorado said of her discipleship training: "I've never been able to build relationships with family or friends; I've kept them at arm's length. [The program] showed me God's love. It opened me to reach out to people."

Experiencing Jesus's love and being in company with Him and His followers, we find courage to act and speak in ways that honor our Lord.

DAVID MCCASLAND

Witnessing isn't a job to be done but a life to be lived.

United in Christ

MARK 3:13–19

[Jesus] appointed twelve that they might be with him
and that he might send them out to preach.

MARK 3:14

When we come across a list of names in the Bible, we might be tempted to skip over it. But we can find treasures there, such as in the list of the twelve apostles Jesus called to serve in His name. Many are familiar—Simon whom Jesus called Peter, the rock. Brothers James and John, fishermen. Judas Iscariot, the betrayer. But we could easily overlook that Matthew the tax collector and Simon the Zealot must once have been enemies.

Matthew collected taxes for Rome, and therefore, in the eyes of his fellow Jews, collaborated with the enemy. Tax collectors were despised for their corrupt practices and for requiring the Jewish people to give money to an authority other than God. On the other hand, before Jesus's call, Simon the Zealot was devoted to a group of Jewish nationalists who hated Rome and sought to overturn it, often through aggressive and violent means.

Although Matthew and Simon held opposing political beliefs, the Gospels don't document them bickering or fighting about them. They must have had at least some success in leaving their previous allegiances behind as they followed Christ.

When we too fix our eyes on Jesus, the God who became Man, we can find increasing unity with our fellow believers through the bond of the Holy Spirit.

AMY BOUCHER PYE

Our strongest allegiance is to Christ,
who gives us unity with each other.

A Family Thing

MARK 3:31–35

Everyone who believes that Jesus is the Christ is born of God,
and everyone who loves the father loves his child as well.

1 JOHN 5:1

When I was growing up, I often heard my pastor read the Ten Commandments and our Lord's command to love God with our whole being and our neighbor as ourselves. I knew I didn't fully live up to those demands, but I took them seriously.

As an eight-year-old, I felt sadness when a six-year-old neighbor boy in a non-Christian family died. But I also felt guilt because I was not as sad as I would have been if this had happened to one of my brothers. And still today, even though my brothers and I all have our own families who come first in our lives, we still take a keen interest in one another.

God is pleased when we cherish these family ties, but He also wants us to love all who have entered our spiritual family by being born again. This is the family Jesus referred to when He responded to a message that His mother and brothers desired to speak with Him. He looked at the audience before Him and said, "Here are my mother and my brothers! Whoever does God's will is my brother and sister and mother" (Mark 3:34–35).

Loving the lost is our duty, but loving those born into God's family, no matter what their faults, should come naturally. It is, after all, a family thing.

HERB VANDER LUGT

We show our love for God when we love His family.

Sow What?

MARK 4:1–20

A wicked person earns deceptive wages,
but the one who sows righteousness reaps a sure reward.
PROVERBS 11:18

On the clock tower of my alma mater is an Art Deco bas-relief sculpture titled *The Sower*. The inscription beneath it is from Galatians 6:7, "Whatsoever a man soweth" (KJV). Michigan State University remains a leader in agricultural research, but despite many improvements in farming techniques and crop production, this fact remains: Seeds of corn will not produce a crop of beans.

Jesus used many farming metaphors to explain the kingdom of God. In the parable of the sower (Mark 4), He compared the Word of God to seeds sown in different types of soil. As the parable indicates, the sower sows indiscriminately, knowing that some seed will fall in places where it will not grow.

Like Jesus, we are to sow good seed in all places at all times. God is responsible for where it lands and how it grows. The important thing is that we sow. God does not want us to reap destruction, so He wants us to sow what is good and right (Proverbs 11:18). The apostle Paul elaborated on the metaphor when he warned believers not to sow seeds of corruption. Instead, we are to sow seeds that will reap eternal life (Galatians 6:8).

The answer to the question, "Sow what?" is "Sow what you want to reap." To reap a good harvest in your life, start sowing seeds of goodness.

JULIE ACKERMAN LINK

A buried seed brings fruit; a selfless life reaps an eternal harvest.

You Never Know

MARK 4:26–32

"All by itself the soil produces grain—first the stalk, then the head, then the full kernel in the head."

MARK 4:28

During my seminary years, I directed a summer day camp for boys and girls at the YMCA. Each morning, I began the day with a brief story in which I tried to incorporate an element of the gospel.

To help illustrate that becoming a Christian means to become a new creation in Christ, I told a story about a moose that wanted to be a horse. The moose had seen a herd of wild horses, thought them elegant creatures, and wanted to be like them. So he taught himself to act like a horse. However, he was never accepted as a horse because he was . . . well, a moose. How can a moose become a horse? Only by being born a horse, of course. And then I would explain how we can all be born again by believing in Jesus.

One summer I had a staff counselor named Henry who was very hostile to the faith. I could do nothing but love him and pray for him, but he left at the end of the summer hardened in unbelief. That was more than fifty years ago. A few years ago I received a letter from Henry. The first sentence said: "I write to tell that I have been born again and now, at last, I am a 'horse.'" This confirmed to me that we need to keep praying and planting the seed of the Word (Mark 4:26) so it will bear fruit one day.

DAVID ROPER

We sow the seed—God produces the harvest.

The Perfect Storm

MARK 4:35–41

They were terrified and asked each other,
"Who is this? Even the wind and the waves obey him!"
MARK 4:41

In his book *The Perfect Storm*, author Sebastian Junger reports astonishing facts about the power of a hurricane: "A mature hurricane is by far the most powerful event on earth; the combined nuclear arsenals of the United States and the former Soviet Union don't contain enough energy to keep a hurricane going for one day. A typical hurricane . . . could provide all the electric power needed by the United States for three or four years."

Seafarers encounter diverse weather conditions. But those who experience a severe storm have one emotion in common—fear. Mark 4:35–41 records a gale that threatened the boat carrying Jesus and His disciples on the Sea of Galilee. In a panic, the disciples awakened Jesus. He calmly rebuked the wind and sea by saying, "Quiet! Be still!" (literally "hush") as if He were quieting an agitated child (v. 39). Immediately, the gale stopped and the water became inexplicably placid. The disciples asked, "Who is this? Even the wind and the waves obey him!" (v. 41).

Do you feel as if your life's circumstances are a mighty storm? Look to the God-man Jesus Christ, who has authority over heaven and earth. He will give you the strength to survive the storm until He ultimately calms it.

DENNIS FISHER

When we trust the power of God, His peace keeps us from panic.

Tell It

MARK 5:1–20

*So the man went away and began to tell in the Decapolis
how much Jesus had done for him. And all the people were amazed.*

MARK 5:20

The year was 1975 and something significant had just happened to me. I needed to find my friend Francis, with whom I shared a lot of personal matters, and tell him about it. I found him in his apartment hurriedly preparing to go out, but I slowed him down. The way he stared at me, he must have sensed that I had something important to tell him. "What is it?" he asked. So I told him simply, "Yesterday I surrendered my life to Jesus!"

Francis looked at me, sighed heavily, and said, "I've felt like doing the same for a long time now." He asked me to share what happened, and I told him how the previous day someone had explained the gospel to me and how I asked Jesus to come into my life. I still remember the tears in his eyes as he too prayed to receive Jesus's forgiveness. No longer in a hurry, he and I talked and talked about our new relationship with Christ.

After Jesus healed the man with an evil spirit, He told him, "Go home to your own people and tell them how much the Lord has done for you, and how he has had mercy on you" (Mark 5:19). The man didn't need to preach a powerful sermon; he simply needed to share his story.

No matter what our conversion experience is, we can do what that man did: "[He] went away and began to tell . . . how much Jesus had done for him" (v. 20).

LAWRENCE DARMANI

**Let the redeemed of the LORD tell their story.
—Psalm 107:2**

Interruptions

MARK 5:21–34

The plans of the LORD stand firm forever,
the purposes of his heart through all generations.

PSALM 33:11

My sister and I were looking forward to our holiday in Taiwan. We had purchased our plane tickets and booked our hotel rooms. But two weeks before the trip, my sister learned she had to stay at home in Singapore to handle an emergency. We were disappointed that our plans were interrupted.

Jesus's disciples were accompanying Him on an urgent mission when their trip was interrupted (Mark 5:21–42). The daughter of Jairus, a ruler of the synagogue, was dying. Time was of the essence, and Jesus was on His way to their home. Then, suddenly, Jesus stopped and said, "Who touched my clothes?" (v. 30).

The disciples seemed irritated by this and said, "You see the people crowding against you . . . , and yet you can ask, 'Who touched me?'" (v. 31). But Jesus saw it as an opportunity to minister to a suffering woman. Her illness had made her ceremonially unclean and unable to participate in community life for twelve years! (see Leviticus 15:25–27).

While Jesus was talking to this woman, Jairus's daughter died. It was too late—or so it seemed. But the delay allowed Jairus to experience an even deeper knowledge of Jesus and His power—even power over death!

Sometimes our disappointment can be God's appointment.

POH FANG CHIA

Look for God's purpose in your next interruption.

Joanie and Jesus

MARK 6:1-6

He could not do any miracles there, except lay his hands on a few sick people and heal them. He was amazed at their lack of faith.

MARK 6:5-6

A child once asked, "What does God do all day?" If the answer to that question depended on how much we allow God to do in our individual lives, some of us would have to reply, "Not much!" In difficult situations, it's easy to say we trust God and yet try to handle things ourselves without turning to Him and His Word. This is masked unbelief. Although God is constantly working, He allows us to set a limit on the degree of work He does on our behalf.

We see this truth demonstrated in Mark 6 when Jesus tried to do mighty things in His hometown. Because the people saw Him merely as a carpenter's son and not as God's Son, they limited what He could do for them (v. 5). So Jesus moved on to other towns.

During my younger years, I tried hard to be a strong Christian, seldom revealing my weaknesses. Then, through a rock-bottom experience, I made this dynamic discovery: Strong Christians are those who unashamedly admit their weaknesses and draw on Christ's power. The more I learned to depend on God, the more opportunity this gave Him to be active in my life. Now, whenever I face a daunting task, I say, "Joanie and Jesus can do it!" So can you and Jesus.

JOANIE YODER

We must admit our weakness to experience God's strength.

Lack Nothing

MARK 6:7–12

God is able to bless you abundantly, so that in all things at all times,
having all that you need, you will abound in every good work.

2 CORINTHIANS 9:8

Imagine going on a trip without luggage. No basic necessities. No change of clothing. No money or credit cards. Sounds both unwise and terrifying, doesn't it?

But that's exactly what Jesus told His twelve disciples to do when He sent them out on their first mission to preach and heal. "Take nothing for the journey except a staff," said Jesus. "No bread, no bag, no money in your belts. Wear sandals but not an extra shirt" (Mark 6:8–9).

Yet later on when Jesus was preparing them for their work after He was gone, He told His disciples, "If you have a purse, take it, and also a bag; and if you don't have a sword, sell your cloak and buy one" (Luke 22:36).

So, what's the point here? It's about trusting God to supply.

When Jesus referred back to that first trip, He asked the disciples, "When I sent you without purse, bag or sandals, did you lack anything?" And they answered, "Nothing" (v. 35). The disciples had everything they needed to carry out God's work. He was able to supply them with the power to do His work (Mark 6:7).

Do we trust God to supply our needs? Are we also taking personal responsibility and planning? Let's have faith that He will give us what we need to carry out His work.

POH FANG CHIA

God's will done in God's way will never lack God's supply.
—Hudson Taylor, founder of China Inland Mission

Running and Rest

MARK 6:30–46

*Then, because so many people were coming and going
that they did not even have a chance to eat, he said to them,
"Come with me by yourselves to a quiet place and get some rest."*

MARK 6:31

The headline caught my eye: "Rest Days Important for Runners." In Tommy Manning's article, the former member of the US Mountain Running Team emphasized a principle that dedicated athletes sometimes ignore—the body needs time to rest and rebuild after exercise. "Physiologically, the adaptations that occur as a result of training only happen during rest," Manning wrote. "This means rest is as important as workouts."

The same is true in our walk of faith and service. Regular times of rest are essential to avoid burnout and discouragement. Jesus sought spiritual balance during His life on earth, even in the face of great demands. When His disciples returned from a strenuous time of teaching and healing others, "he said to them, 'Come with me by yourselves to a quiet place and get some rest'" (Mark 6:31). But a large crowd followed them, so Jesus taught them and fed them with only five loaves and two fish (vv. 32–44). When everyone was gone, Jesus "went up on a mountainside to pray" (v. 46).

If our lives are defined by work alone, then what we do becomes less and less effective. Jesus invites us to regularly join Him in a quiet place to pray and get some rest.

DAVID MCCASLAND

In our life of faith and service, rest is as important as work.

The Beacon

MARK 6:45–52

He saw the disciples straining at the oars, because the wind was against them. Shortly before dawn he went out to them, walking on the lake.
MARK 6:48

When a helicopter crashed in a cold, mountainous wilderness, the pilots survived but were seriously injured. The frozen afternoon stretched toward an even more freezing night. The situation seemed hopeless—until a rescue helicopter appeared, its searchlights illuminating the darkness. It spotted the wreckage, landed nearby, and carried them off to safety.

"How did you know where we were?" an injured man asked.

"The homing device on your aircraft," the rescuers told him. "It went off automatically when you went down. All we had to do was follow it."

The disciples of Jesus also experienced the joy of being rescued. They had been struggling as they rowed their boat against wind and waves in the darkness of night on the Sea of Galilee (Mark 6:45–47). Then Jesus came to them walking on the water and calmed the sea (vv. 48–51).

We may experience similar times when all is dark and foreboding. We can't help ourselves, and it seems that no one else can either. No one knows how terrified and exhausted we are. No one, that is, except Jesus.

When we're trapped, hurt, lonely, or discouraged, Jesus knows it. Our cries of grief are beacons that bring Him to our side—right when we need Him most.

DAVID EGNER

Jesus hears even the faintest cry for help.

Loopholes

MARK 7:1–13

I have hidden your word in my heart that I might not sin against you.
PSALM 119:11

Five-year-old Jenna was not having a good start to her day. Every attempt to arrange the world according to her liking was having the opposite result. Arguing didn't work. Pouting didn't work. Crying didn't work. Finally her mother reminded her of the Bible verse she had been learning: "I have hidden your word in my heart that I might not sin against you" (Psalm 119:11).

Apparently Jenna had been thinking about this verse, because she was quick to answer: "But Mom, it doesn't say that I won't sin; it says that I might not sin."

Her words are all too familiar. I often hear similar arguments in my own mind. There's something very appealing about loopholes, and we look for them wherever there's a command we don't want to obey.

Jesus addressed this problem with religious leaders who thought they had found a loophole in their religious laws (Mark 7:1–13). Instead of honoring their parents with financial or material support, they dedicated all their possessions to God, thereby limiting their use. Although their disobedience was not blatant, Jesus said their behavior was unacceptable.

Whenever we start looking for loopholes, we stop being obedient.

JULIE ACKERMAN LINK

**Even though we make excuses for not obeying God,
He still calls it disobedience.**

The Walking Purchase

MARK 7:5–13

"Woe to you, teachers of the law and Pharisees, you hypocrites!
You give a tenth of your spices—mint, dill and cumin.
But you have neglected the more important matters of the law—
justice, mercy and faithfulness."
MATTHEW 23:23

In colonial North America, William Penn had a reputation as a benevolent Quaker who dealt fairly with Native Americans. When he returned to England, his sons stayed behind. They did not share his integrity. Soon they contrived a scheme to cheat a Delaware tribe. The sons produced an old contract in which the Indians had agreed to sell a portion of land that a man could walk in one and a half days.

When the tribe consented to honor their ancestors' agreement, Penn's sons were delighted. They hired three of the fastest runners they could find. One of the men covered a distance of seventy miles in eighteen hours. They totally disregarded both the letter and the spirit of the agreement.

In Jesus's day, the scribes and Pharisees rationalized their violation of the spirit of God's law. Jesus exposed their hypocritical practice when He cited the commandment to "honor your father and your mother" (Mark 7:10–13). They were declaring a portion of their income as "a gift to God" (v. 11 NKJV) to keep from using it to care for their aged parents.

The Bible is not a tool to get what we want. Instead, we must ask God to help us understand its intended purpose. That way we don't neglect the "more important matters of the law—justice, mercy and faithfulness" (Matthew 23:23).

DENNIS FISHER

Obeying the letter of the law is good;
obeying the spirit of the law is better.

A Remote Location

MARK 8:1–13

*And my God will meet all your needs
according to the riches of his glory in Christ Jesus.*
PHILIPPIANS 4:19

Tristan da Cunha Island is famous for its isolation. It is the most remote inhabited island in the world, thanks to the 264 people who call it home. The island is located in the South Atlantic Ocean, 1,500 miles from South Africa—the nearest mainland. Anyone who might want to drop by for a visit has to travel by boat for seven days because the island has no airstrip.

Jesus and His followers were in a somewhat remote area when He produced a miraculous meal for thousands of hungry people. Before His miracle, Jesus said to His disciples, "[These people] have already been with me three days and have nothing to eat. If I send them home hungry, they will collapse on the way" (Mark 8:2–3). Because they were in the countryside where food was not readily available, they had to depend fully on Jesus. They had nowhere else to turn.

Sometimes God allows us to end up in desolate places where He is our only source of help. His ability to provide for us is not necessarily linked with our circumstances. If He created the entire world out of nothing, God can certainly meet our needs—whatever our circumstances—out of the riches of His glory, in Christ Jesus (Philippians 4:19).

JENNIFER BENSON SCHULDT

We can trust God to do what we cannot do.

Who and How?

MARK 8:27–33

"But what about you?" he asked. "Who do you say I am?"
Peter answered, "You are the Messiah."

MARK 8:29

Whenever I read the Gospels, I identify with the disciples. Like me, they seemed slow to catch on. Jesus kept saying things like "Don't you understand it yet?" and "Are you still so dull?" (see Mark 7:18). Finally, however, Peter "got it," at least one part of it. When Jesus asked, "Who do you say I am?" Peter answered, "You are the Messiah" (8:29).

Peter was right about the "who"—Jesus—but he was still wrong about the "how." When Jesus predicted His own death, Peter rebuked Him for it. Jesus, in turn, rebuked Peter: "Get behind me, Satan! You do not have in mind the concerns of God, but merely human concerns" (v. 33).

Peter was still thinking in human terms about establishing kingdoms. One ruler would overthrow another and set up a new government. He was expecting Jesus to do the same. But Christ's kingdom was going to come in a new way—through service and the sacrifice of His life.

The method God uses today hasn't changed. Whereas Satan's voice tempts us to gain power, Jesus tells us that the meek will inherit the earth (Matthew 5:5). To gain citizens for God's kingdom, we must follow the example of Jesus, who served others, and called people to repent of their sin.

JULIE ACKERMAN LINK

A Christian is an ambassador who speaks for the King of Kings.

"Listen to Him"

MARK 9:1-8

A voice came from the cloud, saying,
"This is my Son, whom I have chosen; listen to him."
LUKE 9:35

On one occasion Peter, James, and John accompanied Jesus to a moun-taintop to pray. As He talked with the heavenly Father, something unusual happened. The glory of His deity shone forth. Then Moses and Elijah appeared, talked with Jesus, and departed. When the two patriarchs were leaving, Peter was so impressed that he immediately proposed to build booths for Moses, Elijah, and Christ. At that point, the voice of God could be heard from a cloud, saying, "This is my Son, whom I love. Listen to him!" (Mark 9:7). The law, represented by Moses, had done its work; the prophecies, symbolized by Elijah, were being fulfilled. But the living Word, Jesus, was with them, and they were to listen closely to what He told them.

God's command "Listen to Him" still applies to us today. But through the course of our Christian lives we often listen to the wrong voices. When we do, trouble follows. We're a little like a teenager I know who has an old car he prizes and is fixing up. His father is an experienced mechanic and is willing to give his son expert advice. But who does the young man listen to? His teenage friends, who don't know any more about cars than he does. The result is a lot of frustration that could be avoided if he would just listen to his dad.

Jesus Christ speaks to us through the written Word. To follow any counsel that contradicts His teaching is to invite disappointment and grief. Jesus is God's divine Son—"Listen to Him!"

DAVID EGNER

Knowing the LIVING Word is the key to
understanding the WRITTEN Word.

Bring the Boy to Me

MARK 9:14–27

*"You unbelieving generation," Jesus replied, "how long shall I stay with you?
How long shall I put up with you? Bring the boy to me."*
MARK 9:19

"I don't believe in God and I won't go," Mark said.

Amy struggled to swallow the lump in her throat. Her son had changed from a happy boy to a surly and uncooperative young man. Life was a battleground, and Sunday had become a day to dread, as Mark refused to go to church with the family. Finally his despairing parents consulted a counselor, who said: "Mark must make his own faith journey. You can't force him into the kingdom. Give God space to work. Keep praying, and wait."

Amy waited—and prayed. One morning the words of Jesus that she had read echoed through her mind. Jesus's disciples had failed to help a demon-possessed boy, but Jesus had the answer: "Bring the boy to me" (Mark 9:19). The sun shone through the window at Amy's side, making a pool of light on the floor. If Jesus could heal in such an extreme situation, then surely He could also help her son. She pictured herself and Mark standing in that light with Jesus. Then she mentally stepped back, leaving her son alone with the One who loved him even more than she did.

Every day Amy silently handed Mark to God, clinging to the assurance that He knew Mark's needs and would in His time and in His way work in his life.

MARION STROUD

Prayer is the voice of faith trusting that God knows and cares.

Candidates for Humility

MARK 9:30–37

Then [Jesus] said to them, "Whoever welcomes this little child in my name welcomes me; and whoever welcomes me welcomes the one who sent me. For it is the one who is least among you all who is the greatest."

LUKE 9:48

"What do you think of the candidates?" That's what a reporter for a newsmagazine asked a young woman at Dartmouth University after a debate among presidential hopefuls. She didn't say a word about their positions on the issues or their skill at debate. She simply remarked, "None of them seems to have any humility."

American statesman Benjamin Franklin (1706–1790) made a list of character qualities he wanted to develop in his life. When he mastered one virtue, he went on to the next. He did pretty well, he said, until he got to humility. Every time he thought he was making significant progress, he would be so pleased with himself that he became proud.

Humility is an elusive virtue. Even Jesus's disciples struggled with it. When Jesus learned that they had been arguing about who was the greatest, He responded, "Anyone who wants to be first must be the very last, and the servant of all" (Mark 9:35). Then He took a little child in His arms and indicated that we need to humbly serve others as if we were serving Christ.

If a news reporter were to talk to our friends, neighbors, or fellow church members and ask them to describe us, would they use the word *humble*?

DAVID EGNER

Humility can be sought but never celebrated.

A Clearer Vision

MARK 9:42–48

*For the time will come when people will not put up with sound doctrine.
Instead, to suit their own desires, they will gather around them a great
number of teachers to say what their itching ears want to hear.*

2 TIMOTHY 4:3

For many years during the 1980s and 1990s, scaffolding in the Sistine
Chapel at the Vatican in Italy partially obscured the view of Michelangelo's
sixteenth-century frescoes. Restorers were carefully removing the dulling
residue of candle smoke, incense, and dust.

Some people were critical of the project and felt that the colors on the
ceiling became too strong as a result of the restoration. But officials insist
that the restoration enables visitors to see what the Renaissance master
wanted them to see.

The debate continued when the even sootier painting *The Last Judgment*
was restored. The renewing of that scene, with its crowded figures crying
out in hell, has a spiritual parallel that is just as soiled. Our generation has
become accustomed to a very dim portrayal of the last judgment described
by Jesus. Countless jokes and profanities have obscured the vivid picture
Christ gave us. And many who believe in Him do not take Him seriously
when He talks about a fire that will never be quenched.

To restore Christ's picture of hell, we need to look at what He said and
sense its reality. When we do, we will be thankful for our salvation and
stimulated to pray for others to escape God's wrath.

Lord, may our vision of hell never become soiled and dull.

MART DEHAAN

A clear vision of hell should give us compassion for all.

Who Are You Defending?

MARK 10:13–16

You see, at just the right time, when we were still powerless,
Christ died for the ungodly.
ROMANS 5:6

When Kathleen's teacher called her to the front of the grammar class to analyze a sentence, she panicked. As a recent transfer student, she hadn't learned that aspect of grammar. The class laughed at her.

Instantly the teacher sprang to her defense. "She can out-write any of you any day of the week!" he explained. Many years later, Kathleen gratefully recalled the moment: "I started that day to try to write as well as he said I could." Eventually, Kathleen Parker would win a Pulitzer Prize for her writing.

As did Kathleen's teacher, Jesus identified with the defenseless and vulnerable. When His disciples kept children away from Him, He grew angry. "Let the little children come to me," He said, "and do not hinder them" (Mark 10:14). He reached out to a despised ethnic group, making the Good Samaritan the hero of His parable (Luke 10:25–37) and offering genuine hope to a searching Samaritan woman at Jacob's well (John 4:1–26). He protected and forgave a woman trapped in adultery (John 8:1–11). And though we were utterly helpless, Christ gave His life for all of us (Romans 5:6).

When we defend the vulnerable and the marginalized, we give them a chance to realize their potential. We show them real love, and in a small but significant way we reflect the very heart of Jesus.

TIM GUSTAFSON

It is impossible to love Christ without loving others.

Knowing and Doing

MARK 10:17–27

Jesus looked at them and said, "With man this is impossible,
but not with God; all things are possible with God."
MARK 10:27

Chinese philosopher Han Feizi made this observation about life: "Knowing the facts is easy. Knowing how to act based on the facts is difficult."

A rich man with that problem once came to Jesus. He knew the law of Moses and believed he had kept the commandments since his youth (Mark 10:20). But he seemed to be wondering what additional facts he might hear from Jesus. " 'Good teacher,' he asked, 'what must I do to inherit eternal life?' " (v. 17).

Jesus's answer disappointed the rich man. He told him to sell his possessions, give the money to the poor, and follow Him (v. 21). With these few words Jesus exposed a fact the man didn't want to hear. He loved and relied on his wealth more than he trusted Jesus. Abandoning the security of his money to follow Jesus was too great a risk, and he went away sad (v. 22).

What was the Teacher thinking? His own disciples were alarmed and asked, "Who then can be saved?" (v. 26). He replied, "With man this is impossible, but not with God; all things are possible with God" (v. 27). It takes courage and faith. "If you declare with your mouth, 'Jesus is Lord,' and believe in your heart that God raised him from the dead, you will be saved" (Romans 10:9).

POH FANG CHIA

Believe in the Lord Jesus, and you will be saved.
—Acts 16:31

True Greatness

MARK 10:35–45

"Whoever wants to become great among you must be your servant."
MARK 10:43

Some people feel like a small pebble lost in the immensity of a canyon. But no matter how insignificant we judge ourselves to be, we can be greatly used by God.

In a sermon early in 1968, Martin Luther King Jr. quoted Jesus's words from Mark 10 about servanthood. Then he said, "Everybody can be great, because everybody can serve. You don't have to have a college degree to serve. You don't have to make your subject and your verb agree to serve. You don't have to know about Plato and Aristotle to serve. . . . You only need a heart full of grace, a soul generated by love."

When Jesus's disciples quarreled about who would get the places of honor in heaven, He told them: "Whoever wants to become great among you must be your servant, and whoever wants to be first must be slave of all. For even the Son of Man did not come to be served, but to serve, and to give his life as a ransom for many" (Mark 10:43–45).

Is this our understanding of greatness—gladly serving in tasks that may be unnoticed? Is the purpose of our serving to please our Lord? If we are willing to be a servant, our lives will point to the One who is truly great.

VERNON GROUNDS

Little things done in Christ's name are great things.

Be Specific

MARK 10:46–52

*"What do you want me to do for you?" Jesus asked [Bartimaeus].
The blind man said, "Rabbi, I want to see."*
MARK 10:51

On the day before I was to have major surgery, I shared with my friend that I was really scared about the procedure. "What part scares you?" she inquired. "I'm just so afraid that I won't wake up from the anesthesia," I replied. Immediately, Anne prayed: "Father, you know all about Cindy's fear. Please calm her heart and fill her with your peace. And, Lord, please wake her up after surgery."

I think God likes that kind of specificity when we talk to Him. When Bartimaeus, the blind beggar, called out to Jesus for help, Jesus said, "What do you want me to do for you?" And the blind man said, "Rabbi, I want to see." Jesus said, "Go, your faith has healed you" (Mark 10:51–52).

We don't need to beat around the bush with God. While there may be a time to pray poetically as David did, there are also times to say bluntly, "God, I'm so sorry for what I just said," or to say simply, "Jesus, I love you because . . . ." Being specific with God can even be a sign of faith, because we are acknowledging that we know we're not talking to a far-off Being but to a real Person who loves us intimately.

God is not impressed by a flurry of fanciful words. He is listening for what our heart is saying.

CINDY HESS KASPER

The heart of prayer is prayer from the heart.

Let It Go

MARK 11:1–11

"If anyone asks you, 'Why are you doing this?' say,
'The Lord needs it and will send it back here shortly.'"

MARK 11:3

Many years ago, when a young friend asked if he could borrow our car, my wife and I were hesitant at first. It was *our* car. We owned it, and we depended on it. But we soon felt convicted to share it with him because we knew that God wanted us to care for others. So we handed the keys over to him, and he traveled to a church thirty miles away to conduct a youth rally. The meeting was used by the Lord to bring teens to Christ.

Jesus instructed His disciples to take another man's donkey. The Son of God told His men to "untie it and bring it" to Him (Mark 11:2). If someone objected, they were to say, "The Lord needs it," and they would then be permitted to lead it away. That donkey carried Christ into Jerusalem on what we call Palm Sunday.

There's a lesson here for us to consider. We all have things we hold dear. We may have thought, *I could never part with that*. It may be a new truck, a coat, some other possession, or our precious few free hours during the week. Will we be open to give when someone obviously needs something we have?

If you sense that the Spirit is speaking to you, let your time or possession go, as the owner released his animal to Jesus. He will then be glorified—just as He deserves!

DAVID EGNER

God gives us all we need, so we can give to others in their need.

Mountains Can Move!

MARK 11:20–24

"Have faith in God," Jesus answered.
MARK 11:22

A familiar slogan about prayer is, "Prayer changes things." But prayer doesn't do this—God does. Some people think that prayer itself is the source of power, so they "try prayer," hoping "it will work" for them. In Mark 11, Jesus disclosed one of the secrets behind all true prayer: "Have faith in God." Not faith in faith, not faith in prayer, but "faith in God" (v. 22).

Jesus told His disciples they could command a mountain to be cast into the sea, and if they believed it would happen, it would. Jesus then gave them His meaning behind that astonishing promise. He said, "Whatever you ask for in prayer, believe that you have received it, and it will be yours" (v. 24). Jesus was speaking about answered prayer. We can ask and receive answers only if our asking is directed to God in faith and according to His will (1 John 5:14).

I've often wished that I could move mountains by faith. Having once lived in Switzerland, I'd like God to move the Alps into my backyard in England. But He has done something much more important: He has removed mountains of worry, fear, and resentment from my heart and cast them into oblivion through my faith in Him. He is still in the mountain-moving business! Have faith in God and pray!

JOANIE YODER

Faith is the key to answered prayer.

A Matter of Love

MARK 12:28–34

Love the LORD your God with all your heart and with all your soul and with all your strength.

DEUTERONOMY 6:5

"Where intellect and emotion clash, the heart often has the greater wisdom," wrote the authors of *A General Theory of Love*. In the past, they say, people believed that the mind should rule the heart, but science has now discovered the opposite to be true. "Who we are and who we become depends, in part, on whom we love."

Those familiar with Scripture recognize this as an ancient truth, not a new discovery. The most important commandment God gave to His people gives the heart the prominent place. "Love the LORD your God with all your heart and with all your soul and with all your strength" (Deuteronomy 6:5). Not until the gospels of Mark and Luke do we learn that Jesus added the word *mind* (Mark 12:30; Luke 10:27). So, what scientists are just now discovering, the Bible taught all along.

Those of us who follow Christ also know the importance of who it is we love. When we obey the greatest commandment and make God the object of our love, we can be assured of having a purpose that transcends anything we could imagine or our strength could achieve. When our desire for God dominates our hearts, our minds will stay focused on ways to serve Him, and our actions will further His kingdom on earth and in heaven.

JULIE ACKERMAN LINK

Count as lost each day you have not used in loving God.
—Brother Lawrence

Two Mites

MARK 12:41–44

*"They all gave out of their wealth; but she,
out of her poverty, put in everything—all she had to live on."*
MARK 12:44

Jesus sat in the temple near the treasury and watched as people walked by and deposited their gifts for the temple (Mark 12). Some made a show of it, perhaps so others could see how much they had given. Just then a poor woman came by and threw in two "mites."

A mite was the least valuable coin in circulation. Thus the widow's gift was very small, amounting to nothing in most folks' eyes. But our Lord saw what others did not see. She had given "all that she had" (Mark 12:44). The widow was simply doing what she was able to do. And Jesus noticed!

Still today our Lord sees what we do, no matter how small. It may be just showing a cheerful countenance in difficult times or an act of kindness to someone who happens to pass by. It may be a brief, silent prayer for a neighbor in need.

Jesus said, "Be careful not to practice your righteousness in front of others to be seen by them. If you do, you will have no reward from your Father in heaven" (Matthew 6:1). "But when you give to the needy, do not let your left hand know what your right hand is doing, so that your giving may be in secret. Then your Father, who sees what is done in secret, will reward you" (vv. 3–4). Jesus sat in the temple and watched as people deposited their gifts (Mark 12). Some made a show of it. Just then a poor woman came by and threw in two "mites." Can you imagine Jesus smiling when He saw her gift?

DAVID ROPER

God looks at the heart, not the hand; the giver, not the gift.

Testimony of Endurance

MARK 13:9–13

Join me in suffering, like a good soldier of Christ Jesus.
2 TIMOTHY 2:3

Christians in every century have astounded the world with their patient endurance under oppression, torture, and even death. For example, Stephen prayed for his murderers, his face shining as the stones fell upon him. Paul and Silas, their feet in stocks and their backs lacerated, sang through the long night of their imprisonment.

Similar examples can be cited from this century. British theologian Michael Green told about the remarkable testimony of three Ugandans who had been sentenced to death. Fellow Christian Festo Kivengere was allowed to visit them, so the men urged him to tell the gospel to their executioners. As the men awaited death, they joyfully bore witness for Christ before the crowd. To the amazement of the firing squad, they continued praising God right up until the moment the shots rang out. News of their faith spread through Uganda like wildfire. Green concluded, "You cannot get the better of that quality of patient endurance. Where it is shown, the church grows. As ever, the blood of martyrs is seed."

We may never be persecuted like that. But we are sure to be faced with such trials as illness, pain, disappointment, or loss. We can triumph through these difficulties in the power of Christ. Then we too will give a shining testimony of endurance to a watching world.

DAVID EGNER

He who waits on the Lord will not be crushed
by the weights of adversity.

Two Calendars

MARK 13:32–37

"Therefore keep watch,
because you do not know on what day your Lord will come."
MATTHEW 24:42

Man has devised various types of calendars with differing days for the new year to start. According to Jewish reckoning, New Year's Day is on Rosh Hashanah, which falls in September or October each year. The Gregorian calendar, instituted by Pope Gregory XIII in 1582, places New Year's on January 1.

God too has a calendar. It starts at an unspecified time called "In the beginning" (Genesis 1:1; John 1:1). It ends when time shall be no more. Somewhere in between are two unprecedented events. The first occurred when God became man. When Jesus was born, God came to earth on a specific day in history (John 1:14). The other event, Christ's second coming, is future. Although no one knows the year, the month, the day, or the hour, its certainty in our calendar, and in God's, is assured.

The Latin word *kalendae* referred to a time in Roman society when accounts became due. So too, at Christ's second coming we will stand before His judgment seat and give a reckoning of what we have done with our lives (2 Corinthians 5:10). Watchfulness, therefore, should characterize every Christian. Interestingly, the name Gregory (the churchman who set up our calendar) means "the watchful one" or "vigilant one."

As we live each day for Christ, we'll be ready and eager for His sure return to earth.

DENNIS DEHAAN

Live as if Christ died yesterday,
rose this morning, and is coming back today.

It's Beautiful

MARK 14:3–9

"Leave her alone," said Jesus. "Why are you bothering her?
She has done a beautiful thing to me."

MARK 14:6

After being away on business, Terry wanted to pick up some small gifts for his children. The clerk at the airport gift shop recommended a number of costly items. "I don't have that much money with me," he said. "I need something less expensive." The clerk tried to make him feel that he was being cheap. But Terry knew his children would be happy with whatever he gave them, because it came from a heart of love. And he was right—they loved the gifts he brought them.

During Jesus's last visit to the town of Bethany, Mary wanted to show her love for Him (Mark 14:3–9). So she brought "an alabaster jar of very expensive perfume made of pure nard" and anointed Him (v. 3). The disciples asked angrily, "Why this waste?" (Matthew 26:8). Jesus told them to stop troubling her, for "she has done a beautiful thing to me" (Mark 14:6). Jesus delighted in her gift, for it came from a heart of love. Even anointing Him for burial was beautiful!

What can we give to Jesus to show our love? Our time? Our talent? Our treasure? It doesn't matter if it's costly or inexpensive, whether others understand or criticize. Whatever is given from a heart of love is beautiful to Him.

ANNE CETAS

A healthy heart beats with love for Jesus.

She Did What She Could

MARK 14:3–9

"She did what she could.
She poured perfume on my body beforehand
to prepare for my burial."

MARK 14:8

When her friends say thoughtless or outrageous things on social media, Charlotte chimes in with gentle but firm dissent. She respects the dignity of everyone, and her words are unfailingly positive.

A few years ago she became Facebook friends with a man who harbored anger toward Christians. He appreciated Charlotte's rare honesty and grace. Over time his hostility melted. Then Charlotte suffered a bad fall. Now housebound, she fretted over what she could do. About that time her Facebook friend died, and then this message arrived from his sister: "[Because of your witness] I know he's now experiencing God's complete and abiding love for him."

During the week in which Christ would be killed, Mary of Bethany anointed Him with expensive perfume (John 12:3; Mark 14:3). Some of those present were appalled, but Jesus applauded her. He said, "She did what she could. She poured perfume on my body beforehand to prepare for my burial" (Mark 14:6–8).

"She did what she could." Christ's words take the pressure off. Our world is full of broken, hurting people. But we don't have to worry about what we can't do. Charlotte did what she could. So can we. The rest is in His capable hands.

TIM GUSTAFSON

Do thy duty, that is best; leave unto the Lord the rest.
—Henry Wadsworth Longfellow

Why Me?

MARK 14:10–21

But God demonstrates his own love for us in this:
While we were still sinners, Christ died for us.

ROMANS 5:8

British pastor Joseph Parker was asked, "Why did Jesus choose Judas to be one of His disciples?" He thought deeply about the question for a while but could not come up with an answer. He said that he kept running into an even more baffling question: "Why did He choose me?"

That's a question that has been asked throughout the centuries. When people become painfully aware of their sin and are overcome with guilt, they cry out to Jesus for mercy. In joyous wonder they experience the truth that God loves them, that Jesus died for them, and that they are forgiven of all their sins. It's incomprehensible!

I too have asked, "Why me?" I know that the dark and sinful deeds of my life were motivated by a heart even darker, and yet God loved me! (Romans 5:8). I was undeserving, wretched, and helpless, yet He opened His arms and His heart to me. I could almost hear Him whisper, "I love you even more than you loved your sin."

It's true! I cherished my sin. I protected it. I denied its wrongdoing. Yet God loved me enough to forgive me and set me free.

"Why me?" It's beyond my understanding. Yet I know He loves me— and He loves you too!

DAVID EGNER

God loves us not because of who we are, but because of who He is.

Remember the Cross

MARK 14:19–20, 33–39

When the centurion, who stood there in front of Jesus,
saw how he died, he said, "Surely this man was the Son of God!"
MARK 15:39

In the church I attend, a large cross stands at the front of the sanctuary. It represents the original cross where Jesus died—the place where our sin intersected with His holiness. There God allowed His perfect Son to die for the sake of every wrong thing we have ever done, said, or thought. On the cross, Jesus finished the work that was required to save us from the death we deserve (Romans 6:23).

The sight of a cross causes me to consider what Jesus endured for us. Before being crucified, He was flogged and spit on. The soldiers hit Him in the head with sticks and got down on their knees in mock worship. They tried to make Him carry His own cross to the place where He would die, but He was too weak from the brutal flogging. At Golgotha, they hammered nails through His flesh to keep Him on the cross when they turned it upright. Those wounds bore the weight of His body as He hung there. Six hours later, Jesus took His final breath (Mark 15:37). A centurion who witnessed Jesus's death declared, "Surely this man was the Son of God!" (v. 39).

The next time you see the symbol of the cross, consider what it means. God's Son suffered and died there and then rose again to make eternal life possible.

JENNIFER BENSON SCHULDT

The cross of Christ reveals our sin
at its worst and God's love at its best.

My Father Is with Me

MARK 14:32–50

*"A time is coming and in fact has come when you will be scattered,
each to your own home. You will leave me all alone.
Yet I am not alone, for my Father is with me."*

JOHN 16:32

A friend struggling with loneliness posted these words on her Facebook page: "It's not that I feel alone because I have no friends. I have lots of friends. I know that I have people who can hold me and reassure me and talk to me and care for me and think of me. But they can't be with me all the time—for all time."

Jesus understands that kind of loneliness. I imagine that during His earthly ministry He saw loneliness in the eyes of lepers and heard it in the voices of the blind. But above all, He must have experienced it himself when His close friends deserted Him (Mark 14:50).

However, as He foretold the disciples' desertion, He also confessed His unshaken confidence in His Father's presence. He said to His disciples: "You will leave me all alone. Yet I am not alone, for my Father is with me" (John 16:32). Shortly after Jesus said these words, He took up the cross for us. He made it possible for you and me to have a restored relationship with God and to be members of His family.

We will all experience times of loneliness. But Jesus helps us understand that we always have the presence of the Father with us. God is omnipresent and eternal. Only He can be with us all the time, for all time.

POH FANG CHIA

If you know Jesus, you'll never walk alone.

Virtue Exemplified

MARK 15:16–20

To this you were called, because Christ suffered for you,
leaving you an example, that you should follow in his steps.

1 PETER 2:21

In the late 1940s, a young mother was stricken with polio and became disabled. She astounded people by the way she accepted her situation as she ran her household from her bed. Her brother-in-law said to me, "I have heard a lot of talk about 'supernatural grace,' but I never knew what it was until I saw it shining through her."

We often do not know the full meaning of a virtue until we see it lived out in a person's life. Think of how Jesus responded when the soldiers mistreated Him. They pressed a crown of thorns into His head, struck Him repeatedly, and mocked Him by clothing Him in a purple robe and bowing before Him in jest (Mark 15:16–20). They were unaware that He had the power to kill every one of them by speaking a single word.

About thirty-five years later, Peter vividly remembered that scene. He told his readers that Christ had set an example for them as they faced persecution (1 Peter 2:18–25). In Jesus, God became a flesh-and-blood human being to show what He is like. Because Jesus lives in us by His Spirit, He expects us to exemplify His goodness and grace.

Whether we suffer like that disabled mother or endure persecution like the Master, we can demonstrate the same virtue He modeled on the cross.

HERB VANDER LUGT

God's love is the blessing in every trial.

Witnessing Wherever

MARK 16:14–20

Then the disciples went out and preached everywhere, and the Lord worked with them and confirmed his word by the signs that accompanied it.
MARK 16:20

It was the 1962 World Series. The San Francisco Giants had a man on second base, which put him near New York Yankee second baseman Bobby Richardson. During one of the games, when the Yanks decided to change pitchers, Richardson, who was a Christian, saw a unique opportunity. While the new pitcher was warming up, he walked over to the man on second and asked him if he knew Jesus as his Savior.

When the runner reached the dugout later, he asked teammate Felipe Alou, who was also a Christian, what was going on. "Even in the World Series," he said to Felipe, "you people are still talking about Jesus." That runner couldn't understand what made Christians so eager to talk about Jesus Christ, even in highly unusual situations.

Bobby Richardson's World Series witness is a great example of what Mark was writing about when he said that the disciples "went out and preached everywhere." Pulpits are not the only places from which to tell the good news of Christ. Richardson did it at second base during a break in a baseball game. Are we as ready and willing to show with our life and tell with our lips the difference Jesus can make?

Lord, help us see and seize opportunities to witness wherever we are.

DAVE BRANON

Any place can be the right place to witness for Christ.

The Snake and the Tricycle

LUKE 1:1–4

*With this in mind, since I myself have carefully investigated
everything from the beginning, I too decided to write an orderly account
for you, most excellent Theophilus.*

LUKE 1:3

For years, I had retold a story from a time in Ghana when my brother and I were toddlers. As I recalled it, he had parked our old iron tricycle on a small cobra. The trike was too heavy for the snake, which remained trapped under the front wheel.

Many years later, after my aunt and my mother had both passed away, we discovered a long-lost letter from Mom recounting the incident. In reality, I had parked the tricycle on the snake, and my brother had run to tell Mom. Her eyewitness account, written close to the actual event, revealed the reality.

The historian Luke understood the importance of accurate records. He explained how the story of Jesus was "handed down to us by those who from the first were eyewitnesses" (Luke 1:2). "I too decided to write an orderly account for you," he wrote to Theophilus, "so that you may know the certainty of the things you have been taught" (vv. 3–4). The result was the gospel of Luke. Then, in his introduction to the book of Acts, Luke said of Jesus, "After his suffering, he presented himself to them and gave many convincing proofs that he was alive" (Acts 1:3).

Our faith is not based on hearsay or wishful thinking. It is rooted in the well-documented life of Jesus, who came to give us peace with God. His story stands.

TIM GUSTAFSON

Genuine faith is rooted in reason.

Our Prayers, God's Timing

LUKE 1:5–17

To him who is able to do immeasurably more than all we ask or imagine, according to his power that is at work within us, to him be glory!
EPHESIANS 3:20–21

Sometimes God takes His time in answering our prayers, and that isn't always easy for us to understand.

That was the situation for Zechariah, a priest the angel Gabriel appeared to one day near an altar in the temple in Jerusalem. Gabriel told him, "Do not be afraid, Zechariah; *your prayer has been heard.* Your wife Elizabeth will bear you a son, and you are to call him John" (Luke 1:13, italics added).

But Zechariah had probably asked God for a child years before, and he struggled with Gabriel's message since Elizabeth was now well beyond the expected age for childbirth. Still, God answered his prayer.

God's memory is perfect. He is able to remember our prayers not just for years but also for generations beyond our lifetime. He never forgets them and may move in response long after we first brought our requests to Him. Sometimes His answer is "no" and other times it is "wait"—but His response is always measured with love. God's ways are beyond us, but we can trust that they are good.

Zechariah learned this. He asked for a son, but God gave him even more. His son John would grow up to be the very prophet who would announce the arrival of the Messiah.

Zechariah's experience demonstrates a vital truth that should also encourage us as we pray: God's timing is rarely our own, but it is always worth waiting for.

JAMES BANKS

When we cannot see God's hand at work, we can still trust His heart.

Trouble for Mary and Joseph

LUKE 1:26–38

*When Joseph woke up, he did what the angel of the Lord
had commanded him and took Mary home as his wife.*

MATTHEW 1:24

When the angel Gabriel appeared to Mary and then to shepherds with good news for the world (Luke 1:26–27; 2:10), was it good news to this teenage girl? Perhaps Mary was thinking: *How do I explain my pregnancy to my family? Will my fiancé Joseph call off the betrothal? What will the townspeople say? Even if my life is spared, how will I survive as a mother all alone?*

When Joseph learned about Mary's pregnancy, he was troubled. He had three options. Go ahead with the marriage; divorce her publicly and allow her to be publicly scorned; or break off the engagement quietly. Joseph chose option three, but God intervened. He told Joseph in a dream, "Do not be afraid to take Mary home as your wife, because what is conceived in her is from the Holy Spirit" (Matthew 1:20).

For Mary and Joseph, the coming of the Messiah began with submitting themselves to God in spite of the unthinkable emotional challenges before them. They entrusted themselves to God and in doing so demonstrated for us the promise of 1 John 2:5: "If anyone obeys his word, love for God is truly made complete in them."

May God's love fill our hearts with the love that comes from obedience as we walk with Him.

ALBERT LEE

Obedience to God flows freely from a heart of love.

The Son Is Given

LUKE 1:26–33

For to us a child is born, to us a son is given,
and the government will be on his shoulders.
And he will be called Wonderful Counselor, Mighty God,
Everlasting Father, Prince of Peace.

ISAIAH 9:6

One of my favorite portions of Handel's *Messiah* is the joyous movement "For unto us a Child is born," from the first part of the oratorio. I especially love how the chorus rises to the phrase, "Unto us a Son is given." Those words, of course, are taken from Isaiah 9:6, "For unto us a Child is born, unto us a Son is given" (NKJV). Handel's majestic music soars with adoration for the Son who came to us in human flesh.

The New Testament clarifies even further who this Son is. In Luke 1, the angelic messenger appeared to Mary and identified the Christ-child in four ways. He would be the son of Mary, which would make Him fully human (1:31). He would be the Son of the Highest, making Him fully divine (1:32). He would also be the Son of David, giving Him royal lineage (1:32). And He would bear the title of Son of God (1:35), giving Him equality with the Father in all things. All of the roles the Messiah was called to fill are made possible in these distinct expressions of His Sonship.

As we worship Him, may our thoughts be filled with joy and wonder at the fullness of what it means for Him to come to earth. Our heavenly Father has given us His perfect, sufficient Son. O come, let us adore Him!

BILL CROWDER

God's love became incarnate at Bethlehem.

Significant Surrender

LUKE 1:26–28

Humble yourselves, therefore, under God's mighty hand,
that he may lift you up in due time.

1 PETER 5:6

Throughout history, Mary the mother of Jesus has been held in high esteem. And rightly so! She was singled out by God to deliver the long-awaited Messiah.

But before we get lost in the significance of her life, let's take a look at what it meant for her to surrender to the assignment. Living in a small backwater Galilean village where everyone knew everyone else's business, she would have to live with the perceived shame of her premarital pregnancy. Explaining to her mother the visits of the angel and the Holy Spirit probably didn't calm things down. To say nothing of the devastating interruption that her pregnancy would bring to her plans to marry Joseph. And while we are thinking about Joseph, what would she tell him? Would he believe her?

In light of these personal crises, her response to the angel who told her the news about her role as Jesus's mother is amazing: "Behold, I am the servant of the Lord; let it be to me according to your word" (Luke 1:38 ESV). Her words remind us that a life of significance is most often preceded by a heart eager to surrender to God's will regardless of the cost.

What significant experience does God have in store for you? It starts with surrender to Him.

JOE STOWELL

Surrender to God precedes His significant work in your life.

Mary's Baby

LUKE 1:26–33; 2:4–7

Mary treasured up all these things and pondered them in her heart.
LUKE 2:19

It was anything but an idyllic, silent night on that cool Bethlehem evening when a scared teenager gave birth to the King of Kings. Mary endured the pain of her baby's arrival without the aid of anything more than the carpentry-roughened hands of Joseph, her betrothed. Shepherds may have been serenaded in nearby fields by angels singing praises to the Baby, but all Mary and Joseph heard were the sounds of animals, birth agony, and the first cries of God in baby form. A high-magnitude star shone in the night sky above the outbuilding, but the manger scene was a dreary place for these two out-of-town visitors.

As Joseph laid the infant in Mary's arms, a combination of wonder, pain, fear, and joy must have coursed through her heart. She knew, because of an angel's promise, that this tiny bundle was "the Son of the Most High" (Luke 1:32). As she peered through the semidarkness into His eyes and then into Joseph's, she must have wondered how she was going to mother this One whose kingdom would never end.

Mary had much to ponder in her heart on that special night. Now, over 2,000 years later, each of us needs to consider the importance of Jesus's birth for ourselves—and especially His subsequent death and resurrection on our behalf.

DAVE BRANON

God came to live with us so that we could live with Him.

The Gift and the Giver

LUKE 1:67–79

"Because of God's tender mercy,
the morning light from heaven is about to break upon us."
LUKE 1:78 (NLT)

It's only a keychain. Five little blocks held together by a shoelace. My daughter gave it to me years ago when she was seven. Today the lace is frayed and the blocks are chipped, but they spell a message that never grows old: "I ♥ DAD."

The most precious gifts are determined not by *what* went into them, but by *who* they are from. Ask any parent who ever received a bouquet of dandelions from a chubby hand. The best gifts are valued not in money but in love.

Zechariah understood that. We hear it in his prophetic song as he praised God for giving him and his wife Elizabeth their son John when they were well past their childbearing years (Luke 1:67–79). Zechariah rejoiced because John was to be a prophet who would proclaim God's greatest gift to all people—the coming Messiah: "Because of God's tender mercy, the morning light from heaven is about to break upon us" (Luke 1:78 NLT). Those words point to a gift given with so much love that it will even "shine on those living in darkness and in the shadow of death" (1:79).

The sweetest gift we can receive is God's tender mercy—the forgiveness of our sins through Jesus. That gift cost Him dearly at the cross, but He offers it freely out of His deep love for us.

JAMES BANKS

Jesus is both the gift and the Giver.

MacPherson Gardens

LUKE 1:69–75

*"Praise be to the Lord, the God of Israel,
because he has come to his people and redeemed them."*

LUKE 1:68

About 230 families and individuals live at MacPherson Gardens, Block 72 in my neighborhood in Singapore. Each person has his or her own life story. On the tenth floor resides an elderly woman whose children have grown up, gotten married, and moved out. She lives by herself now. Just a few doors away from her is a young couple with two kids—a boy and a girl. And a few floors below lives a young man serving in the army. He has been to church before; maybe he will visit again. I met these people one Christmas when our church went caroling in the neighborhood to spread the joy of the season.

Every Christmas—as on the first Christmas—there are many people who do not know that God has entered into our world as a baby whose name is Jesus (Luke 1:68; 2:21). Or they do not know the significance of that event—it is "good news that will cause great joy for all the people" (2:10). Yes, all people! Regardless of our nationality, culture, gender, or financial status, Jesus came to die for us and offer us complete forgiveness so we can be reconciled with Him and enjoy His love, joy, peace, and hope. All people, from the woman next door to the colleagues we have lunch with, need to hear this wonderful news!

When Jesus was born, the angels were the bearers of this joyous news. Today, God desires to work through us to take the story to others.

POH FANG CHIA

The good news of Jesus's birth is a source of joy for all people.

A Thrill of Hope

LUKE 2:11-20

*Today in the town of David a Savior has been born to you;
he is the Messiah, the Lord.*

LUKE 2:11

Reginald Fessenden had been working for years to achieve wireless radio communication. Other scientists found his ideas radical and unorthodox, and they doubted he would succeed. But he claims that on December 24, 1906, he became the first person to ever play music over the radio.

Fessenden held a contract with a fruit company that had installed wireless systems on roughly a dozen boats to communicate about the harvesting and marketing of bananas. On that Christmas Eve in 1906, Fessenden said he told the wireless operators on board all ships to pay attention. At 9 o'clock they heard his voice.

He reportedly played a record of an operatic aria, and then he pulled out his violin, playing "O Holy Night" and singing the words to the last verse as he played. Finally, he read from Luke 2 the story of angels announcing the birth of a Savior to shepherds in Bethlehem.

Both the shepherds in Bethlehem over two thousand years ago and the sailors on board the United Fruit Company ships in 1906 heard an unexpected, surprising message of hope on a dark night. And God still speaks that same message of hope to us today. A Savior has been born for us—Christ the Lord! (Luke 2:11). We can join the choir of angels and believers through the ages who respond with "Glory to God in the highest heaven, and on earth peace to those on whom his favor rests" (v. 14).

AMY PETERSON

Without Christ there is no hope.
—Charles Spurgeon

The Forward Look

LUKE 2:21–35

There was a man in Jerusalem called Simeon,
who was righteous and devout.
He was waiting for the consolation of Israel,
and the Holy Spirit was on him.

LUKE 2:25

When the great Dutch painter Rembrandt died unexpectedly at age sixty-three, an unfinished painting was found on his easel. It focuses on Simeon's emotion in holding the baby Jesus when He was brought to the temple in Jerusalem, forty days after His birth. Yet the background and normal detail remain unfinished. Some art experts believe that Rembrandt knew the end of his life was near and—like Simeon—was ready to be dismissed (Luke 2:29).

The Holy Spirit was upon Simeon (v. 25), so it was no coincidence that he was in the temple when Mary and Joseph presented their firstborn son to God. Simeon, who had been looking for the promised Messiah, took the baby in his arms and praised God, saying: "Sovereign Lord, as you have promised, you may now dismiss your servant in peace. For my eyes have seen your salvation, which you have prepared in the sight of all nations: a light for revelation to the Gentiles, and the glory of your people Israel" (vv. 29–32).

Simeon was not longing for the glory days of Israel's history but was looking ahead for the promised Messiah, who would come to redeem all nations. Like Simeon, we can have an expectant, forward look in life because we know that one day we will see the Lord.

DAVID MCCASLAND

Even so, come, Lord Jesus!
—Revelation 22:20 NKJV

God's Clocks Keep Perfect Time

LUKE 2:36–40

*Coming up to them at that very moment,
she gave thanks to God and spoke about the child to all who
were looking forward to the redemption of Jerusalem.*

LUKE 2:38

I visit two elderly women from time to time. One has no financial worries, is fit for her age, and lives in her own home. But she can always find something negative to say. The other is crippled with arthritis and rather forgetful. She lives in simple accommodations, and she keeps a reminder pad so she won't forget her appointments. But to every visitor to her tiny apartment, her first comment is always the same: "God is so good to me!" Handing her the reminder pad on my last visit, I noticed that she had written the day before "Out to lunch tomorrow! Wonderful! Another happy day."

Anna was a prophetess at the time of Jesus's birth, and her circumstances were hard (Luke 2:36–37). Widowed early and possibly childless, she may have felt purposeless and destitute. But her focus was on God and serving Him. She was yearning for the Messiah, but in the meantime she was busy about God's business—praying, fasting, and teaching others all that she had learned from Him.

Finally the day arrived when she—now in her eighties—saw the infant Messiah in his young mother's arms. All her patient waiting was worthwhile. Her heart sang with joy as she praised God and then passed the glad news on to others.

MARION STROUD

The intersection of God's plan and our part is the best place to be.

Prepared for His Presence

LUKE 3:1–18

As it is written in the book of the words of Isaiah the prophet:
"A voice of one calling in the wilderness, 'Prepare the way for the Lord,
make straight paths for him.'"

LUKE 3:4

Whenever the President of the United States visits a community, local officials cooperate with advance teams to prepare for his coming. His motorcade route is carefully laid out. Streets are repaired and litter is picked up. The offices, auditoriums, and businesses he'll visit are decorated. Those who will meet him put on their finest clothes. Everything possible is done to give him the kind of reception his high position deserves.

If a world leader merits such thorough preparation, certainly the Lord of the universe deserves far more. John the Baptist, "advance man" for Christ, urged the people to get ready for the Messiah. In fulfillment of the prophecy of Isaiah 40:3–4, he called for the removal of spiritual obstacles (Luke 3:10–14).

1. Mountains of pride and abuse must be leveled.
2. Valleys of human need must be filled.
3. Crooked, immoral paths must be straightened.
4. Rough places of oppression must be made smooth.

While such actions don't save us, they do reflect a timeless principle: If our hearts are prepared for the Lord, He'll walk through the streets of our lives with power and peace. I wonder: Is there anything that makes us unprepared for His presence?

MART DEHAAN

Repentance clears the way for our walk with God.

The Gift of Giving

LUKE 3:7–14

*Each of you should give what you have decided in your heart to give,
not reluctantly or under compulsion, for God loves a cheerful giver.*
2 CORINTHIANS 9:7

A pastor breathed life into the phrase "He'd give you the shirt off his back" when he gave this unsettling challenge to his church: "What would happen if we took the coats off our backs and gave them to the needy?" Then he took his own coat and laid it at the front of the church. Dozens of others followed his example. This was during the winter, so the trip home was less comfortable that day. But for dozens of people in need, the season warmed up just a bit.

When John the Baptist roamed the Judean wilderness, he had a stern warning for the crowd that came to hear him. "You brood of vipers!" he said. "Produce fruit in keeping with repentance" (Luke 3:7–8). Startled, they asked him, "What should we do then?" He responded with this advice: "Anyone who has two shirts should share with the one who has none, and anyone who has food should do the same" (vv. 10–11). True repentance produces a generous heart.

Because "God loves a person who gives cheerfully" (2 Corinthians 9:7 NLT), giving should never be guilt-based or pressured. But when we give freely and generously, we find that it truly is more blessed to give than to receive.

TIM GUSTAFSON

Whoever refreshes others will be refreshed.
—Proverbs 11:25

Insignificant

LUKE 3:2–6, 15–18

*During the high-priesthood of Annas and Caiaphas,
the word of God came to John son of Zechariah in the wilderness.*

LUKE 3:2

"Movers and shakers" are people climbing the ladder of influence and success. Luke 3 mentions seven prominent leaders who exercised control in the society of their time. Roman Emperor Tiberius Caesar held the power of life and death over people in his far-flung empire. Pontius Pilate represented Rome as governor of Judea; meanwhile, Herod, Philip, and Lysanias kept people in line at the regional level. Annas and Caiaphas served as high priests, taking their religious authority seriously.

While these power brokers flexed their political muscles, "the word of God came to John son of Zechariah in the wilderness" (v. 2). Who could seem less important than this obscure man living in the desert and listening for God's voice? What could John the Baptist possibly accomplish by "preaching a baptism of repentance for the forgiveness of sins"? (v. 3). Yet multitudes came to John seeking truth, turning from their wrongs, and wondering if he could be the Messiah (vv. 7, 15). John told them, "One who is more powerful than I will come . . . . He will baptize you with the Holy Spirit" (v. 16).

John's life helps us understand what it means to be significant in God's eyes. Like John, may everything we say and do point others to Jesus.

DAVID MCCASLAND

Our surrender to God precedes His significant work in our life.

Being Useful

LUKE 3:21–22

The Holy Spirit descended on [Jesus] in bodily form like a dove.
And a voice came from heaven:
"You are my Son, whom I love; with you I am well pleased."

LUKE 3:22

Jesus emerged from obscurity and was baptized by John the Baptist. When He came out of the water, He heard His Father say, "You are my Son, whom I love; with you I am well pleased" (Luke 3:22).

What had Jesus been doing that merited such unqualified acceptance? He had not yet performed a single miracle; He had not yet preached a sermon; He had not cleansed one leper. In fact, He had not yet done anything that we normally associate with greatness. What had He been doing in Nazareth during those thirty silent years? He was growing "in wisdom and stature, and in favor with God and man" (2:52).

What's done in the silent place with God is what matters. It's in the quiet hours of fellowship with God that we're shaped and molded and made into men and women He can use—people with whom He can be well pleased.

You might be thinking, *I'm in a place where I can't be useful.* You may feel limited and frustrated by the cramping restrictions of age, an illness, a difficult child, an uncooperative spouse. But your place, wherever it is, is a place to grow. Spend time in God's Word and in prayer. Grow and bloom where you are, and your Father will be pleased with you.

DAVID ROPER

Fruitful service grows in the soil of faithful worship.

Focus on Jesus

LUKE 4:1–13

*Therefore, since we are surrounded by such a great cloud of witnesses,
let us throw off everything that hinders and the sin that so easily entangles.
And let us run with perseverance the race marked out for us, fixing our eyes
on Jesus, the pioneer and perfecter of faith. For the joy set before him
he endured the cross, scorning its shame, and sat down at
the right hand of the throne of God.*

HEBREWS 12:1–2

Over and over again, my driver's education instructor said these two words: "Drive ahead." This was his way of telling me to focus on the horizon, not just on my immediate surroundings. Drivers who continually look to the right or to the left may well go into the ditch.

Satan is good at causing "roadside distractions" that tempt us to look at him rather than at Jesus. If he can get our attention, he may be able to get us off track and delay our spiritual progress. He even tried this with Jesus!

After Jesus was baptized, Satan tried to deter Him by suggesting "better" ways to accomplish His work. Satan told Jesus that He could prove He was the Son of God by throwing himself from the temple (Luke 4:9–11). But Jesus knew that proving He was God's Son would come by submitting himself to the cross, not by leaping from a high building. He responded, "Do not put the Lord your God to the test" (v. 12). Jesus had His eyes on our redemption, and He knew there were no detours around the cross.

The way to stay out of spiritual ditches is to fix our eyes on Jesus (Hebrews 12:2) and refuse to even glance at Satan's distractions.

JULIE ACKERMAN LINK

**Let's keep our eyes on Jesus or we won't see
where He wants us to go.**

He Came for You

LUKE 4:14–21

"The Spirit of the Lord is on me, because he has anointed me to proclaim good news to the poor. He has sent me to proclaim freedom for the prisoners and recovery of sight for the blind, to set the oppressed free."

LUKE 4:18

In his novels *The Trial* and *The Castle*, German author Franz Kafka (1883–1924) portrays life as a dehumanizing existence that turns people into a sea of empty faces without identity or worth. Kafka said, "The conveyer belt of life carries you on, no one knows where. One is more of an object, a thing, than a living creature."

Early in Jesus's ministry, He went to a synagogue in Nazareth, stood up in front of the crowd, and read from Isaiah: "The Spirit of the Lord is on me, because he has anointed me to proclaim good news to the poor. He has sent me to proclaim freedom for the prisoners and recovery of sight for the blind, to set the oppressed free, to proclaim the year of the Lord's favor" (Luke 4:18–19).

Then Christ sat down and declared, "Today this scripture is fulfilled in your hearing" (v. 21). Centuries earlier, the prophet Isaiah had proclaimed these words (Isaiah 61:1–2). Now Jesus announced that He was the fulfillment of that promise.

Notice who Jesus came to rescue—the poor, brokenhearted, captive, blind, and oppressed. He came for people dehumanized by sin and suffering, by brokenness and sorrow. He came for us!

BILL CROWDER

No matter how impersonal the world may seem, Jesus loves each of us as if we were His only child.

God Is Here

LUKE 4:16–21

He heals the brokenhearted and binds up their wounds.
PSALM 147:3

Leslie and her two daughters were about to be evicted from their home. Although Leslie believed that God could help them in their situation, so far He hadn't given a clue as to how. She wondered, *Where is God?* As she drove to the courthouse, she prayed for God's intervention. Then she heard a song on the radio proclaiming, "God is here! Let the brokenhearted rejoice." Could this be the assurance from God that she was longing to hear?

Inside the courtroom, Leslie stood before the judge, heard his decision, and signed the legal documents, but still God had not given her an answer.

As Leslie was walking to her car, a truck pulled up beside her. "Ma'am," said the driver, "I heard your testimony inside the courtroom, and I believe God wants me to help you." And he did. Gary helped Leslie get in contact with a woman from a local church who was able to work with the parties involved to reverse the process so she and her girls could stay in their home.

When people ask, "Where is God?" the answer is, "Right here." One way God acts in our lives is through Christians like Gary who are continuing the work Jesus started—healing the brokenhearted and binding up their wounds (Psalm 147:3).

JULIE ACKERMAN LINK

When we love God, we will serve people.

Homecoming

LUKE 4:16-24

"Truly I tell you," [Jesus] continued,
"no prophet is accepted in his hometown."
LUKE 4:24

Homecoming for war heroes, political figures, or famous athletes usually means honor and recognition. Hometown people express their appreciation while sharing in the glory of the moment themselves. This is not always true when God's servants come home, however. Look at what happened to the "prophet of prophets" himself. When Jesus returned from His travels to appear in the synagogue of His own community Nazareth, the people showed their appreciation by trying to push Him over a cliff.

Luke 4 shows how it happened. Our Lord was given a chance to speak in the synagogue, but He said more than His countrymen wanted to hear. He also refused to let them glory in the fact that one of their own had performed miracles in other communities. He was not about to give in to the kind of contempt-breeding familiarity expressed by the person who said in effect, "Hey, wait a minute! Isn't this Joseph's son?" Others picked up on the thought. They said, "Isn't this the carpenter? Isn't this Mary's son and the brother of James, Joseph, Judas and Simon? Aren't his sisters here with us?" (Mark 6:3).

Could we be guilty of making the same mistake with God's servants? Is it possible that we are writing off pastors and Christian leaders because we associate them with someone else in their families? If Jesus's contemporaries did it to Him, we can be sure that we are even more likely to take His servants for granted—right in our own church, right in our own community.

MART DEHAAN

Not every church that wants a courageous minister
would put up with one.

What Simon Said

LUKE 5:1–11

Simon answered,
"Master, we've worked hard all night and haven't caught anything.
But because you say so, I will let down the nets."
LUKE 5:5

A man named Refuge Rabindranath was a youth worker in Sri Lanka for more than ten years. He often interacted with the youth late into the night—playing with them, listening to them, counseling and teaching them. He enjoyed working with the young people, but he found it disheartening when promising students would sometimes walk away from the faith. Some days he felt a bit like Simon Peter in Luke 5.

Simon had been working hard all night but caught no fish (v. 5). He felt discouraged and tired. Yet when Jesus told him to "put out into deep water, and let down the nets for a catch" (v. 4), Simon replied, "Because you say so, I will let down the nets" (v. 5).

Simon's obedience is remarkable. As a seasoned fisherman, he knew that fish move to the bottom of the lake when the sun is up, and the dragnets they used could not go deep enough to catch those fish.

His willingness to trust Jesus, though, was rewarded. Not only did Simon catch a large number of fish but he also gained a deeper understanding of who Jesus is. He moved from calling Jesus "Master" (v. 5) to calling Him "Lord" (v. 8). Indeed, "listening" often allows us to see the works of God firsthand and draw closer to Him.

Perhaps God is calling you to "let down your nets" again. Reply to the Lord as Simon did: "Because you say so, I will."

POH FANG CHIA

Our obedience to God will guide us through the unknown and draw us closer to Him.

Someone to Touch

LUKE 5:12-16

Jesus reached out his hand and touched the man.
"I am willing," he said. "Be clean!" And immediately the leprosy left him.
LUKE 5:13

Commuters on a Canadian Metro train witnessed a heart-moving conclusion to a tense moment. They watched as a seventy-year-old woman gently reached out and offered her hand to a young man whose loud voice and disturbing words were scaring other passengers. The lady's kindness calmed the man, who sank to the floor of the train with tears in his eyes. He said, "Thanks, Grandma," stood up, and walked away. The woman later admitted to being afraid. But she said, "I'm a mother, and he needed someone to touch." While better judgment might have given her reason to keep her distance, she took the risk to love this needy person.

Jesus understands such compassion. He didn't side with the fears of unnerved onlookers when a desperate man, full of leprosy, showed up begging to be healed. Neither was He helpless as other religious leaders were—men who could only have condemned the man for bringing his leprosy into the village (Leviticus 13:45–46). Instead, Jesus reached out to someone who probably hadn't been touched by anyone for years and healed him.

Thankfully for that man and for us Jesus came to offer what no law could ever offer—the touch of His hand and heart.

MART DEHAAN

No one is too troubled or unclean to be touched by Jesus.

Jesus's Prayer Patterns

LUKE 5:12-16

Jesus often withdrew to lonely places and prayed.
LUKE 5:16

Communication is vital to any relationship: parent and child, husband and wife, employer and employee, coach and athlete. And most important—God and those who love Him.

During His time on earth, Jesus showed us the importance of communication. The Gospels tell us of nearly twenty occasions when He prayed to His heavenly Father. He prayed in different circumstances: at His baptism (Luke 3:21), during brief rests from ministry (Luke 6:12), before raising Lazarus (John 11:41). And He prayed for different things: for guidance (Luke 6:12–13), to express His desire to do His Father's will (Matthew 26:39), to give thanks for food (John 6:11).

Jesus was a prayer warrior. Here was God himself in the person of the Son—the One in whom all the power of the universe dwelt. Yet He turned to God the Father in prayer. As hard as that may be to understand, its lesson for us is easy to grasp: If Jesus needed to communicate with God to accomplish His mission, how much more do we need to pray!

Think of what you have to face today. If it is your habit to ask, "What would Jesus do?" you can be sure from His example that He would pray first. That's not a bad pattern to follow.

DAVE BRANON

Pray first!

A Fresh Start

LUKE 5:17–26

Jesus answered them, "It is not the healthy who need a doctor, but the sick."
LUKE 5:31

In many countries, health laws prohibit reselling or reusing old mattresses. Only landfills will take them. Tim Keenan tackled the problem, and today his business employs a dozen people to extract the individual components of metal, fabric, and foam in old mattresses for recycling. But that's only part of the story. In an article in the Colorado Springs *Gazette*, journalist Bill Vogrin wrote, "Of all the items Keenan recycles . . . it's the people that may be his biggest success." Keenan hires men from halfway houses and homeless shelters, giving them a job and a second chance. He says, "We take guys nobody else wants."

Luke 5:17–26 tells how Jesus healed somebody no one wanted. He restored the body and soul of a paralyzed man. Following that miraculous event, Levi answered Jesus's call to follow Him and then invited his fellow tax collectors and friends to a banquet in honor of the Lord (vv. 27–29). When some people accused Jesus of associating with undesirables (v. 30), He reminded them that healthy people don't need a doctor—adding, "I have not come to call the righteous, but sinners to repentance" (v. 32).

To everyone who feels like a "throwaway" headed for the landfill of life, Jesus opens His arms of love and offers a fresh beginning. That's why He came!

DAVID MCCASLAND

Salvation is receiving a new life.

Jesus's Team

LUKE 5:27–35

After this, Jesus went out and saw a tax collector by the name of Levi sitting at his tax booth. "Follow me," Jesus said to him.
LUKE 5:27

In 2002, Major League Baseball's Oakland Athletics built a winning team in an unorthodox way. They had lost three top players after 2001, and the team didn't have money to sign any stars. So Oakland's general manager, Billy Beane, used some often-neglected statistics to assemble a group of lesser-known players either "past their prime" or seen by other teams as not skilled enough. That ragtag team ran off a twenty-game winning streak on the way to winning their division and 103 games.

This reminds me a little of the way Jesus put together His "team" of disciples. He included rough Galilean fishermen, a zealot, and even a despised tax collector named Levi (Matthew). Indeed, God chooses "the foolish things of the world to shame the wise" (1 Corinthians 1:27). God used those dedicated men (minus Judas) to ignite a movement that affected the world so dramatically it has never been the same.

We can learn from this. Sometimes we seek out the familiar, the influential, and the rich. As a result, we can tend to ignore people with less status or those with physical limitations.

Jesus put some of society's less desirable people on His team—treating everyone the same. With the Spirit's power and guidance, we too can honor all people equally.

DAVID EGNER

There are no unimportant people in the body of Christ.

Fly with the Eagles

LUKE 6:12–16

When morning came,
he called his disciples to him and chose twelve of them,
whom he also designated apostles.

LUKE 6:13

A well-known business leader commented on the winners and the losers in his profession. "The winners fly with eagles," he said, "and the losers run with turkeys."

When Jesus selected the small group to whom He would entrust His mission in the world, the men appeared to be anything but "eagles." Jesus knew that by His power and grace they could soar, but first He had to teach them to fly together.

What a strange mix! There was Peter, impetuous and uncouth. Andrew was simple and believing, but Thomas had a question mark for a mind.

Then consider Matthew and Simon. Matthew probably had held his post as tax collector by cooperating with the despised Romans. Simon the Zealot may have belonged to a guerrilla band determined to make life miserable for the foreign overlords of Rome by disrupting their trade or by rioting in the streets. Think of it—it would be a little like having people from the political right and someone from the political left on the same church board.

Why this diversity? Perhaps to teach us that loyalty to Jesus comes first. Discipleship, true to its name, requires us to learn love and obedience and submission in a diverse community of faith under one Head—Jesus Christ.

HADDON ROBINSON

Unity among believers comes from our union with Christ.

Changing Hearts

LUKE 6:27–36

"Be merciful, just as your Father is merciful."
LUKE 6:36

On the last day of the US Civil War, General Joshua Chamberlain was in command of the Union army. His soldiers lined up on both sides of the road that the Confederate army had to march down in surrender. One wrong word or one belligerent act—and the longed-for peace could be turned to slaughter. In an act as brilliant as it was moving, Chamberlain ordered his troops to salute their foe! No taunting here, no vicious words—only guns in salute and swords raised to honor.

When Jesus offered His words about forgiveness in Luke 6, He was helping us understand the difference between people of grace and people without grace. Those who know His forgiveness are to be strikingly unlike everyone else. We must do what others think impossible: Forgive and love our enemies. Jesus said, "Be merciful, just as your Father is merciful" (v. 36).

Imagine the impact in our workplaces and on our families if we were to embrace this principle. If a salute can make armies whole again, what power there must be in Christ's grace reflected through us! Scripture gives evidence of this in Esau's embrace of his deceitful brother (Genesis 33:4), in Zacchaeus's joyful penance (Luke 19:1–10), and in the picture of a father racing to greet his prodigal son (Luke 15).

With the grace of Christ, may we let this be the final day of bitterness and dispute between others and us.

RANDY KILGORE

Anger almost always vanishes in the face of grace.

I'm Right: You Must Be Wrong

LUKE 6:37–42

"Do not judge, and you will not be judged.
Do not condemn, and you will not be condemned.
Forgive, and you will be forgiven."

LUKE 6:37

My friend Ria admires the great blue heron's amazing six-foot spread of wings, and she marvels at his majestic appearance. Ria welcomes the sight of him gliding in for a landing on a small island in the middle of the pond near her home.

Now, I can appreciate that the heron is a marvelous and unique creature. But I don't ever want to spot him in my backyard! That's because I know he won't be there just to admire the garden. No, this not-so-fine-feathered version of persona non grata will be checking out our little pond for a take-out fish dinner!

So, am I right? Or is Ria?

Why can't we agree? Different personalities, history, or knowledge can color people's views. It doesn't mean that one person is right and the other wrong, yet sometimes we can be unkind, rigid, and judgmental if there is not agreement. I'm not talking about sin—but just a difference in opinion or perspective. We need to take care in judging others' thinking, motives, and actions because we too desire that kind of benefit of the doubt (Luke 6:37).

Can we learn from someone who sees things with a different perspective? Do we need to practice a little patience and love? I'm so grateful that God is abundantly patient and loving with me.

CINDY HESS KASPER

A little love can make a big difference.

Table Rock

LUKE 6:46–49

"Why do you call me, 'Lord, Lord,' and do not do what I say?"
LUKE 6:46

A large, illuminated cross stands erect on Table Rock, a rocky plateau overlooking my hometown. Several homes were built on neighboring land, but recently the owners have been forced to move out because of safety concerns. Despite their close proximity to the firm bedrock of Table Rock, these homes aren't secure. They have been shifting atop their foundations—nearly three inches every day—causing risk of major water pipes breaking, which would accelerate the sliding.

Jesus compares those who hear and obey His words to those wise enough to build their homes on rock (Luke 6:47–48). Their homes survive the storms. By contrast, He says homes built without a firm foundation—like people who don't heed His instruction—cannot weather the torrents.

On many occasions, I've been tempted to ignore my conscience when I knew God asked more of me than I had given, thinking my response had been "close enough." Yet the homes in the shifting foothills nearby have depicted for me that being "close" is nowhere near enough when it comes to obeying Him. To be like those who built their homes on a firm foundation and withstand the storms of life that so often threaten us, we must heed the words of our Lord completely.

KRISTEN HOLMBERG

God's Word is the only sure foundation for life.

Becoming a Go-To Person

LUKE 7:1–10

*The centurion heard of Jesus and sent some elders of the Jews to him,
asking him to come and heal his servant.*

LUKE 7:3

"Would you pray for my sister?" the burly worker asked awkwardly. I eyed him suspiciously.

Months earlier, muggy August heat intensified emotions in the pre-strike atmosphere of the assembly plant where I was working that summer. Managers drove production at a frenzied pace, and union members resisted. During breaks, we were coached by union officials on slowing down our output. My faith and idealism got me in the doghouse because I didn't think God would accept anything but my best effort. I naively tried to explain.

My co-workers' response was harassment, and this burly worker who was now asking for prayer had been the ringleader those months earlier as I tried to complete this undesirable task of working under hostile conditions.

So now I greeted this prayer request with suspicion. "Why me?" His answer jarred me: "Because she's got cancer," he said gruffly, "and I need someone God will hear." The bitter rancor between us eased as I prayed for his sister.

Like the centurion in Luke 7, people in the storms of life don't waste time or mince words. They go directly to the people whose faith they've tagged as real. We need to be those people.

RANDY KILGORE

**Even the hardest of souls might ask for help
when someone they love is at risk.**

The Look of Compassion

LUKE 7:11–18

When Jesus landed and saw a large crowd, he had compassion on them,
because they were like sheep without a shepherd.
So he began teaching them many things.

MARK 6:34

At times the world seems to be an uncaring, unsympathetic place. We often don't notice the plight of our suffering neighbors. Perhaps too busy with our own interests, we sometimes fail to see anguish and despair that is at their very doorstep.

This could not be said of our Savior. Time after time He met the needs of suffering people. Luke 7:11–18 tells us that when He saw the widow stricken with grief over the death of her son, He had compassion on her and healed the boy. Earlier, when He saw a man with leprosy—despised, ostracized, and no doubt disfigured—Jesus made him whole (see Luke 5:12–15). Still today, Jesus looks upon human need with compassion.

A little girl's mother had been taken to the hospital, and she was at home with just her father. Soon after the lights were turned out on that first night, the girl asked quietly, "Daddy, are you there?" "Yes," he assured her. A moment later she asked, "Daddy, are you looking at me?" When he said yes, she fell asleep.

We have that kind of assurance from our Savior and His look of love. No matter what we are going through, we know that His eye is fixed on us. While the world may turn its eye from suffering, we know that we are always under the watchful eye of our compassionate Savior.

DAVID EGNER

God loves every one of us as if there were but one of us to love.

It's Okay to Ask

LUKE 7:18-28

[Jesus] replied to the messengers, "Go back and report to John what you have seen and heard: The blind receive sight, the lame walk, those who have leprosy are cleansed, the deaf hear, the dead are raised, and the good news is proclaimed to the poor."

LUKE 7:22

It's perfectly natural for fear and doubt to creep into our minds. *"What if heaven isn't real after all?" "Is Jesus the only way to God?" "Will it matter in the end how I lived my life?"* Questions like these should not be given quick or trite responses.

John the Baptist, whom Jesus called the greatest of the prophets (Luke 7:28), had questions shortly before his execution (v. 19). He wanted to know for sure that Jesus was the Messiah and that his own ministry had therefore been valid.

Jesus's response is a comforting model for us to use. Instead of discounting the doubt or criticizing John, Jesus pointed to the miracles He was doing. As eyewitnesses, John's disciples could return with vivid assurances for their mentor. But He did more—He used words and phrases (v. 22) drawn from Isaiah's prophecies of the coming Messiah (Isaiah 35:4–6; 61:1), which were certain to be familiar to John.

Then, turning to the crowd, Jesus praised John (Luke 7:24–28), removing any doubt that He was offended by John's need for reassurance (Matthew 3:13–17).

Questioning and doubting, which are both understandable human responses, are opportunities to remind, reassure, and comfort those who are shaken by uncertainty.

RANDY KILGORE

Reassurance comes as we doubt our doubts and believe our beliefs.

Winning Friends

LUKE 7:31–35

"The Son of Man came eating and drinking, and you say, 'Here is a glutton and a drunkard, a friend of tax collectors and sinners.'"

LUKE 7:34

In ancient Baghdad lived a merchant named Darius, who had become extremely perplexed. His wares were of the finest quality, and the payment he asked for them was fair; yet he was unable to attract much trade into his well-located shop. In despair he sought the counsel of Aurelius, the philosopher, who advised him, "Darius, the source of your woe is apparent to all but you. You seek trade, but you do not seek friends. You want to be known as the purveyor of fine wares, but by your manner you have built a barrier of cold unfriendliness. Mark this well: good wares are not enough. The secret is good wares together with the good will of men."

As Christians, we offer to lost and dying souls the very best—eternal salvation through faith in Christ. Yet if we don't befriend those who need the Savior—if we are aloof and defensive—we will not attract anyone to Him.

Remember what Jesus did. Although he was criticized for it, the Lord Jesus walked out into the marketplace and made friends of publicans, sinners, and Samaritans. He didn't approve of what they did, but He loved them for who they were.

Imagine following His example. What would it be like to *be* a friend for Jesus to *win* a friend to Jesus?

DAVID EGNER

Kindness has converted more sinners than zeal, eloquence, or learning.

Beautiful

LUKE 7:36–50

*"Leave her alone," said Jesus. "Why are you bothering her?
She has done a beautiful thing to me."*
MARK 14:6

Picture two teenage girls. The first girl is strong and healthy. The other girl has never known the freedom of getting around on her own. From her wheelchair she faces not only the emotional challenges common to life but also a stream of physical pains and struggles.

But both girls are smiling cheerfully as they enjoy each other's company. Two beautiful teenagers—each seeing in the other the treasure of friendship.

Jesus devoted much of His time and attention to people like the girl in the wheelchair. People with lifelong disabilities or physical deformities as well as those who were looked down on by others for various reasons. In fact, Jesus let one of "those people" anoint Him with oil, to the disdain of the religious leaders (Luke 7:39). On another occasion, when a woman showed her love with a similar act, Jesus told her critics, "Leave her alone . . . . She has done a beautiful thing to me" (Mark 14:6).

God values everyone equally; there are no distinctions in His eyes. In reality, we are all in desperate need of Christ's love and forgiveness. Jesus's love compelled Him to die on the cross for each of us.

May we see each person as Jesus did: made in God's image and worthy of His love. Let's treat everyone we meet with Christlike equality and learn to see beauty as He does.

DAVE BRANON

Everyone we meet bears the image of God.

Look What Jesus Has Done

LUKE 8:1-8

*Since you excel in everything—in faith, in speech, in knowledge,
in complete earnestness and in the love we have kindled in you
—see that you also excel in this grace of giving.*

2 CORINTHIANS 8:7

The little boy was only eight when he announced to his parents' friend Wally, "I love Jesus and want to serve God overseas someday." During the next ten years or so, Wally prayed for him as he watched him grow up. When this young man later applied with a mission agency to go to Mali, Wally told him, "It's about time! When I heard what you wanted to do, I invested some money and have been saving it for you, waiting for this exciting news." Wally has a heart for others and for getting God's good news to people.

Jesus and His disciples needed financial support as they traveled from one town and village to another, telling the good news of His kingdom (Luke 8:1–3). A group of women who had been cured of evil spirits and diseases helped to support them "out of their own means" (v. 3). One was Mary Magdalene, who had been freed from the presence of seven demons. Another was Joanna, the wife of an official in Herod's court. Nothing is known about Susanna and "many others" (v. 3), but we know that Jesus had met their spiritual needs. Now they were helping Him and His disciples through giving their financial resources.

When we consider what Jesus has done for us, His heart for others becomes our own. Let's ask God how He wants to use us.

ANNE CETAS

Jesus gave His all; He deserves our all.

Changed by the Book

LUKE 8:4–15

For the word of God is alive and active. Sharper than any double-edged sword, it penetrates even to dividing soul and spirit, joints and marrow; it judges the thoughts and attitudes of the heart.

HEBREWS 4:12

He was trouble. He lived in a home for orphans, but he didn't like it. He was disobedient and miserable, so he ran away. When he did, he took with him the Bible his housemother had given him.

Several years later, the young man returned to the home he had abandoned. He told the people that while he was gone, he had begun reading the Bible. "Now I want to accept Christ," he told his astonished listeners.

What a remarkable book the Bible is! Read by a hurting and troubled young man, this Book was used by God's Spirit to show him his need for salvation.

We live in a world that needs what the Bible offers. People need to read its words of comfort, hope, cleansing, and joy. They need to discover in its pages the good news of salvation in Christ.

Not everyone who reads God's Word turns to Christ. Jesus made this clear in the parable of the sower (Luke 8:4–15). We are to be sowers of God's Word, but we don't decide who will receive it. Our job is to scatter the seed.

Maybe you've been looking for a good witnessing tool and never thought that God's Word is the answer. Why not give a Bible to those you want to reach. Then watch what happens. They can be changed by His Book.

DAVE BRANON

God's Word is an arrow that never misses its mark.

How Do You Hear?

LUKE 8:16–18

"Therefore consider carefully how you listen.
Whoever has will be given more; whoever does not have,
even what they think they have will be taken from them."

LUKE 8:18

A young boy asked his father to solve a riddle. He said, "There were three frogs sitting on a log. One frog *decided* to jump off. How many were left?" The dad replied, "Two, of course." "You're wrong!" gleefully exclaimed the boy. "There were three frogs left. The one frog only decided to jump off, but he didn't jump!"

Take heed how you hear! Before you judge another's remarks, find out just exactly what that person said, and what was meant by what was said.

A local radio station announced that I was going to preach a message titled "Why I Am Looking for the Second Coming of Jesus This Year." I received a scorching letter from a listener who accused me of setting dates and predicting the return of Christ. But I had said nothing of the kind! I said I was *looking* for Christ's return in the coming year. I didn't say He would come, but that I was *looking* for Him to come. And if He doesn't come this year, I will be looking for Him again next year.

Careless listening can result in serious errors. This is especially true as it relates to the Bible, for the misunderstanding of one word can cause a wrong interpretation and keep us from doing what God wants us to do.

Our Lord himself said it: "Consider carefully how you listen."

MART DEHAAN

To hear God speak, read the Bible carefully and study it prayerfully.

Two Daughters

LUKE 8:40–42, 49–56

*While Jesus was still speaking, someone came from the house of Jairus,
the synagogue leader. "Your daughter is dead," he said.
"Don't bother the teacher anymore."*

LUKE 8:49

I had never thought much about Jairus before. Oh, I had heard the story about this synagogue ruler, and I knew he had begged Jesus to come to his house and heal his dying daughter. But I never understood the depth of his sorrow. I never understood how his heart must have shattered in pain when a messenger came to him and announced, "Your daughter is dead."

No, I never comprehended his grief and anguish—until I heard those same words from a police officer who came to our house on June 6, 2002.

Jairus's daughter was twelve, and she died from an illness. Our daughter was seventeen, and it was an auto accident that broke our family's heart.

Jairus's daughter was restored to life by Jesus's touch. My daughter Melissa—though we ache to know she wasn't healed physically—was healed spiritually by Jesus's sacrifice of love when she trusted Him as Savior early in her life. Now our comfort comes from knowing that her eternal existence with the Lord has already begun.

Two daughters. The same Jesus. Two different results. His loving and compassionate touch is a miracle that can bring peace to grieving hearts— like Jairus's, like mine, like yours.

DAVE BRANON

In every desert of trial, God has an oasis of comfort.

Solitude and Service

LUKE 9:1–2, 10–17

The crowds learned about it and followed him. He welcomed them and spoke
to them about the kingdom of God, and healed those who needed healing.

LUKE 9:11

Comedian Fred Allen said, "A celebrity is a person who works hard all his life to become well-known—then wears dark glasses to avoid being recognized." Fame often brings loss of privacy along with a relentless frenzy of attention.

When Jesus began His public ministry of teaching and healing, He was catapulted into the public eye and thronged by people seeking help. Crowds followed Him wherever He went. But Jesus knew that having regular time alone with God was essential to maintaining strength and perspective.

After Jesus's twelve disciples returned from their successful mission "to proclaim the kingdom of God and to heal the sick" (Luke 9:2), He took them to a quiet place to rest (v. 10). Soon, however, crowds of people found them and Jesus welcomed them. He "spoke to them about the kingdom of God, and healed those who needed healing" (v. 11). Instead of sending them away to find food, the Lord provided an outdoor picnic for 5,000 people! (vv. 12–17).

Jesus was not immune to the pressure of curious and hurting people, but He maintained the balance of public service and private solitude by taking time for rest and for prayer alone with His Father (Luke 5:16).

May we follow our Lord's example as we serve others in His name.

DAVID MCCASLAND

Turning down the volume of life allows you to listen to God.

Losing to Find

LUKE 9:18-27

"For whoever desires to save his life will lose it,
but whoever loses his life for My sake will save it."
LUKE 9:24 (NKJV)

When Mother Teresa died in 1997, people marveled again at her example of humble service to Christ and to people in great need. She had spent fifty years ministering to the poor, sick, orphaned, and dying through the Missionaries of Charity in Calcutta, India.

After extensive interviews with her, British journalist Malcolm Muggeridge wrote: "There is much talk today about discovering an identity, as though it were something to be looked for, like a winning number in a lottery; then, once found, to be hoarded and treasured. Actually, . . . the more it is spent the richer it becomes. So, with Mother Teresa, in effacing herself, she becomes herself. I never met anyone more memorable."

I suspect that many of us may be afraid of what will happen if we obey Jesus's words: "If anyone desires to come after Me, let him deny himself, and take up his cross daily, and follow Me. For whoever desires to save his life will lose it, but whoever loses his life for My sake will save it" (Luke 9:23–24 NKJV).

Our Savior reminded His followers that He came to give us life abundantly (John 10:10). We are called to lose our lives for Christ and in so doing discover the fullness of life in Him.

DAVID MCCASLAND

As we give up our life for Jesus, it becomes complete in Him.

Down from the Mountain

LUKE 9:28–42

*The next day, when they came down from the mountain,
a large crowd met him.*
LUKE 9:37

Years ago our family lived in Switzerland. I'll never forget one idyllic afternoon I spent on a mountaintop. The only thing I heard was the sound of silence. The air was clean and sweet. As I lay on the grass, I became still and sensed God's presence in a special way. It was good, even glorious, being there away from people and alone with Him. I longed to cling to this experience, and I resisted going back down to civilization. I recalled Peter's similar reaction on another mountain when Jesus was transfigured before his eyes.

No wonder Peter wanted to stay there! Although his mountaintop experience far exceeded mine, I knew what my response needed to be. Like Peter, I needed to come down from the mountain so I could return refreshed to a multitude of needy people.

I once heard a preacher say, "Great experiences must bring us back to everyday life. They must be related to the heartbreaks of people. Mountaintops don't mean anything without the valleys."

If you're weary from your labors in the valley, the Lord may be saying to you, "Come aside . . . and rest a while" (Mark 6:31 NKJV). But if you're on a mountaintop, don't stay there. God wants to work through you in other people's lives.

JOANIE YODER

The closer you are to God, the more you'll have a heart for people.

Saying Goodbye

LUKE 9:57–62

*Jesus replied, "No one who puts a hand to the plow and looks
back is fit for service in the kingdom of God."*
LUKE 9:62

Saying goodbye is hard—to family and friends, to a favorite and familiar place, to an occupation or livelihood.

In Luke 9:57–62 our Lord describes the cost of being His disciple. A would-be follower says to Jesus, "I will follow you, Lord; but first let me go back and say goodbye to my family" (v. 61). Jesus responds, "No one who puts a hand to the plow and looks back is fit for service in the kingdom of God" (v. 62). Is He asking His followers to say goodbye to everything and every relationship considered precious?

In the Chinese language there is no direct equivalent of the English word *goodbye*. The two Chinese characters used to translate this word really mean, "see you again." Becoming a disciple of Christ may sometimes mean others will reject us, but it does not mean we say goodbye to people in the sense that we are to forget all our past relationships. Saying goodbye means that God wants us to follow Him on His terms—wholeheartedly. Then we will see people again from the right perspective.

God wants the best for us, but we must allow Him to take priority over everything else.

C. P. HIA

When we follow Jesus, we get a new perspective.

Afraid to Fail

LUKE 10:1–12

He told them,
"The harvest is plentiful, but the workers are few.
Ask the Lord of the harvest, therefore,
to send out workers into his harvest field."

LUKE 10:2

Some things haven't changed much in 2,000 years. Jesus observed in His day what a thoughtful Christian observes in ours. "The harvest is plentiful" (Luke 10:2).

Stroll through a bookstore, and you can see shelves of books on "spirituality." But often that simply means an age-old desire to make some sense out of life. Citizens of our age try to satisfy their thirst for significance by drinking too much or spending too much time on social media. What they are truly longing for is Jesus Christ.

The great theologian Augustine took the pulse of his time when he wrote, "O Lord, you have made us for yourself, and our heart is restless until it finds its rest in you."

Today, the harvest has never been greater. But Jesus noted, "The workers are few." But why? Certainly there are enough professing Christians to make a dent in the harvest. Is it a fear that we may fail? Are we afraid that people will reject us and our message?

Let's not be afraid to fail as we go out into the "fields" of our neighborhood, our worksite, our school. We can't control the response—but we can share the message.

HADDON ROBINSON

If faith in Christ is worth having, it's worth sharing.

The Heavenly Manifest

LUKE 10:17–24

"Do not rejoice that the spirits submit to you,
but rejoice that your names are written in heaven."
LUKE 10:20

At the Kenya Airways check-in counter, I presented my passport for verification. When the agents searched for my name on their manifest—the document that lists names of passengers on my flight—my name was missing. The problem? Overbooking and a lack of confirmation. My hope of reaching home that day was shattered.

The episode reminded me of another kind of manifest—the Book of Life. In Luke 10, Jesus sent His disciples on an evangelistic mission. On their return, they happily reported their success. But Jesus told them: "Do not rejoice that the spirits submit to you, but rejoice that your names are written in heaven" (v. 20). The focus of our joy is not merely that we are successful but that our names are inscribed in God's book.

But how can we be sure of that? God's Word tells us, "If you declare with your mouth, 'Jesus is Lord,' and believe in your heart that God raised him from the dead, you will be saved" (Romans 10:9).

In Revelation 21, John gives us a breathtaking description of the Holy City, which awaits those who trust Christ. Then he writes, "Nothing impure will ever enter it, nor will anyone who does what is shameful or deceitful, but only those whose names are written in the Lamb's book of life" (v. 27).

LAWRENCE DARMANI

The Book of Life is God's heavenly manifest.
Is your name written in it?

Neighborly Kindness

LUKE 10:25–37

A Samaritan, as he traveled, came where the man was;
and when he saw him, he took pity on him.

LUKE 10:33

Who is worthy to receive our compassion, and who is not? That kind of thinking is a major obstacle to helping others. Jesus told a parable to answer the question: "Who is my neighbor?" (Luke 10:29). Or, who qualifies as worthy of our neighborly acts?

Jesus told of a man who traveled on the notoriously dangerous road from Jerusalem to Jericho. As he traveled, he encountered some thieves, was robbed and beaten, then left for dead. Religious Jews (one a priest; the other a Levite) noticed him, but they walked by on the other side, probably for fear of being religiously defiled. Eventually a Samaritan came along and had unconditional compassion on the wounded stranger.

Jesus's audience would have gasped at this story, because Jews despised Samaritans. The Samaritan could have limited or qualified his compassion because the injured man was a Jew. But he did not limit his neighborly kindness. Instead, he saw a human being in need and helped him.

Are you limiting your kindness only to the people you deem worthy? As followers of Jesus, it's better to find ways to show neighborly kindness to all people—no matter what their background.

MARVIN WILLIAMS

Our love for Christ is demonstrated by our love for our neighbor.

Battling Distractions

LUKE 10:38–42

"Few things are needed—or indeed only one.
Mary has chosen what is better, and it will not be taken away from her."
LUKE 10:42

Every day I drive the same highway to and from the office, and every day I see an alarming number of distracted drivers. Usually they're talking on the phone or texting, but I have also seen people reading the newspaper, putting on makeup, and eating a bowl of cereal while trying to maneuver a car at 70-plus miles per hour! In some circumstances, distractions are fleeting and harmless. In a moving vehicle, however, they can kill.

Distractions can be a problem in our relationship with God. In fact, that was the concern Jesus had for His friend Martha. She "was distracted by all the preparations that had to be made" for a meal (Luke 10:40). When she complained about her sister Mary's lack of help (apparently due to her devotion to Christ and His teaching), Jesus told her, "Martha, Martha, you are worried and upset about many things, but few things are needed—or indeed only one. Mary has chosen what is better, and it will not be taken away from her" (vv. 41–42).

Martha's distractions were well-intentioned. But she was missing the opportunity to listen to Jesus and enjoy His presence. He is deserving of our deepest devotion, and He alone can enable us to overcome life's distractions.

BILL CROWDER

If you want to be miserable, look within;
distracted, look around; peaceful, look up.

Our Fathers Who Aren't in Heaven

LUKE 11:1–13

*[Jesus] said to them, "When you pray, say:
'Father, hallowed be your name, your kingdom come.'"*
LUKE 11:2

When Jesus taught us to pray, He began with "Father" (Luke 11:2). It is one of many Scriptures that refer to God as a father. I find it both fascinating and instructive that when God wanted us to know what He is like, He chose to emphasize His fatherhood.

What do we know about God as our Father? According to Jesus's prayer, we know that our Father in heaven is available and attentive to us. It is also clear that He provides for us. He forgives us and protects us from evil (vv. 2–4).

What a wonderful pattern for fathers who aren't in heaven! Granted, there is only one perfect Father in the universe, but He sets the pace for the rest of us less-than-perfect fathers. I discovered early in my ministry that my children were not impressed with books I wrote, titles I had, or places I spoke. They craved my time and attention, the provision for basic needs, a love that patiently forgave, and the creation of a safe place for them to grow and mature. It's a short but very profound list of fatherly duties.

And what about people who didn't get a dad in life who met those needs? We can all take heart in this fact: If we have been redeemed through Jesus, we have a perfect heavenly Father—and He's the best Father of all.

JOE STOWELL

The heavenly Father's arms never tire of holding His children.

Jesus Is Greater

LUKE 11:14–23

You, dear children, are from God and have overcome them, because the one who is in you is greater than the one who is in the world.

1 JOHN 4:4

Chinese communities in Southeast Asia and some villages in China celebrate a month-long Ghost Festival. It is believed that during this time the spirits of the dead return to earth to roam among the living. So people burn joss sticks (incense) and phony money, prepare feasts, and perform in street theaters—all to keep the spirits happy.

As a child growing up in Singapore, I was taught to fear those ghosts. One year I had a fever during the festival, and I was told that I must have bumped into some and offended them.

Now that I know what the Bible says about Jesus's power over the real spirit world of Satan and his demons, I have been freed from my former fears. Because I have placed my faith in Christ as my Lord and Savior, I realize that I don't need to try to appease or fight evil spirits by myself.

Jesus showed His power over the spirit world as He cast out demons (Luke 11:14–23). When He died on the cross for us and rose from the grave, Jesus triumphed over Satan and sealed his doom (Colossians 2:15; Revelation 20:10). The Bible assures followers of Christ, "the one who is in you is greater than the one who is in the world" (1 John 4:4).

As believers, we need not fear the devil or demons. Our Lord Jesus is greater!

ALBERT LEE

The power of Satan is no match for the power of Jesus.

Pay Attention to Signs

LUKE 11:29–45

"You foolish people!
Did not the one who made the outside make the inside also?"
LUKE 11:40

The road was smooth and we were making good progress as we headed for my husband Jay's dad's house in South Carolina. As we drove through the mountains in Tennessee, I began seeing detour signs. But Jay kept going, so I assumed that they didn't apply to us. Shortly before we reached the North Carolina border, we came to a sign that said the highway ahead was closed due to a rockslide. We would have to turn around. Jay was surprised. "Why wasn't there any warning?" he wanted to know. "There were lots of warnings," I said. "Didn't you see the signs?" "No," he said. "Why didn't you mention them?" "I assumed that you saw them," I answered. This story is funny now.

Throughout history, God provided plenty of "signs" to show people the way to live, but they kept going their own way. When God finally sent His Son as a sign (Luke 11:30), the religious leaders paid little attention to His warnings. Life for them was good. They were recognized and respected (v. 43). They resented being told that they were wrong (v. 45).

We can be the same way. When life is going well, we tend to ignore warnings that indicate we need to turn around and change our sinful ways. Let's pay attention to the signs.

JULIE ACKERMAN LINK

God sends warnings to protect us, not to punish us.

Sourdough Bread

LUKE 12:1–7

Meanwhile, when a crowd of many thousands had gathered, so that they were trampling on one another, Jesus began to speak first to his disciples, saying: "Be on your guard against the yeast of the Pharisees, which is hypocrisy."
LUKE 12:1

Sourdough bread became popular in California during the Gold Rush of the mid-1800s. In the 1890s, it was a favorite during the great Gold Rush in Alaska and Canada. Prospectors would carry with them a small portion of sourdough mix that contained natural yeast. It could then be used as a starter to make more of their favorite sourdough bread.

In the Bible, though, yeast or leaven can have a negative connotation. For example, in the New Testament, "leaven" is often referred to as a corrupting influence. This is why Jesus said: "Be on your guard against the yeast of the Pharisees, which is hypocrisy" (Luke 12:1).

Hypocrites put on a show of righteousness while hiding sinful thoughts and behavior. Christ warned His disciples and us that secret sins will someday be exposed to full disclosure. He said, "There is nothing concealed that will not be disclosed, or hidden that will not be known" (v. 2). Because of this, we are to reverentially fear God, to ask for His grace to forsake any sin, and to grow as authentic believers.

Yeast may be a blessing in the bakery, but it can also remind us to guard against the permeating influence of sin in our hearts.

DENNIS FISHER

Be sure your sin will find you out.
—Numbers 32:23 (NKJV)

You Fool!

LUKE 12:16–21

The fool says in his heart, "There is no God."
They are corrupt, their deeds are vile; there is no one who does good.

PSALM 14:1

It seems to me rather contradictory that Jesus, who was so gentle at times (Matthew 19:13–15), would call some people fools. Yet, as recorded in the Gospels a number of times, our Lord used this derogatory term to describe those He spoke about—especially the Pharisees (see Matthew 23:17–19; Luke 11:39–40).

Jesus also used the word *fool* in a parable after warning a man about coveting (Luke 12:13–21). What made that man foolish was not the fact that he built bigger barns to store his abundant harvest (vv. 16–18). It would have been more foolish of him to leave it out in the fields where inclement weather would spoil it. Nor was he foolish because of his thought that this unexpected windfall was enough to last him a long time (v. 19). After all, we are urged to follow the example of the ant, which "stores its provisions" for the harvest (Proverbs 6:6–8).

What made the man foolish? He left God out of the picture. He was called a fool because he failed to realize that his life was in God's hands. While he was planning carefully for his comfortable life on earth, he failed to plan for eternity and store up treasures in heaven (Matthew 6:20).

Does your plan for the future have God in it? You won't want to be called foolish by Him in the end.

C. P. HIA

He is no fool who gives what he cannot keep to gain what he cannot lose.
—Jim Elliot

Heart Check

LUKE 12:22-34

"For where your treasure is, there your heart will be also."
Luke 12:34

During the years when I commuted into Chicago on the train every day, I always followed the "unwritten codes of conduct"—such as, no conversations with people sitting next to you if you don't know them. That was tough on a guy like me who has never met a stranger. I love talking to new people!

Although I kept the code of silence, I realized that you can still learn something about people based on the section of the newspaper they read. So I'd watch to see what they turned to first: The business section? Sports? Politics? Current events? Their choices revealed their interests.

Our choices are always revealing. Of course, God doesn't need to wait to see our choices in order for Him to know what's in our hearts. But the things that occupy our time and attention are telling. As Jesus said, "Where your treasure is, there your heart will be also" (Luke 12:34). Regardless of what we want Him to think of us, the true condition of our heart becomes clear based on how we use our time, our money, and our talents. When we invest these resources in the things He cares about, then it reveals that our hearts are in tune with His.

God's heart is with the needs of people and the advancement of His kingdom. What do your choices tell Him and others about where your heart is?

JOE STOWELL

Where is your treasure?

Good News or Bad?

LUKE 12:35–40

"It will be good for those servants whose master finds them watching when he comes. Truly I tell you, he will dress himself to serve, will have them recline at the table and will come and wait on them."

LUKE 12:37

A teacher tells her young students, "Class, I'm going down the hall to the school office for a few minutes. I don't expect to be away long. I'm sure there won't be any trouble. I'm trusting you to work on your assignments while I'm gone."

Fifteen minutes pass, then twenty, then forty. Suddenly the teacher returns. Dennis has just thrown an eraser at Carol, who is doing her math. Steven is standing on the teacher's desk making faces. The students carrying out the teacher's instructions are delighted at the teacher's return, but Dennis and Steven wish she hadn't come back at all.

Jesus is coming back! That stands as both a warning and a promise throughout the New Testament, as in today's reading from Luke 12. It's good news or bad, depending on who hears it.

In church we sing songs like "Come, Thou Long-Expected Jesus." When we partake of the Lord's Supper, we "proclaim the Lord's death till He comes" (1 Corinthians 11:26). On Sunday morning, the second coming of Christ sounds like great news. But during the rest of the week, are we as ready for His return?

Jesus is coming back! Is that good news or bad for you?

HADDON ROBINSON

Watch therefore, for you do not know what hour your Lord is coming.
—Matthew 24:42 (NKJV)

Time to Flourish

LUKE 13:1-9

*"'Sir,' the man replied, 'leave it alone for one more year,
and I'll dig around it and fertilize it.'"*

LUKE 13:8

One spring I decided to cut down the rose bush by our back door. In the three years we had lived in our home, it hadn't produced many flowers, and its ugly, fruitless branches were now creeping in all directions.

But life got busy, and my gardening plan got delayed. It was just as well—only a few weeks later that rose bush burst into bloom like I'd never seen before. Hundreds of big white flowers, rich in perfume, hung over the back door, flowed into our yard, and showered the ground with beautiful petals.

My rose bush's revival reminded me of Jesus's parable of the fig tree in Luke 13:6–9. In Israel, it was customary to give fig trees three years to produce fruit. If they didn't, they were cut down so the soil could be better used. In Jesus's story, a gardener asks his boss to give one particular tree a fourth year to produce. In context (vv. 1–5), the parable implies this: The Israelites hadn't lived as they should, and God could justly judge them. But God is patient and had given extra time for them to turn to Him, be forgiven, and bloom.

God wants all people to flourish and has given extra time so they can. Whether we are still journeying toward faith or are praying for unbelieving family and friends, His patience is good news for all of us.

SHERIDAN VOYSEY

**God has given the world extra time
to respond to His offer of forgiveness.**

Guest List

LUKE 14:7–14

"When you give a banquet, invite the poor, the crippled,
the lame, the blind, and you will be blessed. Although they cannot repay you,
you will be repaid at the resurrection of the righteous."

LUKE 14:13–14

Qumran is the location of a first-century Jewish community that had isolated itself from outside influences to prepare for the arrival of the Messiah. These people took great care in devotional life, ceremonial washings, and strict adherence to rules of conduct. Surviving documents show that they would not allow the lame, the blind, or the crippled into their communities. This was based on their conviction that anyone with a physical "blemish" was ceremonially unclean. During their table fellowship, disabled people were never on their guest lists.

Ironically, at that same time Jesus the Messiah of Israel was at work in the cities and villages of Judea and Galilee. He proclaimed His Father's kingdom, brought teaching and comfort, and worked mighty miracles. Strikingly, He proclaimed: "When you give a banquet, invite the poor, the crippled, the lame, the blind, and you will be blessed" (Luke 14:13–14).

The contrast between Jesus's words and the guest list of the Qumran community's "spiritual elite" is instructive to us. Often we like to fellowship with people who look, think, and act like us. But our Lord exhorts us to be like Him and open our doors to everyone.

DENNIS FISHER

The inclusive gospel cannot be shared by an exclusive people.
—George Sweeting

Killer Plants

LUKE 14:16–26

"If anyone comes to Me and does not hate his father and mother,
wife and children, brothers and sisters, yes, and his own life also,
he cannot be My disciple."

LUKE 14:26 (NKJV)

Some forest workers fight fires. Others battle fast-growing plants. A *Mercury News* article reported about teams of volunteers who worked hard to remove invasive plants from the redwood forests of the Santa Cruz Mountains. Workers point out that many of the non-native species they are fighting are sold in garden stores. The German ivy plant, for example, has become a serious problem in California. This fast-growing exotic houseplant competes with the native species, smothering and shading everything in its path. It can completely cover and destroy a tree.

Thinking about these home-grown invaders can help us understand something even more crucial than saving trees. Jesus warned us that anything that competes with Him for our hearts can choke our spiritual lives. He said that even the natural love of family can be dangerous and keep us from following Him (Luke 14:16–26). Our Lord demands our undivided love and loyalty.

Once we value Christ above everything else, we will learn to love our family with a deeper and healthier love. But until our ultimate loyalty is determined, home-grown affection will do in our hearts what fire or German ivy will do in a forest.

Let's be careful not to allow anything to compete with Christ in our lives.

MART DEHAAN

The more we love Christ, the more we'll love others.

Lost but Found

LUKE 15:1–9

"He calls his friends and neighbors together and says,
'Rejoice with me; I have found my lost sheep.'"
LUKE 15:6

When we discovered that my mother-in-law had gone missing while shopping with a relative, my wife and I were frantic. Mom suffered from memory loss and confusion, and there was no telling what she might do. Would she wander the area or hop onto any bus thinking it would take her home? Worst-case scenarios spun through our minds as we began to search for her, crying out to God, "Please find her."

Hours later, my mother-in-law was spotted stumbling along a road, miles away. How God blessed us in being able to find her! Several months later, He blessed her: at eighty years of age, my mother-in-law turned to Jesus Christ for salvation.

Jesus, comparing humans to lost sheep, gives us this illustration: "Suppose [a shepherd] has a hundred sheep and loses one of them. Doesn't he leave the ninety-nine in the open country and go after the lost sheep until he finds it? And when he finds it, . . . he calls his friends and neighbors together and says, 'Rejoice with me; I have found my lost sheep'" (Luke 15:4–6).

Shepherds counted their sheep to make sure every one was accounted for. In the same way, Jesus, who likens himself to that shepherd, values each of us, young and old. When we're wandering in life, searching, wondering about our purpose, it's never too late to turn to Christ. God wants us to experience His love and blessings.

LESLIE KOH

Amazing grace! . . . I once was lost, but now am found.
—John Newton

Welcome Home!

LUKE 15:11-24

"So he got up and went to his father. But while he was still a long way off, his father saw him and was filled with compassion for him; he ran to his son, threw his arm around him and kissed him."

LUKE 15:20

When we were going through a particularly challenging time with our son, a friend pulled me aside after a church meeting. "I want you to know that I pray for you and your son every day," he said. Then he added: "I feel so guilty."

"Why?" I asked. "Because I've never had to deal with prodigal children," he said. "My kids pretty much played by the rules. But it wasn't because of anything I did or didn't do. Kids," he shrugged, "make their own choices."

I wanted to hug him. His compassion was a reminder, a gift from God, communicating to me the Father's understanding for my struggle with my son.

No one understands the struggle with prodigals better than our heavenly Father. The story of the prodigal son in Luke 15 is our story and God's. Jesus told it on behalf of all sinners who need to come home to their Creator and discover the warmth of a loving relationship with Him.

Jesus is God in the flesh seeing us in the distance and looking on us with compassion. He is God running to us and throwing His arms around us.

God hasn't just left the porch light on for us. He's out on the front porch watching, waiting, calling us home.

JAMES BANKS

Our loved ones may spurn our appeals, reject our message, and oppose our arguments—but they are helpless against our prayers.
—J. Sidlow Baxter

He Would Not Join In

LUKE 15:25–32

"The older brother became angry and refused to go in.
So his father went out and pleaded with him."

LUKE 15:28

Some theologians divide transgressions into "sins of the flesh" and "sins of the spirit." This means that some sins originate in our physical passions; others come from our "heart" or disposition. In the story of the prodigal son, the elder brother's attitude gives us an example of the latter.

We're inclined to single out the prodigal son as worse than his brother. But it's worth noting that when the story ends, the prodigal is restored, forgiven, and full of joy, while the elder brother stands outside and refuses to go in.

The stay-at-home son is more than background filler. He makes us think about the state of our heart, for sour moods create untold misery.

Discontent, jealousy, bitterness, resentment, defensiveness, touchiness, and ingratitude are the dispositions that ruin our marriages, wither our children, alienate our friends, and embitter every life—including our own.

It's easy to defend our bad moods and to slide into deception and hypocrisy. But we must guard our hearts against such destructive attitudes. When they arise, we need to confess them, let them go, and experience God's forgiveness.

A bad attitude can cause us to lose out while others enter into joy.

DAVID ROPER

Resentment comes from looking at others; contentment
comes from looking at God.

Honor System

LUKE 16:1–10

"Whoever can be trusted with very little can also be trusted with much, and whoever is dishonest with very little will also be dishonest with much."
LUKE 16:10

Many homes near ours offer vegetables and flowers for sale on stands by the road. Sometimes we'll drive up to an unattended stand that operates on the "honor system." As we make our selection, we put our money into a cash box or an old coffee can. Then we go home to enjoy the freshly picked produce or perennials.

But the honor system doesn't always work. My friend Jackie has a flower stand in front of her house. One day, as she glanced out her window she saw a well-dressed woman with a big hat loading pots of perennials into the trunk of her car. Jackie smiled as she mentally calculated a $50 profit from her labors in the garden. But when she checked the cash box later, it was empty! The honor system revealed that this woman was not honorable.

Perhaps to her, taking the flowers seemed like a small thing. But being honest in little things indicates how we will respond in the big things (Luke 16:10). Honesty in all areas of our lives is one way we can bring honor to Jesus Christ, our Savior.

The best "honor system" for a follower of Christ is Colossians 3:17, "Whatever you do, whether in word or deed, do it all in the name of the Lord Jesus."

CINDY HESS KASPER

Honesty means never having to look over your shoulder.

Big Money

LUKE 16:1–15

"Use worldly wealth to gain friends for yourselves, so that when it is gone, you will be welcomed into eternal dwellings."

LUKE 16:9

Some athletes and entertainers receive astronomical salaries. I can understand why they would take all they can get, but I wonder about a culture that spends so much to be entertained when countless people in the world are homeless and hungry.

Our attitude toward money and how we use it is a barometer of our spiritual state. It reveals whether we are foolishly thinking only of the present or wisely looking to eternity.

In Luke 16, Jesus told a story about a money manager who knew he would be fired because he had wasted his employer's funds. So he went to the debtors and issued a "paid in full" receipt for a partial payment. This put him in their good graces so that when he lost his job he could go to them for help and not have to beg. No doubt his employer was unhappy about not receiving all that was owed him, but he commended the man for his shrewdness.

That story illustrates the wisdom of spending money with eternity in view. We can use our money now to help spread the gospel, and the people who receive Christ will be our friends forever and will greet us when we enter heaven.

Money can't buy happiness or eternal life. But when invested in Christ's cause, it pays eternal dividends.

HERB VANDER LUGT

The wise use of money pays eternal dividends.

The Options

LUKE 16:19−31

"In Hades, where [a rich man] was in torment, he looked up and saw Abraham far away, with Lazarus by his side."
LUKE 16:23

Last time I checked, nobody likes having problems—problems with money, problems with cars, problems with computers, problems with people, problems with health. We would all prefer a life with as few difficulties as possible.

So, if you were to offer people the choice between (1) a future totally free of problems, sorrow, tears, and pain, and (2) a future full of pain, suffering, regret, and anguish—they would choose option one, right?

Jesus died on the cross so we could experience that option. If we repent of our sins and trust Him as our Savior, He provides us with a life of fellowship with God in a perfect place the Bible calls heaven. A place with no problems. A place where there are no more tears.

People living in a problem-filled world ought to be standing in line to grab that offer. Unfortunately, many haven't heard the good news, and others refuse to trust Christ. When people die without Jesus, it's too late to take the offer, and they go to a place of torment the Bible calls hell.

Do you hate trouble and pain? Turn to Jesus and accept His offer of forgiveness. Your problems in this world won't disappear, but you'll reserve a home in heaven where they will be gone—a place of eternal joy and peace with God.

DAVE BRANON

You must accept God's Son today if you want to live in heaven's sunshine tomorrow.

Crisis of Faith

LUKE 17:1–6

The apostles said to the Lord, "Increase our faith!"
LUKE 17:5

Millions of people are afraid to travel by air. Many of them know very well what the statistics say—that they are safer in an airplane than in the family car, or even in the bathtub. But that doesn't matter. Researchers say that a conscious fear of crashing is usually not the problem. The real root of their anxiety is the fear that they will lose control of their lives once they leave the ground.

A similar crisis of faith may occur when a person puts himself in the care of God. The person of faith leaves what the world considers "solid ground" by trusting an invisible Lord. This can be frightening, especially for a new Christian.

Jesus's disciples experienced such a crisis of faith when He told them they would have to rise to levels of forgiveness and mercy previously unknown to them (Luke 17:3–5). Yet He responded to their lack of faith by pointing out that it takes only a small amount of obedient trust in Him to put the power of heaven at their disposal (v. 6).

That's the key to our journey through life. When we learn what Christ wants from us, we must take the first step of obedience. He will then give us the strength to do what He wants us to do. Lord, increase our faith.

MART DEHAAN

A little faith can dispel big fears.

Forgiving Clubs

LUKE 17:1–10

"Even if they sin against you seven times in a day and seven times come back to you saying 'I repent,' you must forgive them."
LUKE 17:4

If you play golf, you know how important it is to hit the ball at just the right spot on the clubface. More advanced clubs, however, are more forgiving. Ever-changing designs and technology have expanded what is often referred to as the "sweet spot" on the club. Now it is easier than ever to hit the ball off-center and still get good distance.

The idea of a golf club that has a large and forgiving "sweet spot" reminds me of how Christians should respond to one another. Instead of being like the old, unforgiving club that required near-perfect performance, we should be like the new clubs that are generous with the faults of the golfer. We should have a large "sweet spot" that provides plenty of room to forgive any repentant brother or sister in Christ (Luke 17:4).

That's the pattern the Lord Jesus set for us. In fact, He came to earth to die for our sins and to show us, by what He said and did, what forgiveness really means. During His life, and even on the cross, He forgave all who called to Him in faith. We should follow His example. Who should be more forgiving than those of us who have experienced so much forgiveness ourselves?

MART DEHAAN

We can stop forgiving others only if Christ stops forgiving us.

Nothing but Grace

LUKE 17:6–10

"So you also, when you have done everything you were told to do, should say, 'We are unworthy servants; we have only done our duty.'"

LUKE 17:10

In 1914, before the use of insulin injections, Corrie ten Boom's Aunt Jans was diagnosed with diabetes. She knew that she did not have long to live. Yet, within a few days after learning this, she went right back to working in God-honoring causes. Several months later, a blood test indicated that the end was near.

The family was gathered in Aunt Jans's room when Corrie's father gently broke the news to her that she would soon be entering heaven. Then he added, "Jans, some must go to their Father empty-handed, but you will run to Him with hands full."

Jans's response touched them all. She said that her good deeds could be considered "little tricks and trinkets." Then she prayed, "Dear Jesus, I thank you that we must come with empty hands. I thank you that you have done all—*all*—on the cross, and that all we need in life or death is to be sure of this."

Jesus reminded us that even after we've served Him faithfully we have merely done our duty (Luke 17:10). Yet, on another occasion He indicated that one day He would honor us for our faithfulness (12:37). How can this be? Because all that we have, even the ability to serve the Lord, comes to us as a gracious gift from Him.

Remember, from beginning to end, everything is a result of God's grace.

HERB VANDER LUGT

God owes us nothing but gives us everything.

The Greatness of Gratitude

LUKE 17:11-19

One of them, when he saw he was healed, came back,
praising God in a loud voice.

LUKE 17:15

Jesus was on His way to Jerusalem when ten lepers approached Him. Standing at a distance, as lepers were required to do, they called to Him: "Jesus, Master, have pity on us!" (Luke 17:13).

When Jesus saw them, He commanded, "Go, show yourselves to the priests" (v. 14). And as they journeyed, they were healed.

One of them, when he saw that he was healed, came back, threw himself at Jesus's feet, and thanked Him. "Where are the other nine?" Jesus asked. Good question.

Jesus referred to the grateful man as a "foreigner"—an outsider—perhaps to underscore His saying that "the people of this world are more shrewd . . . than are the people of light" (16:8). The word translated *shrewd* means "thoughtful." Sometimes people of the world have better manners than Jesus's followers do.

In the busyness of life, we may forget to give thanks. Someone has done something for us—given a gift, performed a task, delivered a timely sermon, provided a word of counsel or comfort. But we move on without thinking to say thanks.

Has someone done something for you this week? Give that friend a call or email, or send a thank-you note. After all, "Love has good manners" (1 Corinthians 13:5 PHILLIPS).

DAVID ROPER

We don't need more to be thankful for—
we just need to be more thankful.

Always Pray and Don't Give Up

LUKE 18:1–8

*Then Jesus told his disciples a parable to show them that
they should always pray and not give up.*
LUKE 18:1

Are you going through one of those times when it seems every attempt to resolve a problem is met with a new difficulty? You thank the Lord at night that it's taken care of, but then you awake to find that something else has gone wrong.

During an experience like that in my life, I was reading the gospel of Luke and was astounded by the opening words of chapter 18: "Then Jesus told his disciples a parable to show them that they should always pray and not give up" (v. 1). I had read the story of the persistent widow many times but never grasped why Jesus told it (vv. 2–8). Finally, I connected those opening words with the story and saw the obvious lesson: "Always pray and never give up."

Keep in mind that prayer is not a means of coercing God to do what we want. It is a process of recognizing His power and plan for our lives. In prayer we yield our lives and circumstances to the Lord and trust Him to act in His time and in His way.

As we rely on God's grace, we can keep coming to the Lord in prayer, trusting His wisdom and care for us.

Our Lord's encouragement to us is clear: Always pray and don't give up!

DAVID MCCASLAND

Prayer is turning over to God what makes us toss and turn.

Expect and Extend Mercy

LUKE 18:9–14

"The tax collector stood at a distance. He would not even look up to heaven, but beat his breast and said, 'God, have mercy on me, a sinner.'"

LUKE 18:13

When I complained that a friend's choices were leading her deeper into sin—and that her actions affected me—the woman I prayed with weekly placed her hand over mine. "Let's pray for all of us," she gently requested.

I frowned. "All of us?"

"Yes," she said. "Aren't you the one who always says Jesus sets our standard of holiness, so we shouldn't compare our sins to the sins of others?"

"That truth hurts a little," I said, "but you're right. My judgmental attitude and spiritual pride are no better or worse than her sins."

"And by talking about your friend, we're gossiping. So . . ."

". . . we're sinning," I responded. I lowered my head. "Please, pray for us."

In Luke 18, Jesus shared a parable about two men approaching the temple to pray (vv. 9–14). Like the Pharisee, we can become trapped in a circle of comparing ourselves to other people. We can boast about ourselves (vv. 11–12) and live as though we have the right to judge and the responsibility or the power to change others.

But when we look to Jesus as our example of holy living and encounter His goodness firsthand, our desperate need for God's grace is magnified (v. 13). As we experience the Lord's loving forgiveness firsthand, we'll be empowered to expect and extend mercy, not condemnation, to others.

XOCHITL DIXON

When we realize the depth of our need for mercy, we can more readily offer mercy to others.

Bring Them to Jesus

LUKE 18:15–17

*When Jesus saw this, he was indignant. He said to them,
"Let the little children come to me, and do not hinder them,
for the kingdom of God belongs to such as these."*
MARK 10:14

The Scripture reading from Luke 18 about children seemed unusual at the memorial service for David Holquist, the husband of one of my co-workers. After all, he was seventy-seven when he died.

Yet the pastor said the verses fit David, a longtime college professor, perfectly. Part of his legacy was that he took time for children—his own and others'. He made balloon animals and puppets, and he helped in a puppet ministry at church. When planning worship services with others, he frequently asked, "What about the children?" He was concerned about what would help the children—not just the adults—to worship God.

Luke 18 shows us the concern Jesus had for children. When people brought little ones to Him, the disciples wanted to protect Jesus, a busy man, from the bothersome children. But it seems that Jesus was not at all bothered by them. Just the opposite. The Bible says that Jesus was "indignant" at the disciples (Mark 10:14) and said, "Let the little children come to me, and do not hinder them" (Luke 18:16). Mark adds that Jesus took them in His arms and blessed them (10:14–16).

As we examine our own attitude about children, let's follow the example of David Holquist, who helped them come to Jesus.

ANNE CETAS

God has great concern for little children.

Panning for Gold

LUKE 18:18–30

*These have come so that the proven genuineness of your faith—
of greater worth than gold, which perishes even though refined by fire—
may result in praise, glory and honor when Jesus Christ is revealed.*

1 PETER 1:7

While on vacation in Alaska, my husband Jay and I visited the El Dorado Gold Mine near Fairbanks. After a tour and demonstrations of mining techniques during Gold Rush days, we got to do a little panning for gold. Each person was given a pan and a bag of dirt and stones. After pouring the contents into the pan, we added water from a trough and swirled it around to stir up the silt and allow any gold, which is heavy, to sink to the bottom. Even though we had watched experts, we made little progress. The reason? Concerned about discarding something of value, we were unwilling to throw away worthless stones.

This reminded me of how possessions sometimes keep us from finding what is truly valuable. Jesus had an encounter with a rich man for whom this was true. His earthly wealth was more important to him than spiritual treasure (Luke 18:18–30). Jesus said, "How hard it is for the rich to enter the kingdom of God!" (v. 24).

Although money is not evil, it can prevent us from inheriting true riches if accumulating it is the goal of our lives. To hoard wealth is foolish, for it is genuine faith, not gold, that will sustain us through trials and result in praise, honor, and glory to God (1 Peter 1:7).

JULIE ACKERMAN LINK

**Keep your eyes on Jesus so you don't allow earthly riches
to blind you to spiritual riches.**

Divine Interruptions

LUKE 18:35–43

Jesus stopped and ordered the man to be brought to him.
When he came near, Jesus asked him,
"What do you want me to do for you?"
"Lord, I want to see," he replied.

LUKE 18:40–41

Experts agree that a staggering amount of time is consumed each day by interruptions. Whether at work or at home, a phone call or an unexpected visit can easily deflect us from what we feel is our main purpose.

Not many of us like disruptions in our daily lives, especially when they cause inconvenience or a change of plans. But Jesus treated what appeared to be interruptions in a far different way. Time after time in the Gospels, we see the Lord stop what He is doing to help a person in need.

While Jesus was on His way to Jerusalem where He would be crucified, a blind man begging by the side of the road called out, "Jesus, Son of David, have mercy on me!" (Luke 18:38). Some in the crowd told him to be quiet, but he kept calling out to Jesus. Jesus stopped and asked the man, " 'What do you want me to do for you?' 'Lord, I want to see,' he replied. Jesus said to him, 'Receive your sight; your faith has healed you' " (vv. 41–42).

When our plans are interrupted by someone who genuinely needs help, we can ask the Lord for wisdom in how to respond with compassion. What we call an interruption may be a divine appointment the Lord has scheduled for that day.

DAVID MCCASLAND

Interruptions can be opportunities to serve.

A Better View

LUKE 19:1–10

He wanted to see who Jesus was,
but because he was short he could not see over the crowd.

LUKE 19:3

As a child, I loved to climb trees. The higher I climbed, the more I could see. Occasionally, in search of a better view, I might inch out along a branch until I felt it bend under my weight. Not surprisingly, my tree-climbing days are over. I suppose it isn't very safe—or dignified.

Zacchaeus, a wealthy man, set aside his dignity (and perhaps ignored his safety) when he climbed a tree one day in Jericho. Jesus was traveling through the city, and Zacchaeus wanted to get a look at Him. However, "because he was short he could not see over the crowd" (Luke 19:3). Fortunately, that did not stop him from seeing and even talking with Christ. Zacchaeus's plan worked! And when he met Jesus, his life was changed forever. "Salvation has come to this house," Jesus said (v. 9).

We too can be prevented from seeing Jesus. Pride can blind us from seeing Him as the Wonderful Counselor. Anxiety keeps us from knowing Him as the Prince of Peace (Isaiah 9:6). Hunger for status and stuff can prevent us from seeing Him as the true source of satisfaction—the Bread of Life (John 6:48).

What are you willing to do to get a better view of Jesus? Any sincere effort to get closer to Him will have a good result. God rewards people who earnestly seek Him (Hebrews 11:6).

JENNIFER BENSON SCHULDT

To strengthen your faith in God, seek the face of God.

Extreme Measures

LUKE 19:1–10

"For the Son of Man came to seek and to save the lost."
LUKE 19:10

A few years ago, a friend of mine lost track of her young son while walking through a swarm of people at Union Station in Chicago. Needless to say, it was a terrifying experience. Frantically, she yelled his name and ran back up the escalator, retracing her steps in an effort to find her little boy. The minutes of separation seemed like hours, until suddenly—thankfully—her son emerged from the crowd and ran to the safety of her arms.

Thinking of my friend who would have done anything to find her child fills me with a renewed sense of gratitude for the amazing work God did to save us. From the time God's first image-bearers—Adam and Eve— wandered off in sin, He lamented the loss of fellowship with His people. He went to great lengths to restore the relationship by sending His one and only Son "to seek and to save the lost" (Luke 19:10). Without the birth of Jesus, and without His willingness to die to pay the price for our sin and to bring us to God, we would have no hope in this world.

We can be thankful that God took extreme measures by sending Jesus to reclaim our fellowship with Him. Although we once were lost, because of Jesus we have been found!

JOE STOWELL

**Salvation is about God taking extreme measures
to reclaim those who were lost.**

King of Fruits

LUKE 19:12–26

*Therefore, I urge you, brothers and sisters, in view of God's mercy,
to offer your bodies as a living sacrifice, holy and pleasing to God—
this is your true and proper worship.*

ROMANS 12:1

The durian, a tropical fruit, is often called the King of Fruits. Either you love it or you hate it. Those who love it will do almost anything to get it. Those who hate it won't get near it because of its pungent smell. My wife loves it. Recently, a friend who was grateful for something my wife had done for her sent her a box of the finest quality durians. She took great pains to ensure that they were the best.

I asked myself, "If we can give the best to a friend, how can we do less for our Lord who gave His very life for us?"

The nobleman in Jesus's parable in Luke 19 wanted the best from ten servants to whom he gave money, saying, "Put this money to work until I come back" (v. 13). When he returned and asked for an account, he gave the same commendation "Well done!" to all those who had done what they could with the money entrusted to them. But he called "wicked" (v. 22) the one who did nothing with his money.

The primary meaning of this story is stewardship of what we've been given. To be faithful with what God has given to us is to give Him our best in return. As the master gave money to the servants in the parable, so God has given us gifts to use as we serve Him. We lose out if we fail to give Him our best.

C. P. HIA

We are at our best when we serve God by serving others.

The Way to Praise Him

LUKE 19:28–38

"Blessed is the king who comes in the name of the Lord!"
"Peace in heaven and glory in the highest!"
LUKE 19:38

The triumphal entry of Jesus into Jerusalem a few days before His death focused attention on Christ as Lord. When Jesus sent His disciples to get the colt He was to ride, He instructed them to tell its owners, "The Lord needs it" (Luke 19:31). And when the crowds shouted their praise, they quoted Psalm 118:26, saying, "Blessed is the king who comes in the name of the Lord!" (Luke 19:38).

Jesus is Lord. His is "the name that is above every name" (Philippians 2:9). The word *Lord* refers to His sovereignty. He is the King, and every believer in Him is a member of His kingdom.

We make Jesus the Lord of our lives by bowing to His authority as King. This means we live in obedience to Him. It's best not to be like the man who claimed to be a Christian but chose to live in sin. When his minister confronted him, he glibly replied, "Don't worry, pastor. It's okay. I'm just a bad Christian."

It's not okay. Not for a member of Christ's kingdom (Luke 6:43–49).

As we think of Jesus's entrance into Jerusalem, we realize that we honor Him with our deeds as well as with our words. Let's begin by echoing the adoring crowds who shouted, "Blessed is the king!"

DAVID EGNER

Each new day gives us new reasons to sing God's praise.

The Need for Tears

LUKE 19:37–44

As [Jesus] approached Jerusalem and saw the city, he wept over it.
LUKE 19:41

Following the devastating 2010 earthquake in Haiti, we were all overwhelmed by the images of destruction and hardship endured by the people of that tiny nation. Of the many heartbreaking pictures, one captured my attention. It showed a woman staring at the massive destruction—and weeping. Her mind could not process the suffering of her people, and as her heart was crushed, tears poured from her eyes. Her reaction was understandable. Sometimes crying is the only appropriate response to the suffering we encounter.

As I examined that picture, I thought of the compassion of our Lord. Jesus understood the need for tears, and He too wept. But He wept over a different kind of devastation—the destruction brought on by sin. As He approached Jerusalem, marked by corruption and injustice and the pain they create, His response was tears. "As he approached Jerusalem and saw the city, he wept over it" (Luke 19:41). Jesus cried because of His compassion and grief.

As we encounter the inhumanity, suffering, and sin that wreak havoc in our world, how do we respond? If the heart of Christ breaks over the broken condition of our world, shouldn't ours? And shouldn't we then do everything we can to make a difference for those in need, both spiritually and physically?

BILL CROWDER

Compassion offers whatever is necessary to heal the hurts of others.

Examples Anonymous

LUKE 20:45–21:4

[Jesus] also saw a poor widow put in two very small copper coins.
LUKE 21:2

Although some of the "big names" in Christian ministry live out the teachings of Jesus Christ, the vast majority of God-honoring Christians are unknown and unheralded. Think of the faithful pastors struggling in small towns where there is little potential for growth. Think of the missionaries who are hardly known beyond the small circle of people who support them. Think of the Christian couples who take on the responsibility of being foster parents so they can help boys and girls who are having a rough time in life.

I know a man who made his living as a schoolteacher and spent many hours every week starting new churches in areas where there was no testimony for Christ. He never gets to speak at any large churches. He is never singled out for special honor. But he doesn't care. He knows that God knows, and that's what really counts.

In today's Scripture, the widow who gave more than the wealthy people of her day is not named in the biblical record. Similarly, the writer of Hebrews, after citing some great heroes of the faith, refers to a company of anonymous men and women who were true to God through unbelievable persecution and suffering (Hebrews 11:35–40). We won't know who they are until we reach heaven.

You may receive little honor here on earth, but keep doing what you know God wants you to do. Your work has eternal value, and someday God himself will commend you for being an anonymous example.

HERB VANDER LUGT

**If you serve only for the applause of men,
you sacrifice the approval of God.**

Extravagant Gifts

LUKE 21:1–4

"All these people gave their gifts out of their wealth;
but she out of her poverty put in all she had to live on."
LUKE 21:4

When I was pastoring a small church, we faced a huge crisis. Unless we could complete the extensive renovations necessary to bring our building up to the proper safety codes, we would lose our place of worship. A desperate time of fundraising ensued to pay for those renovations. Out of all the money given, one gift captured our leadership's attention.

An elderly woman in the church donated several hundred dollars to the project—money we knew she could not spare. We thanked her for her gift but wanted to return it, feeling that her needs were greater than the church's. However, she refused to take the money back. She had been saving for years in order to buy a stove and was cooking on a hot plate in the meantime. Yet she insisted that she needed a place to worship with her church family more than she needed a stove. We were astounded by her extravagant gift.

When our Lord observed a widow putting two mites (the smallest of coins) into the temple offerings, He praised her for her extravagance (Luke 21:3–4). Why? Not because of how much she gave, but because she gave all she had. It's the kind of gift that not only honors our God but also reminds us of the most extravagant of gifts to us—Christ.

BILL CROWDER

Gratitude of heart can often be seen in a generous spirit.

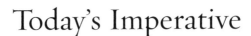

Today's Imperative

LUKE 21:29–38

"Be always on the watch, and pray that you may be able to escape all that is about to happen, and that you may be able to stand before the Son of Man."
LUKE 21:36

In 1857 a money panic hit the United States. Although the entire nation was in a state of perplexity, the main force of the blow was felt in New York City, the center of finance. The now-famous Fulton Street noonday prayer meeting had been organized there a short time before the panic hit. As the uncertainty increased, this gathering grew in size and spiritual intensity. Similar groups began springing up all over the city.

The movement spread across the country, and a great wave of petitions ascended to heaven. Thousands of Americans turned their hearts toward God. This spiritual awakening became known as the "Prayer Meeting Revival," and it is credited with sustaining the nation in an hour of great crisis.

Today the United States and many other nations around the world are facing severe problems. Fear of the future is gripping our hearts. God's people are being challenged again to lift their voices heavenward. "Watch and pray" is a relevant call. Great things could happen if believers from all walks of life would gather to plead for God's mercy! If our concerns were channeled into prayer, the tide could be turned.

Yes, prayer is today's imperative. Imagine how God would be praised if we were all to do our part!

PAUL VAN GORDER

Praying is working with God.

Eliana Level

LUKE 22:7-20

And he took bread, gave thanks and broke it, and gave it to them, saying,
"This is my body given for you; do this in remembrance of me."
LUKE 22:19

When our granddaughter Eliana was a toddler, my wife often babysat for her while her mom taught high school. We did many things to make her feel at home at our house. For example, we would put pictures of her and her parents on our refrigerator at "Eliana level." That way she could see them or take them off and carry them around with her during the day. We wanted her to think of her mom and dad often throughout the day.

Why do this? Was there a chance she would forget them? Of course not. But it was comforting for her to have an ongoing remembrance of them.

Now think about this. Before Jesus was crucified, He created a remembrance of himself. He told His disciples—and us by extension—to "do this [eat the bread and drink from the cup] in remembrance of me" (Luke 22:19). Is this because we might forget Jesus? Of course not! How could we forget the One who died for our sins? Yet He started this way of remembrance—the Lord's Supper—as a comforting reminder of His great sacrifice, His presence, His power, and His promises.

Just as Eliana's photos reminded her of her parents' love, so the celebration of communion provides a valuable reminder of the One who will come again to take us home.

Partake. And remember.

DAVE BRANON

Those who take their sin seriously remember
Christ's cross gratefully.

Another Chance

LUKE 22:24–34

Again Jesus said, "Simon son of John, do you love me?" He answered,
"Yes, Lord, you know that I love you." Jesus said, "Take care of my sheep."
JOHN 21:16

Jesus promised Peter something every repentant believer craves—another chance (Luke 22:31–34). After telling him Satan would sift him as wheat, Jesus reassured Peter that He had prayed that his faith would not fail. Although Peter had insisted he would never forsake Him, Jesus said he would deny Him three times before dawn. In expectation of Peter's restoration, Jesus recommissioned him for future ministry: "When you have turned back, strengthen your brothers" (v. 32).

Preacher George Duncan said, "I don't think many church-vacancy committees would have considered Peter a suitable candidate for a church!" Duncan pointed out that at Pentecost, however, God chose Peter to deliver the most vital sermon in church history. "It would seem," Duncan said, "that some Christians have a message of forgiveness for the unbeliever, but no message of forgiveness for the believer. I'm glad God does!" Because of that forgiveness, a new day of service dawned for Peter.

Indeed, if you are a repentant believer like Peter, you too can trust the Lord to give you another chance. Confess your sin and experience His forgiveness, healing, and restoration (1 John 1:9).

JOANIE YODER

God's forgiveness always comes with another chance.

One Who Serves

LUKE 22:24–27

"For who is greater, the one who is at the table or the one who serves?
Is it not the one who is at the table? But I am among you as one who serves."
LUKE 22:27

"I'm nobody's servant!" I cried out. That morning the demands of my family seemed too much as I frantically helped find my husband's blue tie while feeding the crying baby and recovering the lost toy from under the bed for our two-year-old.

Later on that day, as I was reading the Bible, I came across this verse: "For who is greater, the one who sits at the table or the one who serves? Is it not the one who is at the table? But I am among you as one who serves" (Luke 22:27).

Jesus didn't have to wash His disciples' feet, yet He did (John 13:5). There were servants who did that job, but Jesus chose to serve them. Today's society insists that we should aim to "be somebody." We want the best-paying job, the highest position in the company, the top leadership in church. Yet whatever position we are in, we can learn from our Savior that our job is to serve others.

We hold different roles as parents, children, friends, workers, leaders, or students. Do we carry out those roles with an attitude of service? Even though my everyday routine is sometimes tiring, I'm thankful the Master will help me because I do want to follow His steps and willingly serve.

May God help us to do this each day.

KEILA OCHOA

To be like Jesus, we need a servant's attitude.

Blowing Away the Chaff

LUKE 22:31–34

"Simon, Simon, Satan has asked to sift all of you as wheat.
But I have prayed for you, Simon, that your faith may not fail.
And when you have turned back, strengthen your brothers."

LUKE 22:31–32

In Jesus's day, wheat was separated from the chaff by a process called winnowing. A person would shake a shallow basket with wheat in it back and forth—allowing the wind to blow away the chaff. Jesus used this as an analogy to prepare Peter for the trauma he would face when he would see his Master being led away to the cross. He said, "Simon, Simon! Satan has asked to sift all of you as wheat" (Luke 22:31).

Satan would shake Peter to the core of his being in an attempt to destroy his faith. But Jesus, knowing Peter's weakness, assured him, "I have prayed for you, Simon, that your faith may not fail. And when you have turned back, strengthen your brothers" (v. 32). In spite of this warning and reassurance, Peter still denied that he ever knew Jesus. You might ask, "Wasn't that a failure of his faith?" No, it wasn't his faith that failed, but his courage.

Perhaps you or I have "denied" the Lord. Oh, we didn't lie as Peter did, but by our behavior we denied Him. Like Peter, we may have wept bitterly (v. 62). When we return to the Savior, we receive forgiveness, restoration, and a renewed call to service. Thank you, Lord, for blowing away the chaff!

DENNIS DEHAAN

Satan's ploys are no match for the Savior's power.

Love without Borders

LUKE 22:39–46

Greater love has no one than this: to lay down one's life for one's friends.
JOHN 15:13

During the Boxer Rebellion in China in 1900, missionaries trapped in a home in Taiyuan in northern China decided their only hope for survival rested on running through the crowd that was calling for their deaths. Aided by weapons they held, they escaped the immediate threat. However, Edith Coombs, noticing that two of her injured Chinese students had not escaped, raced back into danger. She rescued one, but stumbled on her return trip for the second student and was killed.

Meanwhile, missionaries in Hsin Chou district had escaped and were hiding in the countryside, accompanied by their Chinese friend Ho Tsuen Kwei. But he was captured while scouting an escape route for his friends in hiding and was martyred for refusing to reveal their location.

In the lives of Edith Coombs and Tsuen Kwei we see a love that rises above cultural or national character. Their sacrifice reminds us of the greater grace and love of our Savior.

As Jesus awaited His arrest and subsequent execution, He prayed earnestly, "Father, if you are willing, take this cup from me" (Luke 22:42). But He concluded that request with this resolute example of courage, love, and sacrifice: "Yet not my will, but yours be done" (v. 42). His death and resurrection made our eternal lives possible.

RANDY KILGORE

Only the light of Christ's love can eliminate the darkness of hatred.

Mistakes Made Beautiful

LUKE 22:39–51

But Jesus answered, "No more of this!"
And he touched the man's ear and healed him.
LUKE 22:51

Early in his career, jazz player Herbie Hancock was invited to play in the quintet of Miles Davis, already a musical legend. In an interview, Hancock admitted being nervous but described it as a wonderful experience because Davis was so nurturing. During one performance, when Davis was near the high point of his solo, Hancock played the wrong chord. He was mortified, but Davis continued as if nothing had happened. "He played some notes that made my chord right," Hancock said.

What an example of loving leadership! Davis didn't scold Hancock or make him look foolish. He didn't blame him for ruining the performance. He simply adjusted his plan and turned a potentially disastrous mistake into something beautiful.

What Davis did for Hancock, Jesus did for Peter. When Peter cut off the ear of one of the crowd who had come to arrest Jesus, Jesus reattached the ear (Luke 22:51), indicating that His kingdom was about healing, not hurting. Time after time Jesus used the disciples' mistakes to show a better way.

What Jesus did for His disciples, He also does for us. And what He does for us, we can do for others. Instead of magnifying every mistake, we can turn them into beautiful acts of forgiveness, healing, and redemption.

JULIE ACKERMAN LINK

Jesus longs to turn our mistakes into amazing examples of His grace.

Speak Up

LUKE 22:54–65

Then seizing [Jesus], they led him away and took him into the house of the high priest. Peter followed at a distance.

LUKE 22:54

When I hear stories about young people who have been bullied, I notice there are always at least two levels of hurt. The first and most obvious comes from the mean-spirited nature of those actually doing the bullying. That's terrible on its own. But there's another, deeper hurt that may end up being even more damaging than the first: The silence of everyone else.

It hurts the one being bullied because he or she is stunned that no one will help. That often makes bullies more brazen, leading them to intensify their meanness. Worse, it heightens the embarrassment, false shame, and loneliness of the victim. So it is imperative to speak up for others and speak out against the behavior (see Proverbs 31:8).

Jesus knows precisely what it feels like to be bullied and to be left to suffer completely alone. Without cause, He was arrested, beaten, and mocked (Luke 22:63–65). Matthew 26:56 says that "all the disciples deserted him and fled." Peter, one of His closest friends, even denied three times that he knew Him (Luke 22:61). While others may not understand fully, Jesus does.

When we see others being hurt, we can ask Him for the courage to speak up.

RANDY KILGORE

The voice of a courageous Christian is an echo of the voice of God.

Unfailing Mercy

LUKE 22:54–62

*Because of the LORD's great love we are not consumed,
for his compassions never fail. They are new every morning;
great is your faithfulness.*
LAMENTATIONS 3:22–23

As I strolled through Chicago's O'Hare Airport, something caught my eye—a hat worn by someone racing through the concourse. What caught my attention was the message it conveyed in just two words: "Deny Everything." I wondered what it meant. Don't ever admit to guilt? Or deny yourself the pleasures and luxuries of life? I scratched my head at the mystery of those two simple words, "Deny Everything."

One of Jesus's followers, Simon Peter, did some denying. In a critical moment, he denied three times that He even knew Jesus! (Luke 22:57, 58, 60). His fear-filled act of denial caused him such guilt and heartache that, broken by his spiritual failure, he could only go out and weep bitterly (v. 62).

But Peter's denial of Christ, like our own moments of spiritual denial, could never diminish the compassion of God. The prophet Jeremiah wrote, "Because of the LORD's great love we are not consumed, for his compassions never fail. They are new every morning; great is your faithfulness" (Lamentations 3:22–23). We can take heart that even when we fail, our faithful God comes to us in mercy and compassion that never fails!

BILL CROWDER

Being imperfect emphasizes our dependence on God's mercy.

Calm in an Age of Rage

LUKE 23:1–12

A gentle answer turns away wrath, but a harsh word stirs up anger.

PROVERBS 15:1

When our daughter Melissa was at the "learning to drive" stage, she had to listen to our numerous safety speeches. On one occasion, I told her, "If someone cuts you off, stay calm. Don't make the other driver angry. You don't know what he or she might do."

That comment seemed so natural. But as I thought later about its implications, I realized how much has changed over time. When I was learning to drive, there was never any mention of "road rage" or being "cut off." Angry drivers weren't a big problem.

But now angry outbursts are so much a part of our lives that we almost expect them. Hateful, spiteful words are common on TV or on social media. Students and teachers get into heated arguments. People who don't even know each other trade insults in public places. Athletes and fans shout in irate tones at sporting events.

We live in an age of rage. But we can help solve the problem—one person at a time. When we're on the receiving end of someone's wrath, we can return a soft answer (Proverbs 15:1). A calm, reasoned approach can stop anger in its tracks.

Christ stayed calm in the face of hateful accusations at His trial (Luke 23:1–12), and we can follow His example by staying calm in an age of rage.

DAVE BRANON

He who conquers his anger conquers a strong enemy.

Who's to Blame

LUKE 23:13–33

We all, like sheep, have gone astray, each of us has turned to our own way;
and the LORD has laid on him the iniquity of us all.

ISAIAH 53:6

What is the worst of all evils? It's not homicide or even genocide. No, it's deicide, the murder of God's Son! Unimaginable as it may be, that is what occurred at a place called Calvary (Luke 23:33).

Whom does God the Father hold responsible for what happened there? Shall we indict the religious leaders who plotted the Savior's execution? Pilate, the spineless Roman governor? The callous soldiers who nailed Jesus to the cross? The fickle multitude who clamored for His blood? All these, to be sure, share the guilt.

The great artist Rembrandt captured the truth of Scripture in one of his paintings. It depicts Christ on the cross with a mob surrounding Him. In the shadows at the edge of that appalling scene stands a man. Who is it? Rembrandt himself! By including himself, the artist confessed that he too was responsible for the Savior's death.

Have we acknowledged that Jesus bore our guilt on the cross? (Isaiah 53:6). Because we all have sinned, the whole race of rebellious transgressors is responsible for the crucifixion as much as the soldiers who did the grisly execution.

Let us, then, take our place alongside Rembrandt. Only let's not stand there. Let's kneel in contrite gratitude.

VERNON GROUNDS

The only people God forgives are those who confess their guilt.

Why Forgive?

LUKE 23:32–34

Jesus said, "Father, forgive them, for they do not know what they are doing."
And they divided up his clothes by casting lots.
LUKE 23:34

When a friend betrayed me, I knew I would need to forgive her, but I wasn't sure I could. Her words pierced deeply inside me, and I felt stunned with pain and anger. Although we talked about it and I told her I forgave her, for a long time whenever I'd see her I felt tinges of hurt, so I knew I was still clinging to some resentment. One day, however, God answered my prayers and gave me the ability to let go completely. I was finally free.

Forgiveness lies at the heart of the Christian faith, with our Savior extending forgiveness even while He was dying on the cross. Jesus loved those who had nailed Him there, uttering a prayer asking His Father to forgive them. He didn't cling to bitterness or anger, but He showed grace and love to those who had wronged Him.

This is a fitting time to consider before the Lord any people we might need to forgive as we follow Jesus's example in extending His love to those who hurt us. When we ask God through His Spirit to help us forgive, He will come to our aid—even if we take what we think is a long time to forgive. When we do, we are freed from the prison of unforgiveness.

AMY BOUCHER PYE

Even on the cross, Jesus forgave those who hurt Him.

War, Then Peace

LUKE 23:32-43

The peace of God, which transcends all understanding,
will guard your hearts and your minds in Christ Jesus.
PHILIPPIANS 4:7

On December 7, 1941, a Japanese warplane piloted by Mitsuo Fuchida took off from the aircraft carrier *Akagi*. Fuchida led the surprise attack on the US Pacific Fleet at Pearl Harbor, Hawaii.

Through the war years to follow, Fuchida continued to fly—often narrowly escaping death. At war's end, he was disillusioned and bitter.

A few years later, he heard a story that piqued his spiritual curiosity: A Christian young woman whose parents had been killed by the Japanese during the war decided to minister to Japanese prisoners. Impressed, Fuchida began reading the Bible.

As he read Jesus's words from the cross, "Father, forgive them, for they do not know what they are doing" (Luke 23:34), he understood how that woman could show kindness to her enemies. That day Fuchida gave his heart to Christ.

Becoming a lay preacher and evangelist to his fellow citizens, this former warrior demonstrated "the peace of God, which transcends all understanding" (Philippians 4:7)—a peace enjoyed by those who have trusted Christ and who "present [their] requests to God" (v. 6).

Have you found this peace? No matter what you have gone through, God makes it available to you.

DENNIS FISHER

True peace is not the absence of war; it is the presence of God.
—Anonymous

Behind the Parted Curtain

LUKE 23:39–43

Jesus answered him,
"Truly I tell you, today you will be with me in paradise."
LUKE 23:43

Pastor and author Erwin Lutzer wrote: "One minute after you slip behind the parted curtain, you will either be enjoying a personal welcome from Christ or catching your first glimpse of gloom as you have never known it. Either way, your future will be irrevocably fixed and eternally unchangeable."

Luke recorded a short yet powerful narrative that pictures two men about to go behind that curtain of death. When Jesus was being crucified, two thieves hung alongside Him. According to Mark, both men hurled insults at Jesus (15:32).

One of the thieves, however, had a change of heart as he realized Jesus's innocence, his own sin, and his destiny. He rebuked the other thief and asked Jesus to remember him when He came into His kingdom. These words were a sign of repentance and simple faith. Jesus responded, "Truly I tell you, today you will be with me in paradise" (Luke 23:43). Salvation for the man was immediate. He knew that day where he would spend eternity.

Realizing that we are sinners and placing our trust in Jesus's death and resurrection assures us that we can immediately know where we will spend our eternal tomorrows when we slip behind the parted curtain.

MARVIN WILLIAMS

To prepare for tomorrow, trust Jesus today.

The Good Story

LUKE 23:44–24:3

*They found the stone rolled away from the tomb,
but when they entered, they did not find the body of the Lord Jesus.*

LUKE 24:2–3

People tend to remember negative images more than they do positive ones, according to an experiment conducted at the University of Chicago. While people claim that they want to turn away from the barrage of bad news in the media—reports on tragedies, diseases, political turmoil—the Chicago study suggests that their minds are drawn to the stories.

Katherine Hankey (1834–1911) was more interested in the "good news." She had a great desire to see young women come to know Christ. In 1866, she became very ill. As she lay in bed, she thought about all the people with whom she had shared the story of Jesus's redemption, and she wished that someone would visit and comfort her with "the old, old story." That's when she wrote the poem that later became a hymn, "Tell Me the Old, Old Story":

Tell me the story slowly, that I may take it in—
That wonderful redemption, God's remedy for sin.
Tell me the story often, for I forget so soon;
The early dew of morning has passed away at noon.

We never tire of hearing this story: Because of God's great love, He sent His only Son to this earth (John 3:16). Jesus lived a perfect life, took our sin upon himself when He was crucified, and three days later rose again (Luke 23:44–24:3). When we receive Him as our Savior, we are given eternal life (John 1:12).

Tell someone the old, old story of Jesus's love. They need some good news.

ANNE CETAS

The good news of Christ is the best news in the world.

Too Good to Be True?

LUKE 24:1–12

*But they did not believe the women, because their words
seemed to them like nonsense.*

LUKE 24:11

In the 1980s, John Knoll and his brother Thomas began experimenting with a computer program to manipulate images. Software companies thought they were crazy, because photographers didn't use computers at that time. Initially the brothers called their program Display, then Imaginator, and finally they settled on Photoshop. Today Photoshop is used by amateurs at home and professionals in business around the world. A *San Jose Mercury News* article noted its place in popular language. When something looks too good to be true, people say, "It must have been Photoshopped."

On the first Easter morning, the women who took spices to anoint the body of Jesus found the tomb empty and heard angels say, "He is not here; He has risen!" (Luke 24:6). When the women told this to the disciples, "Their words seemed to them like nonsense" (v. 11). Nonsense! Mind-boggling! Too good to be true!

If someone had manipulated the evidence at that gravesite, then millions of people around the world gather on Easter Sunday to celebrate a myth. But if Jesus conquered death, then all He said about forgiveness, power to change, and eternal life is real.

Because Christ has risen and lives today, this news is *too good not to be true*!

DAVID MCCASLAND

**The resurrection is a fact of history that
demands a response of faith.**

Connecting the Dots

LUKE 24:13–32

*Beginning with Moses and all the Prophets, he explained to them
what was said in all the Scriptures concerning himself.*
LUKE 24:27

In the 1880s French artist Georges Seurat introduced an art form known
as pointillism. As the name suggests, Seurat used small dots of color, rather
than brush strokes of blended pigments, to create an artistic image. Up
close, his work looks like groupings of individual dots. Yet as the observer
steps back, the human eye blends the dots into brightly colored portraits
or landscapes.

The big picture of the Bible is similar. Up close, its complexity can
leave us with the impression of dots on a canvas. As we read it, we might
feel like Cleopas and his friend on the road to Emmaus. They couldn't
understand the tragic "dotlike" events of the Passover weekend. They had
hoped that Jesus "was the one who was going to redeem Israel" (Luke
24:21), but they had just witnessed His death.

Suddenly a man they did not recognize was walking alongside them.
After showing an interest in their conversation, He helped them connect
the dots of the suffering and death of their long-awaited Messiah. Later,
while eating a meal with them, Jesus let them recognize Him—and then
He left as mysteriously as He came.

Was it the scarred dots of the nail wounds in His hands that caught
their attention? We don't know. What we do know is that when we connect
the dots of Scripture and Jesus's suffering (vv. 27, 44), we see a God who
loves us more than we can imagine.

MART DEHAAN

Jesus laid down His life to show His love for us.

Going Away

LUKE 24:36–53

Then they worshiped him and returned to Jerusalem with great joy.
LUKE 24:52

It was the most unusual "going-away party" ever. There stood Jesus, who had recently risen from the grave. And there stood His followers, listening to His teaching as they had on so many occasions. Jesus spoke about the coming of the Holy Spirit (Luke 24:49), and He told them that it would be their task to be His witnesses.

Then an unusual thing happened. Luke said that Jesus led His disciples to Bethany (v. 50), and as He was blessing them He was "taken up into heaven" (v. 51). Mark recorded, "He was taken up into heaven and he sat at the right hand of God" (16:19).

To see Jesus ascend to heaven was amazing, but what happened next was also remarkable. Instead of being downcast because He had gone away, the disciples responded with renewed purpose. They worshiped Him (Luke 24:52). They joyfully returned to Jerusalem, where they prayed (Acts 1:12–14). Then, after receiving the Holy Spirit (Acts 2), "they went out and preached everywhere" (Mark 16:20).

Although Jesus has gone away, the Holy Spirit makes real to us His presence so that we too can worship, pray, and witness as His disciples did centuries ago. These are still the best ways to celebrate what Jesus has done for us: Worship. Pray. Witness.

DAVE BRANON

Jesus had to go away so the Holy Spirit could come to stay.

Deep Roots

LUKE 24:44–49

Then he opened their minds so they could understand the Scriptures.
LUKE 24:45

The sequoia tree, one of three species of redwoods, is among the world's largest and most enduring organisms. It can grow to 300 feet in height, weigh over 2.5 million pounds, and live for 3,000 years. But the majestic sequoia owes much of its size and longevity to what lies below the surface. A twelve- to fourteen-foot-deep matting of roots, spreading over as much as an acre of earth, firmly grounds its towering height and astonishing weight.

A redwood's expansive root system, however, is small compared to the reach of the national history, religion, and anticipation that undergird Jesus's life. On one occasion He told a group of religious leaders that the Scriptures they loved and trusted told His story (John 5:39). In the synagogue of Nazareth He opened the scroll of Isaiah, read a description of Israel's Messiah, and said, "Today this scripture is fulfilled in your hearing" (Luke 4:21).

Later, after His resurrection, Jesus helped His disciples understand how the words of Moses, the prophets, and even the songs of Israel showed why it was necessary for Him to suffer, die, and rise from the dead (24:46).

What grace and grandeur—to see Jesus rooted in the history and Scriptures of a nation, and to see how extensively our own lives are rooted in our need of Him.

MART DeHAAN

All Scripture helps us see our need of Jesus.

More Than a Hero

JOHN 1:1–5, 9–14

Children born not of natural descent, nor of human decision or a husband's will, but born of God.

JOHN 1:13

As Star Wars fans around the world eagerly awaited the release of Episode 8, *The Last Jedi*, in late 2017, people continued to analyze the remarkable success of these films dating back to 1977. Frank Pallotta, media reporter for *CNNMoney*, said that Star Wars connects with many who long for "a new hope and a force of good at a time when the world needs heroes."

At the time of Jesus's birth, the people of Israel were oppressed and longing for their long-promised Messiah. Many anticipated a hero to deliver them from Roman tyranny, but Jesus did not come as a political or military hero. Instead, He came as a baby to the town of Bethlehem. As a result, many missed who He was. The apostle John wrote, "He came to that which was his own, but his own did not receive him" (John 1:11).

More than a hero, Jesus came as our Savior. He was born to bring God's light into the darkness and to give His life so everyone who receives Him could be forgiven and freed from the power of sin. John called Him "the one and only Son, who came from the Father, full of grace and truth" (v. 14).

"To all who did receive him, to those who believed in his name, he gave the right to become children of God" (v. 12). Indeed, Jesus is the one true hope the world needs.

DAVID McCASLAND

At Bethlehem, God demonstrated that to love is to give.

Son Reflector

JOHN 1:1–9

He came as a witness to testify concerning that light,
so that through him all might believe.

JOHN 1:7

The cozy little village of Rjukan, Norway, is a delightful place to live—except during the dark days of winter. Located in a valley at the foot of the towering Gaustatoppen Mountain, the town receives no direct sunlight for nearly half of the year. Residents had long considered the idea of placing mirrors at the top of the mountain to reflect the sun. But the concept was not feasible until recent years. In 2005, a local artist began "The Mirror Project" to bring together people who could turn the idea into reality. Eight years later, in October 2013, the mirrors went into action. Residents crowded into the town square to soak up the reflected sunlight.

In a spiritual sense, much of the world is like the village of Rjukan—mountains of troubles keep the light of Jesus from getting through. But God strategically places His children to act as reflectors. One such person was John the Baptist, who came "as a witness to the light"—Jesus—who shines "on those living in darkness and in the shadow of death" (John 1:7; Luke 1:79).

Just as sunlight is essential for emotional and physical health, so exposure to the light of Jesus is essential for spiritual health. Thankfully, every believer is in a position to reflect His light into the world's dark places.

JULIE ACKERMAN LINK

A world in darkness needs the light of Jesus.

Theory of Everything

JOHN 1:1–13

For in him all things were created: things in heaven and on earth,
visible and invisible, whether thrones or powers or rulers or authorities;
all things have been created through him and for him.

COLOSSIANS 1:16

Scientists have been looking for the "Theory of Everything." One person who thinks he found it is physicist Brian Greene, who wrote *The Elegant Universe: Superstrings, Hidden Dimensions, and the Quest for the Ultimate Theory*. Greene's "string theory" is a complicated concept suggesting that at its tiniest level everything consists of combinations of vibrating strands, or strings. He described his theory as "a framework with the capacity to explain every fundamental feature upon which the world is constructed."

Over the years, thinkers from Newton to Einstein to Hawking to Greene have spent the greater portion of their lives trying to figure out how the universe works—and they have proposed fascinating theories.

In reality, for any theory to explain everything in the universe adequately it must begin and end with God. "All things . . . visible and invisible" (Colossians 1:16) have their origin in Him and exist for His glory (Psalm 72:19). The first few verses of John's gospel tell us that our Lord created the universe—and that without His hand of creation nothing would exist.

That's why when we consider the world and everything in it, we can exclaim with Isaiah: "The whole earth is full of his glory" (6:3). Praise His holy name!

DAVID EGNER

All creation is an outstretched finger pointing toward God.

The View from 400 Miles

JOHN 1:1–14

The true light that gives light to everyone was coming into the world.
JOHN 1:9

"My perspective on earth changed dramatically the very first time I went into space," says former Space Shuttle astronaut Charles Frank Bolden Jr. From four hundred miles above the earth, all looked peaceful and beautiful to him. Yet Bolden recalled later that as he passed over the Middle East, he was "shaken into reality" when he considered the ongoing conflict there. During an interview with film producer Jared Leto, Bolden spoke of that moment as a time when he saw the earth with a sense of how it ought to be—and then sensed a challenge to do all he could to make it better.

When Jesus was born in Bethlehem, the world was not the way God intended it. Into this moral and spiritual darkness Jesus came bringing life and light to all (John 1:4). Even though the world didn't recognize Him, "to all who did receive him, to those who believed in his name, he gave the right to become children of God" (v. 12).

When life is not the way it ought to be, we are deeply saddened—when families break up, children go hungry, and the world wages war. But God promises that through faith in Christ anyone can begin to move in a new direction. Jesus, the Savior, gives the gift of life and light to everyone who will receive and follow Him.

DAVID MCCASLAND

God is at work to make us who He intends us to be.

Always Accepted

JOHN 1:6-13

He came to that which was his own, but his own did not receive him.
JOHN 1:11

Financial expert Warren Buffet, one of the richest people in the world, was rejected by Harvard's Business School at age nineteen. After a failed admissions interview, he recalls a "feeling of dread," along with concern over his father's reaction to the news. In retrospect, Buffet says, "[Everything] in my life . . . that I thought was a crushing event at the time has turned out for the better."

Rejection, though undeniably painful, does not have to hold us back from accomplishing what God wants us to do. The citizens of Jesus's hometown denied that He was the Messiah (John 1:11), and many of His followers later rejected Him (6:66). Just as Jesus's rejection was part of God's plan for His Son (Isaiah 53:3), so was Jesus's continued ministry. Enduring earthly rejection and knowing that the Father would turn away from Him at Calvary (Matthew 27:46), Jesus went on to cure the sick, cast out demons, and preach good news to the masses. Before His crucifixion, Jesus said, "[Father], I have brought you glory on earth by finishing the work you gave me to do" (John 17:4).

If rejection has become a hindrance to the work God has given you to do, don't give up. Remember that Jesus understands, and those who come to Him will always be accepted by Him (6:37).

JENNIFER BENSON SCHULDT

No one understands like Jesus.

Too Good Not to Share

JOHN 1:6–14

He came as a witness to testify concerning that light,
so that through him all might believe.

JOHN 1:7

During court proceedings, witnesses are more than onlookers or spectators. They are active participants who help determine the outcome of a case. The same is true of our witness for Christ. We are to be active participants in a matter of absolute importance—the truth of Jesus's death and resurrection.

When John the Baptist arrived to tell people about Jesus, the Light of the World, he did so by declaring his knowledge of Jesus. And John the disciple, who recorded the events, testified of his experience with Jesus: "We have seen his glory, the glory of the one and only Son, who came from the Father, full of grace and truth" (John 1:14). The apostle Paul would elaborate on this idea as he told young Timothy, "The things you have heard me say in the presence of many witnesses entrust to reliable people who will also be qualified to teach others" (2 Timothy 2:2).

All Christians have been summoned before the courtroom of the world. The Bible says we are not mere spectators but active participants. We testify to the truth about Jesus's death and resurrection. John the Baptist was the voice of one calling in the desert. Our voices can be heard in our workplace, neighborhood, church, and among our family and friends. We can be active witnesses, telling them about the reality of Jesus in our lives.

LAWRENCE DARMANI

The gospel is too good not to share.

Earth Walk

JOHN 1:11-18

The Word became flesh and made his dwelling among us.
We have seen his glory, the glory of the one and only Son,
who came from the Father, full of grace and truth.

JOHN 1:14

After the *Apollo XV* mission—the eighth successful manned excursion to the moon—Colonel James Irwin (1930–1991) related some of the high points of his and fellow moon walker David Scott's experience. He told of their weightless bodies floating free in the space capsule, the rising crescent of the earth as seen from the moon, and the triumphal splashdown before a watching world.

Irwin also spoke of the impact the experience had on his spiritual life. He said that from the lunar surface he sensed both the glory of God and the plight of earthbound man. As he came back to earth, he realized he couldn't content himself with being merely a celebrity. He would have to be a servant, telling his fellowman of a better way to live. Irwin concluded by saying that if we think it a great event to go to the moon, how much greater is the wonder that God came to earth in the person of Jesus Christ!

Because man walked on the moon, science and technology have made tremendous advances. But because God walked on earth, we know both our origin and our destiny. We can know our Creator personally (John 1:1, 14, 18), and we can live in His light (v. 9). Through Jesus's sinless life and sacrificial death, we can know the joy of having our sins forgiven and experience the fullness of an abundant life—all because God walked on the earth.

MART DEHAAN

God made His home with us so that we might
make our home with God.

Sign Language

JOHN 1:14–18

*May the Lord make your love increase and overflow for each other
and for everyone else, just as ours does for you.*

1 THESSALONIANS 3:12

A friend of mine pastors a church in a small mountain community not far from Boise, Idaho. The community is nestled in a wooded valley through which a pleasant little stream meanders. Behind the church and alongside the stream is a grove of willows, a length of grass, and a sandy beach. It's an idyllic spot that has long been a place where members of the community gather to picnic.

One day, a man in the congregation expressed concern over the legal implications of "outsiders" using the property. "If someone is injured," he said, "the church might be sued." Although the elders were reluctant to take any action, the man convinced them that they should post a sign on the site informing visitors that this was private property. So the pastor posted a sign. It read: "Warning! Anyone using this beach may, at any moment, be surrounded by people who love you." I read his sign the week after he put it up and was charmed. "Exactly," I thought. "Once again grace has triumphed over law!"

This love for one's neighbor springs from God's kindness, forbearance, and patience with us. It's not the law, but the goodness of God that draws men and women to repentance (Romans 2:4) and to saving faith in His Son Jesus Christ.

DAVID ROPER

**Love is the magnet that draws believers together
and attracts unbelievers to Christ.**

What's in a Name?

JOHN 1:35–42

"I tell you that you are Peter, and on this rock I will build my church, and the gates of Hades will not overcome it."
MATTHEW 16:18

My friend wrote a letter to his newborn child that he wanted him to read when he was older: "My dear boy, Daddy and Mummy wish that you will find and stay focused on the Light. Your Chinese name is Xin Xuan. *Xin* means 'faithfulness, contentment, and integrity'; *Xuan* stands for 'warmth and light.'" He and his wife carefully chose a name based on their hopes for their baby boy.

When Jesus renamed Simon as Peter/Cephas (John 1:42), it wasn't a random choice. *Peter* means "the rock." But it took a while for him to live up to his new name. The account of his life reveals him as a fisherman known for his rash ways—a shifting-sand kind of guy. Peter disagreed with Jesus (Matthew 16:22–23), struck a man with a sword (John 18:10–11), and even denied knowing Jesus (John 18:15–27). But in Acts, we read that God worked in and through him to establish His church. Peter truly became a rock.

If you, like Peter, are a follower of Jesus, you have a new identity. In Acts 11:26, we read, "The disciples were called Christians first at Antioch." The name *Christians* means "Christ-ones." You now are one of the Christ-ones. This title lifts up who you are and calls you to become what you are not yet. God is faithful, and He will complete His good work in you (Philippians 1:6).

POH FANG CHIA

**We honor God's name when we call Him
our Father and live like His children.**

Come and See

JOHN 1:35–46

"Come," he replied, "and you will see."
JOHN 1:39

"Can you tell me where I can find the light bulbs?"

"Sure. Come with me, and I'll take you to them."

In many large stores, employees are instructed to take customers to find what they are looking for rather than simply giving them verbal directions. This common act of courtesy and walking alongside an inquiring person may help us expand our concept of what it means to lead others to Christ.

In John 1, the phrase "come and see" occurs twice. When two curious disciples of John the Baptist asked Jesus where He was staying, the Lord said, "Come and see" (v. 39). After spending the day with Him, Andrew found his brother, Simon Peter, and brought him to Jesus (vv. 40–41). Later, Philip told Nathanael he had found the Messiah. To Nathanael's skeptical reply, Philip said, "Come and see" (v. 46).

Witnessing for Christ can be a one-time event when we speak the good news about Him to others. But it may also involve walking alongside people who are seeking help and wholeness. Our genuine interest in their spiritual welfare, our prayers, and our involvement with them says without words, "Come and see. Let's walk together, and I'll take you to Him."

DAVID MCCASLAND

**Kindness and compassion have led more people
to Christ than proclamation alone.**

The Servants Knew

JOHN 2:1–11

His mother said to the servants, "Do whatever he tells you."
JOHN 2:5

Few weddings are matters of life and death, but they often feel that way to the people involved. After giving three daughters in marriage, I can appreciate the concern parents have over proper arrangements for their guests. So whenever I read about the wedding in Cana in John 2:1–11, I find myself smiling at every turn.

Although the events strike me as lighthearted, Jesus's miracle of turning water into wine had the serious purpose of revealing to His disciples that He is the Son of God.

Many people at the wedding may have seen the large stone jars being filled with water. But it was the servants, who had poured every gallon, to whom the Lord said, "Now draw some out, and take it to the master of the banquet" (v. 8). The Bible says simply, "They did so." Their unhesitating obedience is a model for us in our daily God-given tasks.

The master praised the bridegroom, saying, "You have saved the best until now." He didn't know its origin (v. 10), "though the servants who had drawn the water knew" (v. 9).

Like them, we recognize that whenever God uses our meager efforts to help others, it's a miracle of His power. The servants at Cana who drew the water knew that the praise belonged to Jesus. And so do we.

DAVID MCCASLAND

God's great power deserves our grateful praise.

Garbage in the Temple

JOHN 2:13–22

Do you not know that your bodies are temples of the Holy Spirit,
who is in you, whom you have received from God? You are not your own.

1 CORINTHIANS 6:19

A number of years ago, a government investigation discovered that some truckers were hauling garbage in the same refrigerated trucks that were used to transport food. Part of the problem was that trucks making long trips could not afford to return empty.

According to the truckers, some considered garbage a dream commodity. They were paid to transport something that couldn't be damaged. At the same congressional hearings, a food science professor likened the problem to serving potato salad from a cat's litter box.

This "pollution for profit" scandal is nothing compared to the one described in John 2:13–22. Jesus cast out the money changers from the temple because their schemes for financial gain had desecrated His Father's house. But just as bad is polluting the temple of our bodies with thoughts and practices that don't belong there (1 Corinthians 6:19).

In many ways, we are no better than those truckers or the temple merchants of Jesus's day. We think it would be more profitable for us to carry the garbage of this world's values in our minds. May God forgive us, cleanse us, and help us to cast out everything that defiles the temple in which He alone has the right to dwell.

MART DEHAAN

Christians must live in the world, but not let the world live in them.

Straight to Heaven

JOHN 3:1–8

"Salvation is found in no one else, for there is no other name under heaven given to mankind by which we must be saved."

ACTS 4:12

An old spiritual warns, "Everybody talkin' 'bout heaven ain't goin' there." Since heaven is God's dwelling place where His presence and glory are manifested in all their splendor, He has the sovereign right to determine who will be admitted and under what conditions. Any other beliefs about the how and why of admission into heaven are sadly mistaken.

Take, for example, the confidence expressed by a well-known actress. Questioned about her faith, she replied, "I pray. I read the Bible. It's the most beautiful book ever written. I should go to heaven; otherwise it's not nice. I haven't done anything wrong. My conscience is very clean. My soul is as white as those orchids over there, and I should go straight, straight to heaven."

God alone determines who goes straight to heaven. In the Bible, God's holy Word, He tells us that only those who have trusted in Jesus Christ as their personal Savior will be admitted. The apostle Peter said, "Salvation is found in no one else, for there is no other name under heaven given to mankind by which we must be saved" (Acts 4:12).

Self-judgment regarding the purity of one's soul and one's heaven-deserving character is not the criterion. Only God's Word gives us the standard for admission.

VERNON GROUNDS

Christ believed is salvation received and heaven gained.

New: Inside and Out

JOHN 3:1–9, 13–16

Jesus answered and said to him, "Most assuredly, I say to you,
unless one is born again, he cannot see the kingdom of God."

JOHN 3:3 (NKJV)

A few years ago a publisher made a big mistake. A book had been on the market for several years, so it was time for a makeover. The author rewrote the book to bring it up-to-date. But when the revision was published, there was a problem. The publisher gave the book a nice new cover but printed the old book inside.

The exterior was fresh and new, but the interior was old and out-of-date. This "reprint" was not really new at all.

Sometimes that kind of thing happens with people. They realize a change needs to be made in life. Things are heading in the wrong direction. So they may put on a new exterior without making a vital change in their heart. They may change a behavior on the outside but may not realize that it is only God who can change us on the inside.

In John 3, Nicodemus sensed that because Jesus came "from God" (v. 2), He offered something very different. What Jesus told Nicodemus made him realize that He offered nothing short of a rebirth (v. 4): He needed to be "born again," to be made totally new (v. 7).

That change comes only through faith in Jesus Christ. That's when "the old has gone, the new is here!" (2 Corinthians 5:17). Do you need a change? Put your faith in Jesus. He's the one who changes your heart and makes all things new.

DAVE BRANON

Only God can make us new.

Retronyms

JOHN 3:1–17

"You should not be surprised at my saying, 'You must be born again.'"
JOHN 3:7

What do the terms *regular coffee*, *acoustic guitars*, and *black-and-white television* have in common? All are what journalist Frank Mankiewicz calls retronyms—words or phrases created because a familiar word needs to be distinguished from a term that refers to a new development or invention.

Once, all coffee was regular, all guitars were acoustic, and all TVs were black and white. Not so today. Thus the need for a growing list of retronyms, including decaf mocha java, electric guitar, and high-def television.

It could be said that Jesus turned the phrase physical birth into a retronym when He told an inquiring man named Nicodemus, "Unless one is born again, he cannot see the kingdom of God" (John 3:3, NKJV).

Nicodemus was a religious person who didn't grasp the idea of second birth. "How can a man be born when he is old?" he asked Jesus. "Can he enter a second time into his mother's womb and be born?" (v. 4 NKJV). Jesus further explained the difference between being born of the flesh and being born of the Spirit, then concluded, "You should not be surprised at my saying, 'You must be born again'" (v. 7).

DAVID MCCASLAND

**Our Christian life begins when we invite Jesus to live within us.
It's a miracle! We're born again.**

Ambassador of Love

JOHN 3:9–21

*For God did not send his Son into the world to condemn the world,
but to save the world through him.*

JOHN 3:17

In my work as a chaplain, some people occasionally ask if I am willing to give them some additional spiritual help. While I'm happy to spend time with anyone who asks for help, I often find myself doing more learning than teaching. This was especially true when one painfully honest new Christian said to me with resignation, "I don't think it's a good idea for me to read the Bible. The more I read what God expects from me, the more I judge others who aren't doing what it says."

As he said this, I realized that I was at least partly responsible for instilling this judgmental spirit in him. At that time, one of the first things I did with those new to faith in Jesus was to introduce them to things they should no longer be doing. In other words, instead of showing them God's love and letting the Holy Spirit reshape them, I urged them to "behave like a believer."

I gained a new appreciation for John 3:16–17. Jesus's invitation to believe in Him in verse 16 is followed by these words. "For God did not send his Son into the world to condemn the world, but to save the world through him."

Jesus didn't come to condemn us. But by giving these new Christians a checklist of behaviors, I was teaching them to condemn themselves, which then led them to judge others. Instead of being agents of condemnation, we are to be ambassadors of God's love and mercy.

RANDY KILGORE

**If Jesus didn't come to condemn the world,
that's probably not our mission either!**

One Size Fits All

JOHN 3:10-21

For God so loved the world that he gave his one and only Son,
that whoever believes in him shall not perish but have eternal life.
JOHN 3:16

Like most children, I thoroughly enjoyed Christmas. I enjoy it so much, I'm going to talk about it in October!

With great anticipation, I would snoop under the tree to see what toys and games awaited my eager grasp. I felt deflated when I started getting things like shirts and pants. Grownup gifts were no fun! One Christmas, my own kids gave me some cool socks with bright colors and designs. I almost felt young again! Even grownups could wear these socks, as the label reassured me: "One size fits all."

That welcome phrase "one size fits all" reminds me of the best gift of Christmas—the good news that Jesus is for everyone. The point was proven when the first invitation sent by angel choirs was to shepherds on the bottom rung of the social ladder. The news was underscored further when the VIPs—the wealthy and powerful Magi—followed the star to come and worship the Christ-child.

After Jesus began His ministry, an influential member of the Jewish ruling council came to Him at night. In the course of their conversation, Jesus invited "whoever believes" to come to Him. The simple act of faith in Christ grants eternal life to everyone who trusts in Him (John 3:16).

Christ is for everyone, regardless of status, financial situation, or social standing. He is the only gift truly fit for all.

JOE STOWELL

God's gift to a dying world is the life-giving Savior.

God So Loved . . .

JOHN 3:13–19

Jesus said, "Father, forgive them, for they do not know what they are doing."
And they divided up his clothes by casting lots.

LUKE 23:34

July 28, 2014, marked the 100th anniversary of the beginning of World War I. In the British media many discussions and documentaries recalled the start of that four-year conflict. Even the TV program *Mr. Selfridge*, which is based on an actual department store in London, included an episode set in 1914 that showed young male employees lining up to volunteer for the army. As I observed these portrayals of self-sacrifice, I felt a lump in my throat. The soldiers they depicted had been so young, so eager, and so unlikely to return from the horror of the trenches.

Although Jesus didn't go off to war to defeat an earthly foe, He did go to the cross to defeat the ultimate enemy—sin and death. Jesus came to earth to demonstrate God's love in action and to die a horrendous death so we could be forgiven of our sins. And He was even prepared to forgive the men who flogged and crucified Him (Luke 23:34). He conquered death by His resurrection, and now we can become part of God's forever family (John 3:13–16).

Anniversaries and memorials remind us of important historical events and heroic deeds. The cross reminds us of the pain of Jesus's death and the beauty of His sacrifice for our salvation.

MARION STROUD

The cross of Jesus is the supreme evidence of the love of God.
—Oswald Chambers

Ring of Invisibility

JOHN 3:16–21

*Everyone practicing evil hates the light and does not come to the light,
lest his deeds should be exposed.*

JOHN 3:20 (NKJV)

The Greek philosopher Plato (c. 427–c. 348 BC) found an imaginative way of shining light on the dark side of the human heart. He told the story of a shepherd who innocently discovered a golden ring that had been hidden deep in the earth. One day a great earthquake opened up an ancient mountainside tomb and revealed the ring to the shepherd. By accident he also discovered that the ring had the magical ability to enable the wearer to become invisible at will. Thinking about invisibility, Plato raised this question: If people didn't have to worry about being caught and punished, would they resist doing wrong?

In John's gospel we find Jesus taking this idea in a different direction. Jesus, the Good Shepherd, speaks of hearts that stay in the cover of darkness to hide what they are doing (John 3:19–20). He isn't calling attention to our desire for cover-up to condemn us, but to offer us salvation through Him (v. 17). As the Shepherd of our hearts, He brings the worst of our human nature to light to show us how much God loves us (v. 16).

God in His mercy calls us out of our darkness and invites us to follow Him in the light.

MART DeHAAN

No day is dark when you live in the light of God's Son.

Behind the Scenes

JOHN 3:22–31

"He must become greater; I must become less."
JOHN 3:30

The outreach activities of our church culminated with a citywide service. As the team that had organized and led the events—comprised of our youth music group, counselors, and church leaders—walked onto the stage, we all excitedly applauded and poured out our appreciation for their hard work.

One man, however, was hardly noticeable, yet he was the leader of the team. When I saw him a few days later, I thanked and congratulated him for his work and said, "We hardly noticed you during the program."

"I like to work in the background," he said. He was not concerned with getting recognition for himself. It was time for those who did the work to receive appreciation.

His quiet demeanor was an entire sermon to me. It was a reminder that when serving the Lord, we need not seek to be recognized. We can give honor to God whether or not others openly appreciate us. A Christ-first attitude can subdue any petty jealousies or unhealthy competition.

Jesus, who is "above all" (John 3:31), "must become greater." John then said, "I must become less" (v. 30). When we have this attitude, we will seek the progress of God's work. It is Christ, not us, who should be the focus of all we do.

LAWRENCE DARMANI

The spotlight should be on Jesus—not on us.

Generous Receivers

JOHN 4:1–15

The Samaritan woman said to him,
"You are a Jew and I am a Samaritan woman.
How can you ask me for a drink?"
(For Jews do not associate with Samaritans.)

JOHN 4:9

In John 4:1–15, we read that Jesus was weary, hungry, and thirsty. As the Son of God, He could have met all His own physical needs. He could have gotten His own food to eat and water to drink. But Jesus did not insist on doing everything for himself.

On this occasion His disciples had gone to a nearby city to buy food while He sat by the well to rest and wait. And when a Samaritan woman of questionable character came to draw water, He did what many of us might hesitate to do—He asked her for a drink.

For years I missed an important lesson in our Lord's vulnerability—until He taught me the subtle selfishness of not letting others help me. One day a friend tried to do a kindness for me, and as usual I resisted. In frustration she said, "You know what? You're an ungenerous receiver!"

Instantly I saw it! Quite rightly, I had always tried to live by Jesus's words, "It is more blessed to give than to receive" (Acts 20:35). The trouble was, in my attempts to be unselfish, I always had to be the giver.

Others desire to experience the blessedness of giving, but we often frustrate them by refusing their help. Let's learn to be generous receivers—just like Jesus.

CINDY HESS KASPER

Be as gracious in receiving as you are in giving.

Resting and Waiting

JOHN 4:4–14

"My food," said Jesus,
"is to do the will of him who sent me and to finish his work."
JOHN 4:34

It was high noon. Jesus, foot-weary from His long journey, was resting beside Jacob's well. His disciples had gone into the city of Sychar to buy bread. A woman came out of the city to draw water . . . and found her Messiah. The account tells us that she quickly went into the city and invited others to come hear "a man who told me everything I ever did" (John 4:29).

The disciples came back bringing bread. When they urged Jesus to eat, He said to them, "My food . . . is to do the will of him who sent me and to finish his work" (v. 34).

Now I ask you: What work had Jesus been doing? He'd been resting and waiting by the well.

I find great encouragement in this story for I live with physical limitations. This passage tells me that I do not have to scurry about— worrying myself about doing the will of my Father and getting His work done. In this season of life, I can rest and wait for Him to bring His work to me.

Similarly, your tiny apartment, your work cubicle, your prison cell, or your hospital bed can become a "Jacob's well," a place to rest and to wait for your Father to bring His work to you. I wonder who He'll bring to you today?

DAVID ROPER

If you want a field of service, look around you.

The Drinkable Book

JOHN 4:7–15

*"Whoever drinks of the water that I shall give him will never thirst.
But the water that I shall give him will become in him a fountain
of water springing up into everlasting life."*
JOHN 4:14 (NKJV)

Because it is so difficult in some parts of the world to find clean drinking water, an organization called Water Is Life developed a wonderful resource called "The Drinkable Book." The paper in the book is coated in silver nanoparticles that filter out almost 99.9 percent of harmful bacteria! Each tear-out page can be used and reused to filter up to 100 liters of water at the cost of only four pennies per page.

The Bible is also an unusually "drinkable" Book. In John 4, we read of a particular kind of thirst and a special kind of water. The woman at the well needed much more than to quench her physical thirst with clean, clear liquid. She was desperate to know the source of "living water." She needed the grace and forgiveness that comes from God alone.

God's Word is the ultimate "drinkable" Book that points to God's Son as the sole source of "living water" (v. 10). And those who accept the water that Jesus gives will experience "a spring of water welling up to eternal life" (v. 14).

CINDY HESS KASPER

Jesus is the sole source of living water.

Refreshing Candor

JOHN 4:7–26

*Whoever looks intently into the perfect law that gives freedom,
and continues in it—not forgetting what they have heard,
but doing it—they will be blessed in what they do.*

JAMES 1:25

Of the many things I love about my mom, chief among them may be her candor. Many times I have called to ask her opinion on a matter and she has consistently responded, "Don't ask my opinion unless you want to hear it. I'm not going to try to figure out what you want to hear. I'll tell you what I really think."

In a world where words are carefully parsed, her straightforwardness is refreshing. It is also one of the characteristics of a true friend. Real friends speak the truth to us in love—even if it isn't what we want to hear. As the proverb says, "Wounds from a friend can be trusted" (Proverbs 27:6).

This is one of the reasons Jesus is the greatest of friends. When He encountered the woman at the well (John 4:7–26), He refused to be pulled into a tug-of-war over secondary issues but instead drove to the deepest issues and needs of her heart. He challenged her about the character of the Father and lovingly spoke to her of her broken dreams and deep disappointments.

As we walk with our Lord, may we allow Him to speak candidly to the true condition of our hearts through the Scriptures—that we might turn to Him and find His grace to help us in our times of need.

BILL CROWDER

Jesus always tells us truth.

Secret Menu

JOHN 4:31–34

[Jesus] said to them, "I have food to eat that you know nothing about."
JOHN 4:32

Meat Mountain is a super-sandwich layered with six kinds of meat. Stacked with chicken tenders, three strips of bacon, two cheeses, and much more, it looks like it should be a restaurant's featured item.

But Meat Mountain isn't on any restaurant's published menu. The sandwich represents a trend in off-menu items known only by social media or word of mouth. It seems that competition is driving fast-food restaurants to offer a secret menu to in-the-know customers.

When Jesus told His disciples that He had "food" they knew nothing about, it must have seemed like a secret menu to them (John 4:32). He sensed their confusion and explained that His food was to do the will of His Father and to finish the work given to Him (v. 34).

Jesus had just spoken to a Samaritan woman at Jacob's well about living water she had never heard of. As they talked, he revealed a supernatural understanding of her unquenched thirst for life. When he disclosed who He was, she left her water pot behind and ran to ask her neighbors, "Could this be the Messiah?" (v. 29).

What was once a secret can now be offered to everyone. Jesus invites all of us to trust His ability to satisfy the deepest needs of our hearts. As we do, we discover how to live not just by our physical appetites but also by the soul-satisfying Spirit of our God.

MART DEHAAN

Only Christ the Living Bread can satisfy the world's spiritual hunger.

The Waggle Dance

JOHN 4:27–36

"Come, see a man who told me everything I ever did.
Could this be the Messiah?"
JOHN 4:29

How do bees lead one another to nectar? Scientists say it's all about the "waggle" dance. The theory was regarded with skepticism when Nobel Prize-winning zoologist Karl von Frisch first proposed it in the 1960s. But now, researchers in the United Kingdom have used tiny radar responders attached to worker bees to support von Frisch's theory. They've confirmed that the bee orients its body toward the food source and uses the intensity of its waggle dance to signal the distance to other bees.

The woman who met Jesus at Jacob's well also found a way to lead the rest of her community to what she had found—living water (John 4:10). They were drawn to discover why this woman with five ex-husbands and a current live-in was saying, "Come, see a man who told me everything I ever did" (v. 29).

As the crowd was on its way, the One who on other occasions had called himself "the bread of life" (6:48) was telling His disciples that His food was found in doing the will of God (4:32, 34).

Jesus is living water and food for our soul. Joining Him to do the will of God and finish the work He has given us to do is the ultimate source of nourishment.

MART DeHAAN

When you have found food for your soul, lead others to the Source.

Ripe for Harvest

JOHN 4:35–38

"Don't you have a saying, 'It's still four months until harvest'?
I tell you, open your eyes and look at the fields! They are ripe for harvest."

JOHN 4:35

In late summer, we went for a walk in the New Forest in England and had fun picking wild blackberries while watching horses frolicking nearby. As I enjoyed the bounty of the sweet fruit planted by others perhaps many years before, I thought of Jesus's words to His disciples: "I sent you to reap what you have not worked for" (John 4:38).

I love the generosity of God's kingdom reflected in those words. He lets us enjoy the fruits of someone else's labors, such as when we share our love for Jesus with a friend whose family—unbeknown to us—has been praying for her for years. I also love the implied limits of Jesus's words, for we may plant seeds that we will never harvest but someone else may. Therefore, we can rest in the tasks before us, not being hoodwinked into thinking that we are responsible for the outcomes. God's work, after all, doesn't depend on us. He has all of the resources for a bountiful harvest, and we are privileged to play a role in it.

I wonder what fields ready for harvest are before you? Before me? May we heed Jesus's loving instruction: "Open your eyes and look at the fields!" (v. 35).

AMY BOUCHER PYE

We can reap what others have sown.

Eyes of Faith

JOHN 4:46–54

We live by faith, not by sight.
2 CORINTHIANS 5:7

God sometimes answers our prayers in marvelous ways, but He does not want us to become preoccupied with the miraculous. That's why Jesus gently rebuked the nobleman who begged Him to come and heal his son (John 4:48). But in response to the father's repeated appeal He said, "Go, your son will live" (v. 50). The father came to "believe" on the basis of Jesus's word alone. The reality of his faith is seen in the fact that he obeyed Christ's simple command and "took Jesus at his word and departed."

Upon returning home, the nobleman discovered that his son had been healed "at one in the afternoon" on the previous day. From his servants he learned exactly what had taken place and when. His son was made well at the same instant that Jesus said, "Your son will live" (vv. 50–53).

At times we are amazed by God's perfect timing and miraculous intervention when He answers our prayers. We must be careful, though, not to become so preoccupied with the miracle that we forget the One who performed it. We need to remain focused on Christ, whether a miracle takes place or not.

Sooner or later we will be called upon to trust God as we endure sickness, grief, or disappointment. That's when "we live by faith, not by sight" (2 Corinthians 5:7).

HERB VANDER LUGT

Believing is seeing what our eyes cannot see.

Just Like Dad

JOHN 5:17–20

*Jesus gave them this answer: "Very truly I tell you,
the Son can do nothing by himself;
he can do only what he sees his Father doing,
because whatever the Father does the Son also does."*

JOHN 5:19

Isn't it endearing to see a child mimicking his parents? How often we've seen the young boy in a car seat, gripping his imaginary steering wheel intently while keeping a close eye on the driver to see what Daddy does next.

I remember doing the same thing when I was young. Nothing gave me greater pleasure than doing exactly what my dad did—and I'm sure he got an even bigger kick out of watching me copy his actions.

I would like to think God felt the same way when He saw His Son doing exactly what the Father did—reaching out to the lost, helping the needy, and healing the sick. Jesus said, "the Son can do nothing by himself; he can do only what he sees his Father doing, because whatever the Father does the Son also does" (John 5:19).

We are called to do the same—to "follow God's example, therefore, as dearly loved children and walk in the way of love" (Ephesians 5:1–2). As we continue growing to be more like Jesus, may we seek to live in ways that please Him. It is a delight to copy His actions in the power of the Spirit—knowing that our reward is the affectionate, tender smile of a loving Father.

LESLIE KOH

Nothing looks better on you than Christlikeness.

Victory over Death!

JOHN 5:24–30

"Do not be amazed at this, for a time is coming when all who are in their graves will hear his voice and come out—those who have done what is good will rise to live, and those who have done what is evil will rise to be condemned."

JOHN 5:28–29

An ancient painting I saw recently made a deep impression on me. Its title, *Anastasis*, means "resurrection," and it depicts the triumph of Christ's victory over death in a stunning way. The Lord Jesus, newly emerged from the tomb, is pulling Adam and Eve out of their coffins to eternal life. What is so amazing about this artwork is the way it shows how spiritual and physical death, the result of the fall, were dramatically reversed by the risen Christ.

Prior to His death on the cross, the Lord Jesus predicted a future day when He will call believers into a new and glorified existence: "A time is coming when all who are in their graves will hear His voice and come out" (John 5:28–29).

Because of Christ's victory over death, the grave is not final. We naturally feel intense sorrow and grief when people we love die and we are separated from them in this life. But the believer does not grieve as one who has no hope (1 Thessalonians 4:13). The witness of Jesus's resurrection is that all Christians will one day be taken from their graves to be clothed with glorified resurrection bodies (1 Corinthians 15:42–44). And so "we will be with the Lord forever" (1 Thessalonians 4:17).

DENNIS FISHER

Because Christ is alive, we too shall live.

Not Interested in Religion

JOHN 5:18, 37–47

"Jerusalem, Jerusalem, you who kill the prophets and stone those sent to you, how often I have longed to gather your children together, as a hen gathers her chicks under her wings, and you were not willing."

MATTHEW 23:37

A radio ad for a church caught my attention: "Because you've heard about Christianity, you might not be interested in religion. Well, it might surprise you—Jesus wasn't interested in religion either. But He was big on relationship and teaching us to love one another." It continued, "You may not like everything about our church, but we offer authentic relationship, and we're learning to love God and each other. You're welcome to visit."

This church may have overstated things about Jesus and religion because Scripture does speak of "true religion" in James 1:27 as helpful deeds toward others. But Jesus did have difficulties with religious people of His day. He said to the Pharisees, guided by tradition and rules not by love for the Lord, "on the outside you appear to people as righteous but on the inside you are full of hypocrisy and wickedness" (Matthew 23:28). They didn't have the love of God in their hearts (John 5:42). Jesus wanted a relationship with them, but He concluded, "you refuse to come to me to have life" (v. 40).

If being "religious" means following a set of rules so we can look good—instead of enjoying a relationship with the Savior—Jesus isn't interested. He offers forgiveness and love to all who want an intimate relationship with Him.

ANNE CETAS

There is a longing in every heart that only Jesus can satisfy.

Beyond the Status Quo

JOHN 5:35–47

"You refuse to come to me to have life."
JOHN 5:40

Dr. Jack Mezirow, professor emeritus at Columbia Teachers College, believes that an essential element in adult learning is to challenge our own ingrained perceptions and examine our insights critically. Dr. Mezirow says that adults learn best when faced with what he calls a "disorienting dilemma"—something that "helps you critically reflect on the assumptions you've acquired," according to an article by Barbara Strauch in *The New York Times*. This is the opposite of saying, "My mind is made up—don't confuse me with the facts."

When Jesus healed on the Sabbath, He challenged the deeply held beliefs of many religious leaders, and they sought to silence Him (John 5:16–18). Jesus said to them: "You study the Scriptures diligently because you think that in them you have eternal life. These are the very Scriptures that testify about me, yet you refuse to come to me to have life" (vv. 39–40).

Oswald Chambers observed, "God has a way of bringing in facts which upset a man's doctrines if these stand in the way of God getting at his soul."

Unsettling experiences that cause us to question our assumptions about the Lord can also lead us to a deeper understanding and trust in Him—if we're willing to think it through and come to Him.

DAVID MCCASLAND

The unexamined life is not worth living.
—Socrates

Small Things

JOHN 6:4–14

*"Here is a boy with five small barley loaves and two small fish,
but how far will they go among so many?"*
JOHN 6:9

Skeptical about the usefulness of a small lunch, Andrew said to Jesus, "How far will [these five loaves and two fish] go among so many?" (John 6:9). Yet the little lunch in the hands of Jesus turned out to be a huge blessing. So, before you think you don't have much to offer Jesus, consider this:

Edward Kimball, a Sunday school teacher in Boston, decided to visit a young man in his class to be sure he was a Christian. That day he led that man, Dwight L. Moody, to the Lord.

Moody, who went on to be a great evangelist in the nineteenth century, had a major impact on Wilbur Chapman. Chapman, a prominent evangelist, recruited Billy Sunday to join in his evangelistic campaigns. In turn, Sunday launched a national ministry that had great results in cities like Charlotte, North Carolina. An organization that started as a result of Sunday's revival invited evangelist Mordecai Ham to Charlotte. In one of those meetings, Billy Graham received Christ as his Savior and later became the most prominent evangelist of the twentieth century.

When you think you don't have much to offer, remember Sunday school teacher Edward Kimball, who spent a Saturday afternoon reaching out to someone in his class. God has a special way of using routine faithfulness in the "small things" to accomplish great things!

JOE STOWELL

God uses small things to accomplish great things for His glory.

What Do You Fear?

JOHN 6:16–21

But he said to them, "It is I; don't be afraid."
JOHN 6:20

One of the stories in *Grimm's Fairy Tales* is about a rather dimwitted young man who didn't understand what it meant to shudder in fear. People attempted to shock him by putting him in all sorts of terrifying situations—but to no avail. He finally did shudder, though not out of fear. He was asleep when someone poured a bucket of cold water and wiggling fish on top of him.

Something is wrong with us if we're never afraid. Fear is the natural human reaction to any difficult or dangerous undertaking, and God doesn't condemn it. Neither does He want us to be crippled by fear. Jesus's words to His disciples on more than one occasion were, "Do not be afraid" (Luke 5:10; 12:4; John 6:20). In each case He used a verb tense that suggests continuance. In other words, He told them, "Don't keep on fearing."

We need not be overcome by our fear, nor should we ever say no to doing what we know God wants us to do merely because we are fearful. God can turn our fear into fortitude. We can trust God and say, I "am not afraid" (Psalm 56:11).

Courage is not the absence of fear but the mastery of it. So let's resist our fear and meet it with faith in our Lord, for He has said, "Never will I leave you; never will I forsake you" (Hebrews 13:5).

DAVID ROPER

We can face any fear when we know the Lord is near.

Baking with Jess

JOHN 6:22–34

*"Do not work for food that spoils, but for food that endures to eternal life,
which the Son of Man will give you.
For on him God the Father has placed his seal of approval."*

JOHN 6:27

One morning as Lilia prepared for work, her four-year-old daughter Jess set to work too. The family had purchased a conveyor toaster, and the concept of cycling bread through the small countertop oven fascinated Jess. Minutes later, Lilia discovered a loaf and a half of toast piled on the counter. "I'm a very good baker!" Jess declared.

It's no miracle that an inquisitive girl could turn bread into toast. But when Jesus transformed a boy's five loaves and two fish into a meal for thousands, the crowd on the hillside recognized the miraculous nature of the event and wanted to make Him king (see John 6:1–15).

Jesus's kingdom, of course, is "not of this world" (John 18:36), so He slipped away. When the crowd found Him the next day, Christ identified a flaw in their motives: "You are looking for me, not because you saw the signs I performed but because you ate of the loaves and had your fill" (6:26). They mistakenly thought "King" Jesus would give them full stomachs and national freedom. But Jesus counseled them, "Do not work for food that spoils, but for food that endures to eternal life" (v. 27).

An earthbound view will cause us to treat Jesus as a means to an end. Instead, we should see Him as our Bread of Life.

TIM GUSTAFSON

**Seek first the kingdom of God,
and all these things will be added to you.**
—Jesus

Come to Me

JOHN 6:30–40

Jesus declared, "I am the bread of life. Whoever comes to me will never go hungry, and whoever believes in me will never be thirsty."
JOHN 6:35

When Jesus lived on this earth, He invited people to come to Him, and He still does today (John 6:35). But what do He and His Father in heaven have that we need?

Salvation. Jesus is the only way to have forgiveness of sin and the promise of heaven. "Everyone who believes may have eternal life in him" (John 3:15).

Purpose. We are to give all of our heart, soul, mind, and strength to following Jesus. "Whoever desires to come after Me, let him deny himself, and take up his cross, and follow Me" (Mark 8:34 NKJV).

Comfort. In trial or sorrow, the "God of all comfort . . . comforts us in all our troubles" (2 Corinthians 1:3–4).

Wisdom. We need wisdom beyond our own for making decisions. "If any of you lacks wisdom, you should ask God, . . . and it will be given to you" (James 1:5).

Strength. When we're weary, "the LORD gives strength to his people" (Psalm 29:11).

Abundant life. The fullest life is found in a relationship with Jesus. "I have come that they may have life, and have it to the full" (John 10:10).

Jesus said, "Whoever comes to me I will never drive away" (John 6:37). Come!

ANNE CETAS

Jesus invites us to come to Him for life.

"Bread!"

JOHN 6:34–51

"I am the bread of life."
JOHN 6:48

In the small Mexican city where I'm from, every morning and evening you can hear a distinctive cry: "Bread!" A man with a huge basket on his bike offers a great variety of fresh sweet and salty breads for sale. I enjoy having fresh bread brought to my door.

Moving from the thought of feeding physical hunger to spiritual hunger, I think of Jesus's words: "I am the living bread that came down from heaven. Whoever eats this bread will live forever" (John 6:51).

Someone has said that evangelism is really one beggar telling another beggar where he found bread. Many of us can say, "Once I was spiritually hungry, spiritually starving because of my sins. Then I heard the good news. Someone told me where to find bread: in Jesus. And my life changed!"

Now we have the privilege and the responsibility of pointing others to this Bread of Life. We can share Jesus in our neighborhood, in our workplace, in our school, in our places of recreation. We can talk about Jesus in the waiting room, on the bus, or on the train. We can take the good news to others through doors of friendship.

Jesus is the Bread of Life. Let's tell everybody the great news.

KEILA OCHOA

Share the Bread of Life wherever you are.

Jesus's Difficult Words

JOHN 6:44–58

From this time many of his disciples turned back and no longer followed him.
JOHN 6:66

Recently, a company advertised a "huggable, washable, and talking" Jesus doll that recites "actual Scripture verses to introduce children of all ages to the wisdom of the Bible." Its sayings include, "I have an exciting plan for your life," and "Your life matters so much to Me." Who wouldn't want to follow a Jesus like this?

Jesus does offer a wonderful plan for our lives. But He doesn't serve as a cosmic genie or cuddly doll to meet our every whim. John 6 gives us a picture of a Jesus who is not so cuddly; in fact, He's often offensive. Instead of fulfilling the selfish desires of His followers, He disturbed their expectations. He offered himself as spiritual bread from heaven and said, "Whoever eats my flesh and drinks my blood has eternal life" (v. 54).

This message was offensive and difficult. The image of eating flesh and drinking blood did not give His hearers "warm fuzzies." Many stopped following Him (v. 66). He wasn't the conquering Messiah-King they had expected.

Sometimes we want a Jesus who meets our selfish needs. But the wonderful life He offers is found only in radical obedience to His commands. Let's ask Jesus to show us what His words mean—and for the courage to act on His truth.

MARVIN WILLIAMS

The way of Jesus is not always easy.

Beyond Time

JOHN 6:53–69

*Simon Peter answered him, "Lord, to whom shall we go?
You have the words of eternal life. We have come to believe
and to know that you are the Holy One of God."*

JOHN 6:68–69

During 2016, theater companies in Britain and around the world staged special productions to mark the 400th anniversary of the death of William Shakespeare. Concerts, lectures, and festivals drew crowds who celebrated the enduring work of the man widely considered to be the greatest playwright in the English language. Ben Jonson, one of Shakespeare's contemporaries, wrote of him, "He was not of an age, but for all time."

While the influence of some artists, writers, and thinkers may last for centuries, Jesus Christ is the only person whose life and work will endure beyond time. He claimed to be "the bread that came down from heaven . . . whoever feeds on this bread will live forever" (v. 58).

When many people who heard Jesus's teaching were offended by His words and stopped following Him (John 6:61–66), the Lord asked His disciples if they also wanted to leave (v. 67). Peter replied, "Lord, to whom shall we go? You have the words of eternal life. We have come to believe and to know that you are the Holy One of God" (vv. 68–69).

When we invite Jesus to come into our lives as our Lord and Savior, we join His first disciples and all those who have followed Him in a new life that will last forever—beyond time.

DAVID McCASLAND

**Jesus is the Son of God, the Man beyond time,
who gives us eternal life.**

Popularity

JOHN 6:60–69

He asked this only to test him,
for he already had in mind what he was going to do.
JOHN 6:6

Popularity is fickle. Just ask a politician. Many of them watch their ratings to see how their constituents view their policies. They may start with a high rating, but then it steadily declines during their term.

Jesus also experienced a sharp decline in popularity. His popularity reached its peak after He fed the 5,000 (John 6:14–15). It plummeted when He told His listeners that He had "come down from heaven" (v. 38). Their response to His stupendous claim was, essentially, "Who does this guy think He is?" (see v. 41).

Jesus's popularity continued to dip when He explained how they could have Him as spiritual bread (vv. 51–52). Perplexed by what they heard, they said, "This is a hard teaching. Who can accept it?" (v. 60). As a result, many left Him.

The crowds followed Jesus conditionally. They were happy only as long as Jesus supplied their needs and met their wants. They balked when He asked for commitment.

Jesus's question to His disciples was this: "You do not want to leave too, do you?" (v. 67). Peter answered, "Lord, to whom shall we go? You have the words of eternal life" (v. 68). Like Peter, let's ignore the world's rating of Jesus and follow Him daily.

C. P. HIA

Commitment to Christ is a daily calling that challenges us.

First Impressions

JOHN 7:14–24

"Stop judging by mere appearances, but instead judge correctly."
JOHN 7:24

A while back, *Our Daily Bread* published an article I wrote about a young woman who wore a T-shirt that said, "Love Is for Losers." In it, I commented on what a sad message that was, and I wrote about the hurt this motto represented.

To my surprise, one of our readers gave that message a completely different slant. She sent a note informing me that her daughter and her daughter's friends—all tennis players—wear shirts with that slogan. In tennis, a "love" score is zero. If your score in a game is "love," you lose—so in tennis, love really is for losers. That mom's note gave me a new perspective on that saying.

This incident reminded me how easy it is to make wrong first judgments. Based on incomplete or inaccurate information, we can jump to wrong conclusions and make poor value judgments about people and situations. And that can cause great hurt to others.

Speaking to people who had misjudged Him, Jesus warned, "Stop judging by mere appearances, but instead judge correctly" (John 7:24). We need to be careful that our judgments are backed up by the right information (the truth) and the right attitude (the compassion of Christ). Try this motto: "Righteous judgment is for winners."

BILL CROWDER

A snap judgment has a way of becoming unfastened.

Avoid Dehydration

JOHN 7:37–39

On the last and greatest day of the festival, Jesus stood and said in a loud voice, "Let anyone who is thirsty come to me and drink."
JOHN 7:37

A couple of times in the past few years I've experienced dehydration and, believe me, it is not something I want to repeat. It happened once after I suffered a torn hamstring while cross-country skiing, and another time in the 115-degree heat of an Israeli desert. Both times I experienced dizziness, disorientation, loss of clear vision, and a host of other symptoms. I learned the hard way that water is vital to maintaining my well-being.

My experience with dehydration gives me a new appreciation for Jesus's invitation: "Let anyone who is thirsty come to me and drink" (John 7:37). His announcement was dramatic, particularly in terms of the timing. John notes that it was the last day of the "festival"—the annual event commemorating the wandering of the Jews in the wilderness. The event climaxed with a ceremonial pouring of water down the temple steps to recall God's provision of water for the thirsty wanderers. At that point, Jesus rose and proclaimed that He is the water we all desperately need.

Living like we really need Jesus—talking to Him and depending on His wisdom—is vital to our spiritual well-being. So, stay connected to Jesus, for He alone can satisfy your thirsty soul!

JOE STOWELL

Come to Jesus for the refreshing power of His living water.

Embarrassing Moments

JOHN 8:1-11

"No one, sir," she said. "Then neither do I condemn you,"
Jesus declared. "Go now and leave your life of sin."
JOHN 8:11

The flashing lights of the police car drew my attention to a motorist who had been pulled over for a traffic violation. As the officer, ticket book in hand, walked back to his car, I could clearly see the embarrassed driver sitting helplessly behind the wheel of her car. With her hands, she attempted to block her face from the view of passersby—hoping to hide her identity. Her actions were a reminder to me of how embarrassing it can be when we are exposed by our choices and their consequences.

When a guilty woman was brought before Jesus and her immorality was exposed, the crowd did more than just watch. They called for her condemnation. But Jesus showed mercy. The only One with the right to judge sin responded to her failure with compassion. After dispatching her accusers, Jesus said to her, "Neither do I condemn you. . . . Go now and leave your life of sin" (John 8:11). His compassion reminds us of His forgiving grace, and His command to her points to His great desire that we live in the joy of that grace. Both elements show the depth of Christ's concern for us when we stumble and fall.

Even in our most embarrassing moments of failure, we can cry out to Him and find that His grace is truly amazing.

BILL CROWDER

Jesus alone can supply the grace we need for each trial we face.

The Gift of Light

JOHN 8:12–20

When Jesus spoke again to the people, he said,
"I am the light of the world. Whoever follows me will never walk in darkness,
but will have the light of life."

JOHN 8:12

Sir Christopher Wren designed and built more than fifty church buildings in London during the late 1600s. His design style had two prominent features—the first of which was sturdy, tall steeples. The second, however, was more profound. Wren was convinced that all of the windows in his churches must use clear glass as opposed to the stained glass so popular in churches of that era. In part, his reason for the clear glass is found in words attributed to him: "God's greatest gift to man is light." Allowing light to bathe people as they worshiped was, to Wren, a celebration of that gift.

In the Genesis account, on the first day of creation God made light (1:3). The light God created is even more than just a means by which to see. It's a picture of what Christ brought when He entered this darkened world. In John 8:12, our Lord said, "I am the light of the world. Whoever follows me will never walk in darkness, but will have the light of life." To the follower of Christ, light is one of the great reminders of the character of our Savior and the quality of the life He has given us through His sacrifice on the cross.

Wren was right. God's greatest gift to man is light—Jesus Christ, the Light of the World!

BILL CROWDER

Jesus came to give light to a dark world.

Truth Is Liberating

JOHN 8:28–36

"Then you will know the truth, and the truth will set you free."
JOHN 8:32

A Christian friend shared several problems with me over the phone. He was particularly concerned about his frustration and anger. But talking seemed to help. The next day he emailed this message to me: "After our talk, I read my Bible notes and found several pages that spoke to me. But what helped me most was the realization that Christianity really is the truth. I suppose that for a Christian this should be obvious. But for me it was a fresh revelation that Jesus in fact is the Son of God and He loves me." He added, "Just knowing the truth was very liberating. Suddenly, all the frustration and anger left me."

Writer Os Guinness tells about a young, searching Christian who exclaimed, "I always knew the Christian faith was true, but I never realized it was *this* true!"

As these believers searched for greater understanding of the gospel, they rediscovered what Jesus promised: "You will know the truth, and the truth will set you free" (John 8:32).

Do you need a fresh realization of truth in your life? Then spend time searching the Scriptures (the written truth), and earnestly seek Jesus Christ (the living truth). Soon the old, familiar truth of Jesus and His love will become refreshingly new to you and will make you free indeed.

JOANIE YODER

The truth of Christ is the only path to freedom.

What's Your Father's Name?

JOHN 8:39–47

*Yet to all who did receive him, to those who believed in his name,
he gave the right to become children of God.*
JOHN 1:12

When I went to buy a cell phone in the Middle East, I was asked the typical questions: name, nationality, address. But then as the clerk was filling out the form, he asked, "What's your father's name?" That surprised me, and I wondered why it was important. Knowing my father's name would not be important in my culture, but here it was necessary in order to establish my identity. In some cultures, ancestry is vital.

The Israelites believed in the importance of ancestry too. They were proud of their patriarch Abraham, and they thought being part of Abraham's clan made them God's children. Their human ancestry was connected, in their opinion, to their spiritual family.

Hundreds of years later when Jesus was talking with the Jews, He pointed out that this was not so. They could say Abraham was their earthly ancestor, but if they didn't love Him—the One sent by the Father—they were not part of God's family.

The same applies today. We don't choose our human family, but we can decide the spiritual family we belong to. If we believe in Jesus's name, God gives us the right to become His children (John 1:12).

Who is your spiritual Father? Have you decided to follow Jesus? Let this be the day you trust in Jesus for the forgiveness of your sins and become part of God's family.

KEILA OCHOA

God is our eternal Father.

Timeless Savior

JOHN 8:48–59

"Very truly I tell you," Jesus answered, "before Abraham was born, I am!"
JOHN 8:58

Jeralean Talley died in June 2015 as the world's oldest living person—116 years of age. In 1995, the city of Jerusalem celebrated its 3,000th birthday. One hundred sixteen is old for a person, and 3,000 is old for a city, but there are trees that grow even older. A bristlecone pine tree in California's White Mountains has been determined to be more than 5,000 years old. That precedes the patriarch Abraham by 1,000 years!

Jesus, when challenged by the Jewish religious leaders about His identity, also claimed to predate Abraham. He told them, "Very truly I tell you, . . . before Abraham was born, I am!" (John 8:58). His bold assertion shocked those who were confronting Him, and they sought to stone Him. They knew He wasn't referring to a chronological age but was actually claiming to be eternal by taking the ancient name of God, "I am" (see Exodus 3:14). But as a member of the trinity, He could make that claim legitimately.

In John 17:3, Jesus prayed, "This is eternal life: that they know you, the only true God, and Jesus Christ, whom you have sent." The timeless One entered into time so we could live forever. He accomplished that mission by dying in our place and rising again. Because of His sacrifice, we anticipate a future not bound by time, where we will spend eternity with Him. He is the timeless one.

BILL CROWDER

Christ holds all things together.

The Why Question

JOHN 9:1–7

"Neither this man nor his parents sinned," said Jesus, "but this happened so that the works of God might be displayed in him."

JOHN 9:3

The fact that some people come into the world with severe disabilities disturbs us. We feel a deep sense of compassion for them, and we instinctively wonder why they must suffer in this way.

Those who believe in reincarnation say such disabilities are penalties for things done in previous lives. But this theory is completely contrary to the teaching of the Bible.

We must be careful about placing blame when someone has a disability. When Jesus encountered the man born blind, His disciples asked, "Who sinned, this man or his parents?" (John 9:2). But Jesus answered, "Neither," and added that the inability happened so "the works of God might be displayed in him" (v. 3). Then He did what He could to help—He healed the man.

We are not able to heal people as Jesus did, but we can make their lives more pleasant through acts of kindness. There are numerous opportunities to show love by offering practical help or a listening ear, not in a patronizing manner but in genuine friendship. When we show respect for others, we display the spirit of Christ.

Lord, help us to remember and uphold the dignity of every person. Help us to focus on what we can do when we can't explain why bad things happen.

HERB VANDER LUGT

It's better to lend a helping hand than to point an accusing finger.

Living in Darkness

JOHN 9:1-7, 24-39

*Jesus said, "For judgment I have come into this world,
so that the blind will see and those who see will become blind."*
JOHN 9:39

Anna Mae Pennica was born with cataracts that left her blind. But in October 1981, when Anna was sixty-two years old, Dr. Thomas Pettit of the Jules Stein Eye Institute at UCLA removed the cataract from Anna Mae's left eye—and for the first time she could see! She even passed a driver's test.

But there is a sad postscript to this surgical triumph. The technique for correcting Mrs. Pennica's eye condition had been in use since the 1940s. She could have been enjoying forty years of sight but instead had remained blind needlessly.

Here's a greater tragedy: To stumble through this world with sightless souls and be lost in impenetrable night forever! That was the condition of the Pharisees when Jesus healed the man born blind (John 9). They were so blinded by their slavish devotion to outward religious appearances and traditions that they could not recognize the Light of the World. Their stubborn refusal to see their own sins kept them in spiritual darkness, and they rejected the Lord's offer of forgiveness.

Jesus said, "I am the light of the world. Whoever follows me will never walk in darkness, but will have the light of life" (John 8:12). Have you let the Light of the World into your life, or are you needlessly living in darkness?

VERNON GROUNDS

When you trust God's Son, darkness gives way to light.

Curiosity or Compassion?

JOHN 9:1–12

*His disciples asked him,
"Rabbi, who sinned, this man or his parents,
that he was born blind?"*

JOHN 9:2

Why is it that when we hear about someone who is suffering, we are more interested in the details of what, why, when, and where than we are about how we can help?

When the disciples passed the blind beggar (John 9:1), their curiosity about why he was suffering outweighed the prospect of reaching out to help him. "Who sinned, this man or his parents, that he was born blind?" they asked (v. 2). Their pop-quiz for Jesus revealed that they were dreadfully out of step with their Master's heart. In fact, lurking beneath their question was a judgmental spirit—a desire to know who to blame—as if that would make anyone feel better!

Thankfully, Jesus modeled a compassionate response. Rather than speculation and condemnation, He marshaled His resources to help, which in this case meant complete healing. He made it clear that the man's blindness was intended to provide a moment for God to be magnified through Jesus's compassionate touch.

Feeling curious about somebody's problem? Shift into Jesus's mode and move past the point of curiosity to his or her point of need. Reach out and touch someone's pain. Show the compassionate love of Jesus in action.

JOE STOWELL

Do you want to be like Jesus? Replace curiosity with compassion.

Our Best Defense

JOHN 9:13–25

He replied, "Whether he is a sinner or not, I don't know.
One thing I do know. I was blind but now I see!"
JOHN 9:25

Thrown together as seatmates for an eight-hour train ride, a retired US ambassador and I quickly clashed as he sighed when I pulled out my Bible.

I took the bait. At first, we traded one-liners aimed at goading the other or scoring points. Gradually, though, bits and pieces of our respective life stories started creeping into the discussion. Curiosity got the better of both of us and we found ourselves asking questions instead of feuding. A political science major in college and a political junkie by hobby, I was intrigued with his career, which included two prominent ambassadorships.

Strangely enough, his questions to me were about my faith. How I became "a believer" was what interested him most. The train ride ended amicably, and we even traded business cards. As he left the train, he turned to me and said, "By the way, the best part of your argument isn't what you think Jesus can do for me. It's what He's done for you."

In John 9, as on that train, God reminds us that the best story is the one we know intimately: Our own encounter with Jesus Christ. Practice telling your story of faith to loved ones and close friends so you'll be able to tell it clearly to others.

RANDY KILGORE

People know true faith stories when they hear them.

A Glimpse of God's Love

JOHN 9:24–34

"Let the one who boasts boast in the Lord."
2 CORINTHIANS 10:17

Nadine was in the last stages of cancer when I met her. The doctor said chemotherapy would no longer help. She was a dedicated Christian and had a wonderful peace from God. She spent her last weeks making scrapbooks for her adult daughters and planning her memorial service.

Nadine's joyful spirit was inviting to be around, and people looked forward to spending time with her. She kept her sense of humor and always shared the ways the Lord was meeting her needs. She gave everyone around her a glimpse of God's loving character.

When a man who had been born blind was healed by Jesus, he too had the opportunity to show others a glimpse of who God is (John 9:1–41). Neighbors asked, "How then were your eyes opened?" (v. 10). He told them about Jesus. When Pharisees questioned him, he told them how Jesus had given him sight and concluded, "If this man were not from God, he could do nothing" (v. 33).

We may wonder how we can show others what God is like. God can be clearly seen in the way we handle life's difficulties, such as problems at work or home, or perhaps a serious illness. We can share with others how He is comforting us—and let them know that the Lord cares for them too.

Who in your life needs to see the love of God?

ANNE CETAS

You can be a glimpse of God's love to someone.

Called by Name

JOHN 10:1–11

"The gatekeeper opens the gate for him, and the sheep listen to his voice. He calls his own sheep by name and leads them out."

JOHN 10:3

When I first meet a new group of university students in the writing class I teach, I already know their names. I take the time to familiarize myself with their names and photos on my student roster, so when they walk into my classroom for the initial class I can say, "Hello, Jessica," or "Welcome, Trevor." I do this because I know how meaningful it is when someone knows us and calls us by name.

Yet to truly know someone, we need to know more than that person's name. In John 10, we can sense the warmth and care Jesus, the Good Shepherd, has for us when we read that He "calls his own sheep by name" (v. 3). But He knows even more than our name. He knows our thoughts, longings, fears, wrongs, and deepest needs. Because He knows our deepest needs, He has given us our very life—our eternal life—at the cost of His own. As He says in verse 11, He "lays down his life for the sheep."

You see, our sin has separated us from God. So Jesus, the Good Shepherd, became the Lamb and sacrificed himself, taking our sin on himself. When He gave His life for us and then was resurrected, He redeemed us. As a result, when we accept His gift of salvation through faith, we are no longer separated from God.

Give thanks to Jesus! He knows your name and your needs!

DAVE BRANON

God's knowledge of us knows no bounds.

I'm Bored

JOHN 10:7–14

"The thief comes only to steal and kill and destroy;
I have come that they may have life, and have it to the full."
JOHN 10:10

When our kids were teens, we repeatedly had the following discussion after their church youth group meeting: I asked, "How was youth group tonight?" And they responded, "It was boring." After several weeks of this, I decided to find out for myself. I slipped into the gym where their meeting was held, and I watched. I saw them participating, laughing, listening—having a great time. That night on the way home I asked about their evening and, once again, they said, "It was boring." I responded, "I was there. I watched. You had a great time!" They responded, "Maybe it wasn't as bad as usual."

I recognized that behind their reluctance to admit they were enjoying youth group were things such as peer pressure and a fear of not appearing "cool." But then I wondered, *Am I similarly afraid to get too excited about spiritual things?*

Indeed, there is nothing in this universe more worthy of our enthusiasm than who Christ is and what He did for us. Jesus said, "I have come that they may have life, and have it to the full" (John 10:10). That's the opposite of boring! At any age, we have a gift from the Savior—a gift that is worth celebrating. Our salvation is something to get excited about!

BILL CROWDER

If you know Christ, you always have a reason to celebrate.

Knowing and Loving

JOHN 10:7–16

"I am the good shepherd; I know my sheep and my sheep know me."
JOHN 10:14

"Jesus loves me, this I know, for the Bible tells me so" is the message of one of Christian music's most enduring songs, particularly for children. Written by Anna B. Warner in the 1800s, this lyric tenderly affirms our relationship with Him—we are loved.

Someone gave my wife a plaque for our home that gives these words a fresh twist by flipping that simple idea. It reads, "Jesus *knows* me, this I *love*." This provides a different perspective on our relationship with Him—we are known.

In ancient Israel, loving and knowing the sheep distinguished a true shepherd from a hired hand. The shepherd spent so much time with his sheep that he developed an abiding care for and a deep knowledge of his lambs. Little wonder then that Jesus tells His own, "I am the good shepherd; I know my sheep and my sheep know me. . . . My sheep listen to my voice; I know them, and they follow me" (John 10:14, 27).

He knows us and He loves us! We can trust Jesus's purposes for us and rest in the promise of His care because His Father "knows what [we] need before [we] ask him" (Matthew 6:8). As you deal with the ups and downs of life today, be at rest. You are known and loved by the Shepherd of your heart.

BILL CROWDER

The wonder of it all —just to think that Jesus loves me!

Listening to His Voice

JOHN 10:25-30

"My sheep listen to my voice; I know them, and they follow me."
JOHN 10:27

I'm hard of hearing—"deaf in one ear and can't hear out of the other," as my father used to say. So I wear a set of hearing aids.

Most of the time the devices work well, except in environments where there's a lot of surrounding noise. In those settings, my hearing aids pick up every voice in the room, and I cannot hear the person in front of me.

So it is with our culture: a cacophony of sounds can drown out God's quiet voice. "Where shall the Word be found, where will the Word resound?" poet T. S. Eliot asks. "Not here, there is not enough silence."

Fortunately, my hearing aids have a setting that cuts out the surrounding sounds and enables me to hear only the voices I want to hear. In the same way, despite the voices around us, if we quiet our souls and listen, we will hear God's "still small voice" (1 Kings 19:11–12 KJV).

He speaks to us every day, summoning us in our restlessness and our longing. He calls to us in our deepest sorrow and in the incompleteness and dissatisfaction of our greatest joys.

But primarily God speaks to us in His Word (1 Thessalonians 2:13). As you pick up His book and read it, you too will hear His voice. He loves you more than you can ever know, and He wants you to hear what He has to say.

DAVID ROPER

God speaks through His Word when we take time to listen.

The Death of Doubt

JOHN 11:1–16

So the other disciples told [Thomas], "We have seen the Lord!"
But he said to them, "Unless I see the nail marks in his hands and put my
finger where the nails were, and put my hand into his side,
I will not believe."

JOHN 20:25

We know him as Doubting Thomas (see John 20:24–29), but the label isn't entirely fair. After all, how many of *us* would have believed that our executed leader had been resurrected? We might just as easily call him "Courageous Thomas." After all, Thomas displayed impressive courage as Jesus moved purposefully into the events leading to His death.

At the death of Lazarus, Jesus had said, "Let us go back to Judea" (John 11:7), prompting a protest from the disciples. "Rabbi," they said, "a short while ago the Jews there tried to stone you, and yet you are going back?" (v. 8). It was Thomas who said, "Let us also go, that we may die with him" (v. 16).

Thomas's intentions proved nobler than his actions. Upon Jesus's arrest, Thomas fled with the rest (Matthew 26:56), leaving Peter and John to accompany Christ to the courtyard of the high priest. Only John followed Jesus all the way to the cross.

Despite having witnessed the resurrection of Lazarus (John 11:38–44), Thomas still could not bring himself to believe that the crucified Lord had conquered death. Not until Thomas the doubter—the human—saw the risen Lord, could he exclaim, "My Lord and my God!" (John 20:28). Jesus's response gave assurance to the doubter and immeasurable comfort to us: "Because you have seen me, you have believed; blessed are those who have not seen and yet have believed" (v. 29).

TIM GUSTAFSON

Real doubt searches for the light;
unbelief is content with the darkness.

Jesus Wept

JOHN 11:1–4, 38–44

The sting of death is sin, and the power of sin is the law. But thanks be to God! He gives us the victory through our Lord Jesus Christ.

1 CORINTHIANS 15:56–57

I was engrossed in a book when a friend bent over to see what I was reading. Almost immediately, she recoiled and looked at me aghast. "What a gloomy title!" she said.

I was reading the story "The Glass Coffin" in *Grimm's Fairy Tales*, and the word *coffin* disturbed her. Most of us don't like to be reminded of our mortality. But the reality is that out of one thousand people, one thousand people will die.

Death always elicits a deep emotional response. It was at the funeral of one of His dear friends that Jesus displayed strong emotions. When He saw Mary, whose brother had recently died, "he was deeply moved in spirit and troubled" (John 11:33). Another translation says, "a deep anger welled up within him" (NLT).

Jesus was troubled—even angry—but at what? Possibly, He was indignant at sin and its consequences. God didn't make a world filled with sickness, suffering, and death. But sin entered the world and marred God's beautiful plan.

The Lord comes alongside us in our grief, weeping with us in our sorrow (v. 35). But more than that, Christ defeated sin and death by dying in our place and rising from the dead (1 Corinthians 15:56–57).

Jesus promises, "He who believes in Me, though he may die, he shall live" (John 11:25 NKJV). As believers we enjoy fellowship with our Savior now, and we look forward to an eternity with Him where there will be no more tears, pain, sickness, or death.

POH FANG CHIA

Christ's empty tomb guarantees our victory over death.

A Chuckle in the Darkness

JOHN 11:17–27

For God so loved the world that he gave his one and only Son,
that whoever believes in him shall not perish but have eternal life.

JOHN 3:16

In a *Washington Post* article titled "Tech Titans' Latest Project: Defy Death," Ariana Cha wrote about the efforts of Peter Thiele and other tech moguls to extend human life indefinitely. They're prepared to spend billions on the project.

They are a little late. Death has already been defeated! Jesus said, "I am the resurrection and the life. He who believes in Me, though he may die, he shall live. And whoever lives and believes in Me shall never die" (John 11:25–26 NKJV). Jesus assures us that those who put their trust in Him will never, ever, under any circumstances whatever, die.

To be clear, our bodies will die—and there is nothing anyone can do to change that. But the thinking, reasoning, remembering, loving, adventuring part of us that we call "me, myself, and I" will never, ever die. We will live in on in God's presence.

And here's the best part: It's a gift! All you have to do is receive the salvation Jesus offers. C. S. Lewis, musing on this notion, describes it as something like "a chuckle in the darkness"—the sense that something that simple is the answer.

Some say, "It's too simple." I say, "If God loved you even before you were born and wants you to live with Him forever, why would He make it hard?"

DAVID ROPER

Christ has replaced the dark door of death
with the shining gate of life.

In Transition

JOHN 11:17–27

After that, we who are still alive and are left will be caught up together with them in the clouds to meet the Lord in the air. And so we will be with the Lord forever.

1 THESSALONIANS 4:17

People post obituary notices on billboards and concrete block walls in Ghana regularly. Headlines such as "Gone Too Soon," "Celebration of Life," and "What a Shock!" announce the passing away of loved ones and the approaching funerals. One I read—"In Transition"—points to life beyond the grave.

When a close relative or friend dies, we sorrow as Mary and Martha did for their brother Lazarus (John 11:17–27). We miss the departed so much that our hearts break and we weep, as Jesus wept at the passing of His friend (v. 35).

Yet, it was at this sorrowful moment Jesus made a delightful statement on life after death: "I am the resurrection and the life. The one who believes in me will live, even though they die; and whoever lives by believing in me will never die" (v. 25).

On the basis of this we give departed believers only a temporary farewell. For they "will be with the Lord forever," Paul emphasizes (1 Thessalonians 4:17). Of course, farewells are painful, but we can rest assured that they are in the Lord's safe hands.

"In Transition" suggests that we are only changing from one situation to another. Though life on earth ends for us, we will continue to live forever and better in the next life where Jesus is. "Therefore encourage one another with these words" (v. 18).

LAWRENCE DARMANI

Because of Jesus, we can live forever.

If Only . . .

JOHN 11:21–35

When Mary reached the place where Jesus was and saw him, she fell at his feet and said, "Lord, if you had been here, my brother would not have died."
JOHN 11:32

As we exited the parking lot, my husband slowed the car to wait for a young woman riding her bike. When Tom nodded to indicate she could go first, she smiled, waved, and rode on. Moments later, the driver from a parked SUV threw his door open, knocking the young bicyclist to the pavement. Her legs bleeding, she cried as she examined her bent-up bike.

Later, we reflected on the accident: If only we had made her wait . . . If only the driver had looked before opening his door. If only . . . Difficulties catch us up in a cycle of second-guessing ourselves. If only I had known my child was with teens who were drinking . . . If only we had found the cancer earlier . . .

When unexpected trouble comes, we sometimes question the goodness of God. We may even feel the despair that Martha and Mary experienced when their brother died. Oh, if Jesus had only come when He first found out that Lazarus was sick! (John 11:21, 32).

Like Martha and Mary, we don't always understand why hard things happen to us. But we can rest in the knowledge that God is working out His purposes for a greater good. In every circumstance, we can trust the wisdom of our faithful and loving God.

CINDY HESS KASPER

**To trust God in the light is nothing,
but to trust Him in the dark—that is faith.**
—Charles Spurgeon

Let Down Your Hair

JOHN 12:1–8

*Then Mary took about a pint of pure nard, an expensive perfume;
she poured it on Jesus' feet and wiped his feet with her hair. And the house
was filled with the fragrance of the perfume.*

JOHN 12:3

Shortly before Jesus was crucified, a woman named Mary poured a bottle of expensive perfume on His feet. Then, in what may have been an even more daring act, she wiped His feet with her hair (John 12:3). Not only did Mary sacrifice what may have been her life's savings but she also sacrificed her reputation. In first-century Middle Eastern culture, respectable women never let down their hair in public. But true worship is not concerned about what others think of us (2 Samuel 6:21–22). To worship Jesus, Mary was willing to be thought of as immodest, perhaps even immoral.

Some of us may feel pressured to be perfect when we go to church so people will think highly of us. Metaphorically speaking, we work hard to make sure we have every hair in place. But a healthy church is a place where we can let down our hair and not hide our flaws behind a façade of perfection. In church, we should be able to reveal our weaknesses to find strength rather than conceal our faults to appear strong.

Worship doesn't involve behaving as if nothing is wrong; it's making sure everything is right—right with God and with one another. When our greatest fear is letting down our hair, perhaps our greatest sin is keeping it up.

JULIE ACKERMAN LINK

Our worship is right when we are right with God.

Fickle Followers

JOHN 12:12-19; 19:14-19

*"Do not be afraid, Daughter Zion; see, your king is coming,
seated on a donkey's colt."*

JOHN 12:15

How quickly public opinion can change! When Jesus entered Jerusalem for the Passover feast, He was welcomed by crowds cheering to have Him made king (John 12:13). But by the end of the week, the crowds were demanding that He be crucified (19:15).

I recognize myself in those fickle crowds. I love cheering for a team that's winning, but my interest wanes when they start losing. I love being part of a movement that is new and exciting, but when the energy moves to a new part of town, I'm ready to move on. I love following Jesus when He is doing the impossible, but I slink away when He expects me to do something difficult. It's exciting to follow Jesus when I can do it as part of the "in" crowd. It's easy to trust Him when He outsmarts the smart people and outmaneuvers the people in power (see Matthew 12:10; 22:15–46). But when He begins to talk about suffering and sacrifice and death, I hesitate.

I like to think that I would have followed Jesus all the way to the cross—but I have my doubts. After all, if I don't speak up for Him in places where it's safe, what makes me think I would do so in a crowd of His opponents?

How thankful I am that Jesus died for fickle followers like me so we can become devoted followers.

JULIE ACKERMAN LINK

Christ deserves full-time followers.

Helicopter Seeds

JOHN 12:23–33

"Very truly I tell you, unless a kernel of wheat falls to the ground and dies, it remains only a single seed. But if it dies, it produces many seeds."
JOHN 12:24

When our children were young, they loved trying to catch the "helicopter seeds" that fell from our neighbor's silver maple trees. Each seed resembles a wing. In late spring they twirl to the ground like a helicopter's rotor blades. The seed's purpose is not to fly, but to fall to earth and grow into a tree.

Before Jesus was crucified, He told His followers, "The hour has come for the Son of Man to be glorified. . . . unless a kernel of wheat falls to the ground and dies, it remains only a single seed. But if it dies, it produces many seeds" (John 12:23–24).

While Jesus's disciples wanted Him to be honored as the Messiah, He came to give His life so we could be forgiven and transformed through faith in Him. As Jesus's followers, we hear His words: "Anyone who loves their life will lose it, while anyone who hates their life in this world will keep it for eternal life. Whoever serves me must follow me; and where I am, my servant also will be. My Father will honor the one who serves me" (vv. 25–26).

Helicopter seeds can point us to the miracle of Jesus, the Savior, who died that we might live for Him.

DAVID McCASLAND

Jesus calls us to give our lives in serving Him.

Rejected Light

JOHN 12:35-46

"I have come into the world as a light, so that no one who believes in me should stay in darkness."
JOHN 12:46

In the early hours of December 21, 2010, I witnessed an event that last occurred in 1638—a total lunar eclipse on the winter solstice. Slowly the shadow of the earth slipped across the bright full moon and made it appear a dark red. It was a remarkable and beautiful event. Yet it reminded me that while physical darkness is part of God's created design, spiritual darkness is not.

Scottish pastor Alexander Maclaren said: "Rejected light is the parent of the densest darkness, and the man who, having the light, does not trust it, piles around himself thick clouds of obscurity and gloom." Jesus described this self-imposed spiritual eclipse of heart and mind when He said, "If then the light within you is darkness, how great is that darkness!" (Matthew 6:23).

The great invitation from God is to open our hearts to the Savior who came to end our darkness. Jesus said, "While you have the light, believe in the light, that you may become sons of light. . . . I have come as a light into the world, that whoever believes in Me should not abide in darkness" (John 12:36, 46 NKJV).

The way out of our spiritual night is to walk in the light with Him.

DAVID McCASLAND

**When we walk in the Light,
we won't stumble in the darkness.**

Light in the Darkness

JOHN 12:42–50

"I have come into the world as a light,
so that no one who believes in me should stay in darkness."
JOHN 12:46

During a trip to Peru, I visited one of the many caves found throughout that mountainous country. Our guide told us that this particular cave had already been explored to a depth of nine miles—and it went even deeper. We saw fascinating bats, nocturnal birds, and interesting rock formations. Before long, however, the darkness of the cave became unnerving—almost suffocating. I was greatly relieved when we returned to the surface and the light of day.

That experience was a stark reminder of how oppressive darkness can be and how much we need light. We live in a world made dark by sin—a world that has turned against its Creator. And we need the Light.

Jesus, who came to restore all of creation—including humanity—to its intended place, referred to himself as that "light" (John 8:12). "I have come into the world as a light," He said, "so that no one who believes in me should stay in darkness" (12:46).

In Him, we not only have the light of salvation but also the only light by which we can find our way—His way—through this world's spiritual darkness.

BILL CROWDER

Sometimes we must experience the darkness
to appreciate the light.

A Picture of Humility

JOHN 13:1-11

He gives us more grace. That is why Scripture says:
"God opposes the proud but shows favor to the humble."

JAMES 4:6

During one Easter season, my wife and I attended a church service where the participants sought to model the events that Jesus and His disciples experienced on the night before He was crucified. As part of the service, the church staff members washed the feet of some of the church volunteers. As I watched, I wondered which was more humbling in our day—to wash another person's feet or to have someone else wash yours. Both those who were serving and those being served were presenting distinct pictures of humility.

When Jesus and His disciples were gathered for the Last Supper (John 13:1–20), Jesus, in humble servanthood, washed His disciples' feet. But Simon Peter resisted, saying, "You shall never wash my feet!" Then Jesus answered, "Unless I wash you, you have no part with me" (13:8). Washing their feet was not a mere ritual. It could also be seen as a picture of our need of Christ's cleansing—a cleansing that will never be realized unless we are willing to be humble before the Savior.

James wrote, "God opposes the proud but shows favor to the humble" (James 4:6). We receive God's grace when we acknowledge the greatness of God, who humbled himself at the cross (Philippians 2:5–11).

BILL CROWDER

**The most powerful position on earth
is kneeling before the Lord of the universe.**

Angels at Work

JOHN 13:1–17

*Are not all angels ministering spirits sent to
serve those who will inherit salvation?*
HEBREWS 1:14

Hanging in a Paris museum is a painting of an old-fashioned kitchen. The unique thing about it is that instead of showing people at work, the artist depicted angels busily engaged in kitchen chores—putting a kettle on the fire, carrying a pail of water, and preparing the table for a meal.

Commenting on this scene, nineteenth-century preacher and song-writer William C. Gannett said, "Somehow you forget that pans are pans, and pots are pots, and only think of the angels, and how very natural and beautiful kitchen work is—just what angels would do, of course."

According to Hebrews 1:14, angels are "ministering spirits sent to serve those who will inherit salvation." They are servants, and we should all be committed to function in that same role.

My wife Margaret has such a serving attitude that I sometimes tell her I must have married an "angel." She is one of the most loving, caring, helpful persons I've ever met. A registered nurse, she does volunteer work in a nursing home, performing foot and hand care, which includes cutting toenails. Not very glamorous. But done in Christ's name, with a loving spirit, it is "angelic" work.

May each of us serve one another so that we might be viewed as "angels at work."

RICHARD DEHAAN

**Little things become great things
when they are done to please God.**

Pay It Forward

JOHN 13:3–15

"I have set you an example that you should do as I have done for you."
JOHN 13:15

Pay It Forward is a movie about a twelve-year-old's plan to make a difference in the world. Motivated by a teacher at his school, Trevor invites a homeless man to sleep in his garage. Unaware of this arrangement, his mother awakens one evening to find the man working on her truck. Holding him at gunpoint, she asks him to explain himself. He shows her that he has successfully repaired her truck and tells her about Trevor's kindness. He says, "I'm just paying it forward."

I think this kind of thing is what Jesus had in mind in one of His last conversations with His disciples. He wanted to show them the full extent of His love. So before their last meal together, He took off His outer garment, wrapped a towel around His waist, and began to wash His disciples' feet. This was shocking because only slaves washed feet. It was an act of servanthood and a symbol that pointed to Jesus's sacrifice, passion, and humiliation on the cross. His request to His disciples was: "Now that I, your Lord and Teacher, have washed your feet, you also should wash one another's feet" (John 13:14). They were to "pay it forward."

Imagine how different our world would look if we gave the kind of love to others that God has given us through Jesus.

MARVIN WILLIAMS

To know love, open your heart to Jesus.
To show love, open your heart to others.

Leaning on Jesus

JOHN 13:12–26

One of them, the disciple whom Jesus loved, was reclining next to him.
JOHN 13:23

Sometimes when I put my head on my pillow at night and pray, I imagine I'm leaning on Jesus. Whenever I do this, I remember something the Word of God tells us about the apostle John. John himself writes about how he was sitting beside Jesus at the Last Supper: "One of them, the disciple whom Jesus loved, was reclining next to him" (John 13:23).

John used the term "the disciple whom Jesus loved" as a way of referring to himself without mentioning his own name. He is also depicting a typical banquet setting in first-century Israel, where the table was much lower than those we use today, about knee height. Reclining without chairs on a mat or cushions was the natural position for those around the table. John was sitting so close to the Lord that when he turned to ask Him a question, he was "leaning back against Jesus" (John 13:25), with his head on His chest.

John's closeness to Jesus in that moment provides a helpful illustration for our lives with Him today. We may not be able to touch Jesus physically, but we can entrust the weightiest circumstances of our lives to Him. He said, "Come to me, all you who are weary and burdened, and I will give you rest" (Matthew 11:28). How blessed we are to have a Savior we can trust to be faithful through every circumstance of our lives! Are you "leaning" on Him today?

JAMES BANKS

Jesus alone gives the rest we need.

Someone to Trust

JOHN 13:33–35

Many claim to have unfailing love, but a faithful person who can find?
PROVERBS 20:6

"I just can't trust anyone," my friend said through tears. "Every time I do, they hurt me." Her story angered me: an ex-boyfriend, whom she thought she could trust completely, had started spreading rumors about her as soon as they broke up. Struggling to trust again after a pain-filled childhood, this betrayal seemed just one more confirmation that people could not be trusted.

I struggled to find words that would comfort. One thing I could *not* say was that she was wrong about how hard it is to find someone to fully trust, that most people are completely kind and trustworthy. Her story was painfully familiar, reminding me of moments of unexpected betrayal in my own life. In fact, Scripture is very candid about human nature. In Proverbs 20:6, the author voices the same lament as my friend, forever memorializing the pain of betrayal.

What I *could* say is that the cruelty of others is only part of the story. Although wounds from others are real and painful, Jesus has made genuine love possible. In John 13:35, Jesus told His disciples that the world would know they were His followers because of their love. Although some people may still hurt us, because of Jesus there will also always be those who, freely sharing His love, will unconditionally support and care for us. Resting in His unfailing love, may we find healing, community, and courage to love others as He did.

MONICA BRANDS

Jesus has made true love possible.

A Place

JOHN 13:36–14:4

"If I go and prepare a place for you, I will come back and take you to be with me that you also may be where I am."
JOHN 14:3

A couple who brought their elderly aunt to live with them was concerned that she would not feel at home. So they transformed a room in their house into an exact replica of her bedroom at the home she left behind. When their aunt arrived, her furniture, wall hangings, and other favorite things felt like a special "Welcome home!" to her.

In John 13:36–14:4, we read that at the Last Supper Jesus spoke to His disciples and tried to prepare them for His death. When Simon Peter asked, "Where are you going?" Jesus replied, "Where I am going you cannot follow now, but you will follow later" (13:36). Jesus was still speaking directly to Peter (and also meant it for all of His followers) when He said, "There is more than enough room in my Father's home. If this were not so, would I have told you that I am going to prepare a place for you? When everything is ready, I will come and get you, so that you will always be where I am" (14:2–3 NLT).

Heaven is a family gathering of believers from every tribe and nation, but it is also our Father's house—and in that house He is preparing a dwelling place just for you.

When you arrive in heaven and Jesus opens the door, you'll know you're home.

DAVID MCCASLAND

For the Christian, heaven is spelled H-O-M-E.

Seeing God

JOHN 14:1–12

Philip said, "Lord, show us the Father and that will be enough for us."
JOHN 14:8

Author and pastor Erwin Lutzer recounts a story about television show host Art Linkletter and a little boy who was drawing a picture of God. Amused, Linkletter said, "You can't do that because nobody knows what God looks like."

"They will when I get through!" the boy declared.

We may wonder, *What is God like? Is He good? Is He kind? Does He care?* The simple answer to those questions is Jesus's response to Philip's request: "Lord, show us the Father." Jesus replied, "Don't you know me, Philip, even after I have been among you such a long time? Anyone who has seen me has seen the Father" (John 14:8–9).

If you ever get hungry to see God, look at Jesus. "The Son is the image of the invisible God," said Paul (Colossians 1:15). Read through the four Gospels in the New Testament: Matthew, Mark, Luke, and John. Think deeply about what Jesus did and said. "Draw" your own mental picture of God as you read. You'll know much more of what He's like when you're through.

A friend of mine once told me that the only God he could believe in is the one he saw in Jesus. If you look closely, I think you'll agree. As you read about Him your heart will leap, for though you may not know it, Jesus is the God you've been looking for all your life.

DAVID ROPER

The clearer we see God, the clearer we see ourselves.
—Erwin Lutzer

The Advance Team

JOHN 14:1–14

"There is more than enough room in my Father's home. If this were not so, would I have told you that I am going to prepare a place for you?"

JOHN 14:2 (NLT)

A friend recently prepared to relocate to a city more than a thousand miles from her current hometown. She and her husband divided the labor of moving to accommodate a short timeline. He secured new living arrangements while she packed their belongings. I was astounded by her ability to move without previewing the area or participating in the house hunt, so I asked her how she could do so. She acknowledged the challenge but said she knew she could trust her husband because of his attention to her preferences and needs over their years together.

In the upper room, Jesus spoke with His disciples of His coming betrayal and death. The darkest hours of Jesus's earthly life, and that of the disciples as well, lay ahead. He comforted them with the assurance that He would prepare a place for them in heaven, just as my friend's husband prepared a new home for their family. When the disciples questioned Jesus, He pointed them to their mutual history and the miracles they had witnessed Him perform. Though they would grieve Jesus's death and absence, He reminded them He could be counted on to do as He had said.

Even in the midst of our own dark hours, we can trust Him to lead us forward to a place of goodness. As we walk with Him, we too will learn to trust increasingly in His faithfulness.

KRISTEN HOLMBERG

We can trust God to lead us through difficult times.

Finding Life

JOHN 14:5–14

"Before long, the world will not see me anymore, but you will see me. Because I live, you also will live."

JOHN 14:19

The words of Ravi's father cut deep. "You're a complete failure. You're an embarrassment to the family." Compared to his talented siblings, Ravi was viewed as a disgrace. He tried excelling in sports, and he did, but he still felt like a loser. He wondered, *What is going to become of me? Am I a complete failure? Can I get out of life some way, painlessly?* These thoughts haunted him, but he talked to no one. That simply wasn't done in his culture. He had been taught to "keep your private heartache private; keep your collapsing world propped up."

So Ravi struggled alone. Then while he was recovering in the hospital after a failed suicide attempt, a visitor brought him a Bible opened to John 14. His mother read these words of Jesus to Ravi: "Because I live, you also will live" (v. 19). *This may be my only hope,* he thought. *A new way of living. Life as defined by the Author of life.* So he prayed, "Jesus, if you are the one who gives life as it is meant to be, I want it."

Life can present despairing moments. But like Ravi, we can find hope in Jesus who is "the way and the truth and the life" (v. 6). God longs to give us a rich and satisfying life.

POH FANG CHIA

Only Jesus can give us new life.

With Us and in Us

JOHN 14:15–27

"I will ask the Father, and he will give you another advocate to help you and be with you forever—the Spirit of truth."

JOHN 14:16–17

My son had just started nursery school. The first day he cried and declared, "I don't like school." My husband and I talked to him about it. "We may not be physically there, but we are praying for you. Besides, Jesus is with you always."

"But I can't see Him!" he reasoned. My husband hugged him and said, "He lives in you. And He won't leave you alone." My son touched his heart and said, "Yes, Jesus lives in me."

Kids are not the only ones who suffer from separation anxiety. In every stage of life we face times of separation from those we love, sometimes because of geographical distance and sometimes because of death. However, we need to remember that even if we feel forsaken by others, God hasn't forsaken us. He has promised to be with us always. God sent the Spirit of truth—our Advocate and Helper—to dwell with us and in us forever (John 14:15–18). We are His beloved children.

My son is learning to trust, but so am I. Like my son, I can't see the Spirit, but I feel His power as each day He encourages me and guides me as I read God's Word. Let us thank God for His wonderful provision, the Spirit of Christ who is with us and in us. We are certainly not alone!

KEILA OCHOA

We are never alone.

Perfect Peace

JOHN 14:25–31

"Peace I leave with you; my peace I give you. I do not give to you as the world gives. Do not let your hearts be troubled and do not be afraid."

JOHN 14:27

A friend shared with me that for years she searched for peace and contentment. She and her husband built up a successful business, so she was able to buy a big house, fancy clothes, and expensive jewelry. But these possessions didn't satisfy her inner longings for peace, nor did her friendships with influential people. Then one day, when she was feeling low and desperate, a friend told her about the good news of Jesus. There she found the Prince of Peace, and her understanding of true peace and contentment was forever changed.

Jesus spoke words of peace to His friends after their last supper together (John 14), as He prepared them for the events that would soon follow: His death, resurrection, and the coming of the Holy Spirit. Describing peace—a peace unlike anything the world can give—He wanted them to learn how to find a sense of well-being even in the midst of hardship.

Later, when the resurrected Jesus appeared to the frightened disciples, He greeted them, saying, "Peace be with you!" (John 20:19). Now He could give them, and us, a new understanding of resting in what He had done for us. As we rest in Him, we can find a confidence far more dependable than our ever-changing feelings.

AMY BOUCHER PYE

Jesus came to usher peace into our lives and our world.

Honoring God

JOHN 15:1–5

"I am the vine; you are the branches. If you remain in me and I in you, you will bear much fruit; apart from me you can do nothing."

JOHN 15:5

The church service was still in progress, and we had some visitors there that morning. The speaker was only halfway through his sermon when I noticed one of our visitors walking out. I was curious and concerned, so I walked out to talk with her.

"You're leaving so soon," I said, approaching her. "Is there a problem I can help with?"

She was frank and forthright. "Yes," she said, "my problem is that sermon! I don't accept what the preacher is saying." He had said that no matter what we accomplish in life, the credit and praise belong to God. "At least," the woman moaned, "I deserve *some* credit for my achievements!"

I explained to her what the pastor meant. People do deserve recognition and appreciation for what they do. Yet even our gifts and talents are from God, so He gets the ultimate glory. Even Jesus, the Son of God, said, "The Son can do nothing by himself; he can do only what he sees his Father doing" (John 5:19). He told His followers, "Apart from me you can do nothing" (15:5).

We acknowledge the Lord as the One who helps us to accomplish everything.

LAWRENCE DARMANI

God's children do His will for His glory.

More Than Information

JOHN 15:1–13

"Remain in me, as I also remain in you.
No branch can bear fruit by itself; it must remain in the vine.
Neither can you bear fruit unless you remain in me."

JOHN 15:4

How is behavior altered? In his book *The Social Animal*, newspaper columnist David Brooks notes that some experts have said people just need to be taught the long-term risks of bad behavior. For example, he writes: "Smoking can lead to cancer. Adultery destroys families, and lying destroys trust. The assumption was that once you reminded people of the foolishness of their behavior, they would be motivated to stop. Both reason and will are obviously important in making moral decisions and exercising self-control. But neither of these character models has proven very effective." In other words, information alone is not powerful enough to transform behavior.

As Jesus's followers, we want to grow and change spiritually. More than two millennia ago, Jesus told His disciples how that can happen. He said, "Remain in me, as I also remain in you. No branch can bear fruit by itself; it must remain in the vine. Neither can you bear fruit unless you remain in me" (John 15:4). Jesus is the Vine and we, His followers, are the branches. If we're honest, we know we're utterly helpless and spiritually ineffective apart from Him.

Jesus transforms us spiritually and reproduces His life in us—as we remain in Him.

MARVIN WILLIAMS

A change in behavior begins when Jesus changes our heart.

Love of Another Kind

JOHN 15:9–17

"My command is this: Love each other as I have loved you."
JOHN 15:12

One of my favorite churches started several years ago as a ministry to ex-prisoners who were transitioning back into society. Now the church flourishes with people from all walks of life. I love that church because it reminds me of what I picture heaven will be like—filled with different kinds of people, all redeemed sinners, all bound together by the love of Jesus.

Sometimes, though, I wonder if church seems more like an exclusive club than a safe-haven for forgiven sinners. As people naturally gravitate into groups of "a certain kind" and cluster around those they feel comfortable with, it leaves others feeling marginalized. But that's not what Jesus had in mind when He told His disciples to "love each other as I have loved you" (John 15:12). His church was to be an extension of His love—mutually shared with all.

If hurting, rejected people can find loving refuge, comfort, and forgiveness in Jesus, they should expect no less from the church. It's important to exhibit the love of Jesus to everyone we encounter. All around us are people Jesus wants to love through us. What a joy it is when people unite to worship together in love—a slice of heaven we can enjoy here on earth!

JOE STOWELL

Share Christ's love with another.

The Way We See Jesus

JOHN 15:12–17

"You are my friends if you do what I command."
JOHN 15:14

Raleigh looks like a powerful dog—he is large and muscular and has a thick coat of fur. And he weighs over one hundred pounds! Despite his appearance, Raleigh connects well with people. His owner takes him to nursing homes and hospitals to bring people a smile.

Once, a four-year-old girl spotted Raleigh across a room. She wanted to pet him but was afraid to get close. Eventually, her curiosity overcame her sense of caution, and she spent several minutes talking to him and petting him. She discovered that he is a gentle creature—even though he is powerful.

The combination of these qualities reminds me of what we read about Jesus in the New Testament. Jesus was approachable—He welcomed little children (Matthew 19:13–15). He was kind to an adulterous woman in a desperate situation (John 8:1–11). Compassion motivated Him to teach crowds (Mark 6:34). At the same time, Jesus's power was astounding. Heads turned and jaws dropped as He subdued demons, calmed violent storms, and resurrected dead people! (Mark 1:21–34; 4:35–41; John 11).

The way we see Jesus determines how we relate to Him. If we focus only on His power, we may treat Him with the detached worship we'd give a comic book superhero. Yet, if we overemphasize His kindness, we risk treating Him too casually. The truth is that Jesus is both at once—great enough to deserve our obedience yet humble enough to call us friends.

JENNIFER BENSON SCHULDT

What we think of Jesus shows in how we relate with Him.

Why Love Begets Hate

JOHN 15:18–27

"If the world hates you, keep in mind that it hated me first."
JOHN 15:18

If there is one thing believers in Jesus should be known for, it is love. The word *love* appears in Scripture more than five hundred times. The essence of the gospel is love, as we see in John 3:16. "For God so loved the world . . . ." The epistle of 1 John 3:16 elaborates: "This is how we know what love is: Jesus Christ laid down his life for us."

Christians are to serve one another in love (Galatians 5:13), love their neighbors as themselves (Galatians 5:14), live a life of love (Ephesians 5:2), and love with actions and in truth (1 John 3:18).

So, if Jesus and His followers are all about love, why do some people love to hate us? Why are there, according to one estimate, two hundred million persecuted believers in the world today?

The apostle John told us why. He said, "Everyone who does evil hates the light, and will not come into the light for fear that their deeds will be exposed" (John 3:20). Jesus is the Light. We are now His light in this world (Matthew 5:14); therefore, the world will also hate us (John 15:19).

Our task is to be channels of God's love and light, even if we are hated in return.

DAVE BRANON

Love in return for love is natural,
but love in return for hate is supernatural.

Debits and Credits

JOHN 16:1–11

"I have told you these things, so that in my you may have peace. In this world you will have trouble. But take heart! I have overcome the world."

JOHN 16:33

When my husband was teaching an accounting class at a local college, I took one of the tests just for fun to see how well I could do. The results were not good. I answered every question wrong. The reason for my failure was that I started with a faulty understanding of a basic banking concept. I reversed debits and credits.

We sometimes get our debits and credits confused in the spiritual realm as well. When we blame Satan for everything that goes wrong—whether it's bad weather, a jammed printer, or financial trouble—we're actually giving him credit that he doesn't deserve. We are ascribing to him the power to determine the quality of our lives, which he does not have. Satan is limited in time and space. He has to ask God's permission before he can touch us (Job 1:12; Luke 22:31).

However, as the father of lies and prince of this world (John 8:44; 16:11), Satan can cause confusion. Jesus warned of a time when people would be so confused that they wouldn't know right from wrong (16:2). But He added this assurance: "The prince of this world now stands condemned" (v. 11).

Problems will disrupt our lives, but they cannot defeat us. Jesus has already overcome the world. To Him goes all the credit.

JULIE ACKERMAN LINK

While Satan accuses and confuses, God overcomes.

Companion and Guide

JOHN 16:5–15

"They will do such things because they have not known the Father or me."
JOHN 16:3

Lisa Marino has a personal fitness coach who gives her daily advice and encouragement. But she's never seen him. As a participant in a program called "Life Practice," Lisa begins each day by sending a report of her diet, exercise, sleep, and stress to a website. Later, she receives an email response from her coach. She says that the daily reporting helps keep her honest and focused on her fitness goals.

As Christians, we know the marvelous yet mysterious experience of having the Holy Spirit as our companion and guide—even though we can't see Him.

Jesus promised His disciples that when He left this earth He would send Someone else to be with them. "It is to your advantage that I go away; for if I do not go away, the Helper will not come to you; but if I depart, I will send Him to you" (John 16:7 NKJV).

The word translated *Helper* (sometimes translated *Comforter*) means "called to one's side or aid." Bible scholar W. E. Vine says that it signifies Someone who can be to us what Christ was to His disciples.

Although He is invisible to our eyes, the Holy Spirit is with us every day, just as Jesus walked with His disciples on earth. He keeps us honest, focused, and encouraged so we too can glorify Christ.

DAVID McCASLAND

The Father gave us the Spirit to make us like His Son.

Foley Artists

JOHN 16:7–15

Satan himself masquerades as an angel of light.
2 CORINTHIANS 11:14

Crunch. Crunch. Whoosh!

In the early days of film, Foley artists created sounds to support the story's action. Squeezing a leather pouch filled with cornstarch made the sound of snow crunching; shaking a pair of gloves sounded like bird wings flapping; and waving a thin stick made a whoosh sound. To make movies as realistic as possible, these artists used creative techniques to replicate sounds.

Like sounds, messages can be replicated. One of Satan's most frequently used techniques is that of replicating messages in spiritually dangerous ways. Paul warns in 2 Corinthians 11:13–14, "For such people are false apostles, deceitful workers, masquerading as apostles of Christ. And no wonder, for Satan himself masquerades as an angel of light." Paul is warning us about false teachers who turn our attention away from Jesus Christ and the message of His grace.

Jesus said that one purpose for the Holy Spirit living in us is that "when he, the Spirit of truth, comes, he will guide you into all the truth" (John 16:13). With the help and guidance of the Spirit, we can find the safety of truth in a world of counterfeit messages.

BILL CROWDER

The Holy Spirit is our ever-present Teacher.

From Grief to Joy

JOHN 16:16–22

"Very truly I tell you, you will weep and mourn while the world rejoices. You will grieve, but your grief will turn to joy."
JOHN 16:20

Kelly's pregnancy brought complications, and doctors were concerned. During her long labor, they decided to whisk her away for a Cesarean section. But despite the ordeal, Kelly quickly forgot her pain when she held her newborn son. Joy had replaced anguish.

Scripture affirms this truth: "A woman giving birth to a child has pain because her time has come; but when her baby is born she forgets the anguish because of her joy that a child is born into the world" (John 16:21). Jesus used this illustration with His disciples to emphasize that though they would grieve because He would be leaving soon, that grief would turn to joy when they saw Him again (vv. 20–22).

Jesus was referring to His death and resurrection—and what followed. After His resurrection, to the disciples' joy, Jesus spent another forty days walking with and teaching them before ascending into heaven and leaving them again (Acts 1:3). Yet Jesus did not leave them grief-stricken. The Holy Spirit would fill them with joy (John 16:7–15; Acts 13:52).

Although we have never seen Jesus face-to-face, as believers we have the assurance that one day we will. In that day, the anguish we experience on this earth will be forgotten. But until then, the Lord has not left us without joy—He has given us His Spirit (Romans 15:13; 1 Peter 1:8–9).

ALYSON KIEDA

One day our sorrow will be turned to joy!

Flight Simulator

JOHN 16:25–33

"I have told you these things, so that in me you may have peace. In this world you will have trouble. But take heart! I have overcome the world."

JOHN 16:33

When airplane pilots are training, they spend many hours in flight simulators. These simulators give the students a chance to experience the challenges and dangers of flying an aircraft—but without the risk. The pilots don't have to leave the ground, and if they crash in the simulation, they can calmly walk away.

Simulators are tremendous teaching tools–helpful in preparing the aspiring pilot to take command of an actual aircraft. The devices, however, have a shortcoming. They create an artificial experience in which the full-blown pressures of handling a real cockpit cannot be fully replicated.

Real life is like that, isn't it? It cannot be simulated. There is no risk-free environment in which we can experience life's ups and downs unharmed. The risks and dangers of living in a broken world are inescapable. That's why the words of Jesus are reassuring. He said, "I have told you these things, so that in me you may have peace. In this world you will have trouble. But take heart! I have overcome the world" (John 16:33).

Although we can't avoid the dangers of life in a fallen world, we can have peace through a relationship with Jesus. He has secured our ultimate victory.

BILL CROWDER

No life is more secure than a life surrendered to God.

The Factory of Sadness

JOHN 16:28–33

"He will wipe away every tear from their eyes. There will be no more death or mourning or crying or pain, for the old order of things has passed away."
REVELATION 21:4

As a lifelong Cleveland Browns football fan, I grew up knowing my share of disappointment. Despite being one of only four teams to have never appeared in the Super Bowl, the Browns have a loyal fan base that sticks with the team year in and year out. But because the fans usually end up disappointed, many of them refer to the home stadium as the "Factory of Sadness."

The broken world we live in can be a "factory of sadness" too. There seems to be an endless supply of heartache and disappointment, whether from our own choices or things beyond our control.

Yet the follower of Christ has hope—not only in the life to come but also for this very day. Jesus said, "I have told you these things, so that in me you may have peace. In this world you will have trouble. But take heart! I have overcome the world" (John 16:33). Notice that without minimizing the struggles or sadness we may experience, Christ counters them with His promises of peace, joy, and ultimate victory.

Great peace is available in Christ, and it's more than enough to help us navigate whatever life throws at us.

BILL CROWDER

Our hope and peace are found in Jesus.

The Beauty of Rome

JOHN 17:1–5

"Now this is eternal life: that they know you, the only true God, and Jesus Christ, whom you have sent."

JOHN 17:3

The glory of the Roman Empire offered an expansive backdrop for the birth of Jesus. In 27 BC Rome's first emperor, Caesar Augustus, ended two hundred years of civil war and began to replace rundown neighborhoods with monuments, temples, arenas, and government complexes. According to Roman historian Pliny the Elder, they were "the most beautiful buildings the world has ever seen."

Yet even with her beauty, the Eternal City and its empire had a history of brutality that continued until Rome fell. Thousands of slaves, foreigners, revolutionaries, and army deserters were crucified on roadside poles as a warning to anyone who dared to defy the power of Rome.

What irony that Jesus's death on a Roman cross turned out to reveal an eternal glory that made the pride of Rome look like the momentary beauty of a sunset!

Who could have imagined that in the public curse and agony of the cross we would find the eternal glory of the love, presence, and kingdom of our God?

Who could have foreseen that all heaven and earth would one day sing, "Worthy is the Lamb, who was slain, to receive power and wealth and wisdom and strength and honor and glory and praise!" (Revelation 5:12).

MART DEHAAN

The Lamb who died is the Lord who lives!

He Wants More

JOHN 17:1–8

*"Now this is eternal life: that they know you, the only true God,
and Jesus Christ, whom you have sent."*

JOHN 17:3

You always sit in the row ahead of Sam in church. You smile and say, "Good morning" when you come in. You say, "See you next Sunday" when you leave. But one morning, you add a little conversation: "Sam, could you give me a hundred dollars?"

Unfortunately, that's the way some people treat the Lord. They have a Sunday-only relationship with Him until they need something. But God desires much more.

The Lord wants us first of all to know Him as our Savior. "This is eternal life: that they know you, the only true God, and Jesus Christ, whom you have sent" (John 17:3).

After we become His child (1:12), God desires an ongoing dialog with us and a growing knowledge of who He is and who we can be with His help. He doesn't want to be a Sunday-only acquaintance or Someone we cry out to only when we're desperate. God wants us to have a personal relationship with Him. He also wants us to grow in our desire to please Him by obeying Him. "We know that we have come to know him if we keep his commands" (1 John 2:3).

God loves you and wants you to know Him. He does answer desperation prayers. But before you start asking, make sure you know Him personally.

CINDY HESS KASPER

**Knowing about God may interest us,
but only knowing God himself will change us.**

The Praying Patient

JOHN 17:6–1

*"I will remain in the world no longer, but they are still in the world,
and I am coming to you."*

JOHN 17:11

The obituary for Alan Nanninga, a man in my city, identified him as "foremost, a dedicated witness for Christ." After a description of his family life and career, the article mentioned nearly a decade of declining health. It concluded by saying, "His hospital stays . . . earned him the honorary title of 'The Praying Patient'" because of his ministry to other patients. Here was a man who, in his times of distress, reached out to pray for and with the people in need around him.

Hours before Judas betrayed Him, Jesus prayed for His disciples. "I will remain in the world no longer, but they are still in the world, and I am coming to you. Holy Father, protect them by the power of your name, the name you gave me, so that they may be one as we are one" (John 17:11). Knowing what was about to happen, Jesus looked beyond himself to focus on His followers and friends.

During our times of illness and distress, we long for and need the prayers of others. How those prayers help and encourage us! But may we also, like our Lord, lift our eyes to pray for those around us who are in great need.

DAVID MCCASLAND

Our troubles can fill our prayers with love and empathy for others.

Mysterious Truth

JOHN 17:20–26

"Precious in the sight of the LORD is the death of his faithful servants."
PSALM 116:15

Sometimes when the infinite God conveys His thoughts to finite man, mystery is the result. For example, there's a profound verse in the book of Psalms that seems to present more questions than answers: "Precious in the sight of the LORD is the death of His faithful servants" (116:15).

I shake my head and wonder how that can be. I see things with earthbound eyes, and I have a tough time seeing what is "precious" about the fact that our daughter was taken in a car accident at the age of seventeen— or that any of us have lost cherished loved ones.

We begin to unwrap the mystery, though, when we consider that what is precious to the Lord is not confined to earthly blessings. This verse examines a heaven-based perspective. For instance, I know from Psalm 139:16 that Melissa's arrival in God's heaven was expected. God was looking for her arrival, and it was precious in His eyes. And think about this: Imagine the Father's joy when He welcomes His children home and sees their absolute ecstasy in being face-to-face with His Son (see John 17:24).

When death comes for the follower of Christ, God opens His arms to welcome that person into His presence. Even through our tears, we can see how precious that is in God's eyes.

DAVE BRANON

A sunset in one land is a sunrise in another.

Hidden Resources

JOHN 18:1–14

I can do all things through Christ who strengthens me.
PHILIPPIANS 4:13 (NKJV)

Did you ever wonder how some Christians handle life so calmly? Perhaps you've observed a young mother with several small children. Somehow, even when things were the most hassled, she kept right on caring for her family. Maybe you've noticed a businessman who learned that his flight had been delayed and that he would miss an important conference—but he wasn't upset. Or you know a couple with an aging parent in their home, and he has become difficult to handle. Yet they care for him without becoming impatient. How do these people do it? They have learned to rely upon the hidden resources of God.

In his book *Be Joyful*, Warren Wiersbe wrote these words: "All of nature depends on hidden resources. The great trees send their roots down into the earth to draw up water and minerals. Rivers have their sources in the snow-capped mountains. The most important part of a tree is the part you cannot see, the root system, and the most important part of the Christian's life is the part that only God sees. Unless we draw upon the deep resources of God by faith, we fail against the pressures of life."

Perhaps you are the kind of Christian who does okay when things are going well but who collapses when life brings adversity. If so, begin to draw upon God's power. Feed upon His Word. Build up your inner strength through regular times of prayer. Ask God to help you depend on His resources. Then, when a crisis comes, the deep roots of faith will enable you to stand.

DAVID EGNER

Lives rooted in God are never uprooted.

Strong Conqueror

JOHN 18:10–14, 36–37

Jesus said, "My kingdom is not of this world.
If it were, my servants would fight to prevent my arrest by the Jewish leaders.
But now my kingdom is from another place."

JOHN 18:36

Most of us hope for good government. We vote, we serve, and we speak out for causes we believe are fair and just. But political solutions remain powerless to change the condition of our hearts.

Many of Jesus's followers anticipated a Messiah who would bring a vigorous political response to Rome and its heavy-handed oppression. Peter was no exception. When Roman soldiers came to arrest Christ, Peter drew his sword and took a swing at the head of the high priest's servant, lopping off his ear in the process.

Jesus halted Peter's one-man war, saying, "Put your sword away! Shall I not drink the cup the Father has given me?" (John 18:11). Hours later, Jesus would tell Pilate, "My kingdom is not of this world. If it were, my servants would fight to prevent my arrest by the Jewish leaders" (v. 36).

The Lord's restraint in that moment, as His life hung in the balance, astonishes us when we ponder the scope of His mission. On a future day, He will lead the armies of heaven into battle. John wrote of that day, "With justice he judges and wages war" (Revelation 19:11).

But as He endured the ordeal of His arrest, trial, and crucifixion, Jesus kept His Father's will in view. By embracing death on the cross, He set in motion a chain of events that truly transforms hearts. And in the process, our Strong Conqueror defeated death itself.

TIM GUSTAFSON

Real restraint is not weakness, for it arises out of genuine strength.

Failure Is Not Final

JOHN 18:15–27

"We have come to believe and to know that you are the Holy One of God."
JOHN 6:69

Prime Minister Winston Churchill knew how to bolster the spirits of the British people during World War II. On June 18, 1940, he told a frightened populace, "Hitler knows that he will have to break us . . . or lose the war. . . . Let us therefore brace . . . and so bear ourselves that, if the British Empire [lasts] for a thousand years, men will still say, 'This was their finest hour!'"

We would all like to be remembered for our "finest hour." Perhaps the apostle Peter's finest hour was when he proclaimed, "You are the Christ, the Son of the living God" (John 6:69 NKJV). Sometimes, however, we let our failures define us. After Peter repeatedly denied that he knew Jesus, he went out and wept bitterly (Matthew 26:75; John 18).

Like Peter, we all fall short—in our relationships, in our struggle with sin, in our faithfulness to God. But "failure is not fatal," as Churchill also said. Thankfully, this is true in our spiritual life. Jesus forgave the repentant Peter for his failure (John 21) and used him to preach and lead many to the Savior.

Failure is not fatal. God lovingly restores those who turn back to Him.

CINDY HESS KASPER

When God forgives, He removes the sin and restores the soul.

What Is Truth?

JOHN 18:28–38

"What is truth?" retorted Pilate. With this he went out again to the Jews
gathered there and said, "I find no basis for a charge against him."
JOHN 18:38

It was the closest Pilate would come to life's greatest discovery. Jesus had just told him that He had come into the world to bear witness to the truth. This prompted Pilate to ask, "What is truth?" (John 18:38). The shrewd Roman politician had asked the right question of the right Person, and his answer was standing before him. But instead of falling to his knees in repentance, confession, and faith, he could only pass off the answer by concluding, "I find no fault in Him" (18:38 NKJV).

Sooner or later, all of us find ourselves in Pilate's position, where we must decide about the unusual Man who claims what no other can claim—that He is the truth.

Throughout history many religious leaders have come and gone, but not one has claimed to be the truth and then proved it by rising from the dead. Millions of people down through the centuries have found Jesus's life, His words, and His resurrection to be convincing evidence of His credibility. And they have concluded that knowing the truth must begin with a personal relationship with Christ.

Have you found the answer to life's most important question: "What is truth?" If not, consider Jesus's statement in John 14:6, "I am the way and the truth and the life. No one comes to the Father except through me."

DENNIS DEHAAN

To know Christ is to know the truth.

Crowns of Honor

JOHN 19:1–8

The soldiers twisted together a crown of thorns and put it on his head.
They clothed him in a purple robe.

JOHN 19:2

The Crown Jewels of the United Kingdom are stored securely and protected within the Tower of London under twenty-four-hour guard. Each year, millions visit the display area to "ooh and aah" over these ornate treasures. The Crown Jewels symbolize the power of the kingdom as well as the prestige and position of those who use them.

Part of the Crown Jewels are the crowns themselves. There are three different types: the coronation crown, which is worn when an individual is crowned monarch; the state crown (or coronet), which is worn for various functions; and the consort crown worn by the wife of a reigning king. Different crowns serve different purposes.

The King of heaven, who was worthy of the greatest crown and the highest honor, wore a very different crown. In the hours of humiliation and suffering that Christ experienced before He was crucified, "the soldiers twisted together a crown of thorns and put it on his head. They clothed him a purple robe" (John 19:2). That day, the crown, which is normally a symbol of royalty and honor, was turned into a tool of mockery and hate. Yet our Savior willingly wore that crown for us, bearing our sin and shame.

The One who deserved the best of all crowns took the worst for us.

BILL CROWDER

Without the cross, there could be no crown.

Jesus's Love for All

JOHN 19:17–24

Carrying his own cross, he went out to the place of the Skull (which in Aramaic is called Golgotha). There they crucified him, and with him two others—one on each side and Jesus in the middle.

JOHN 19:17–18

It was a bit unusual, but three times in one day I heard the same song. In the early afternoon, I attended a hymnsing at a home for the elderly. As part of her prayer at the end of our time together, Willie, one of the residents, said, "Sing with me, 'Jesus Loves Me.'" In the evening, I attended a gathering with young people who sang it while pounding out the beat with their hands and feet. Later that evening, I received a text message on my phone with an audio recording of my two-year-old grandniece with a sweet little voice, singing, "I am weak, but He is strong." People in their nineties, teenagers, and a toddler all sang that song that day.

After hearing that simple song three times, I began to think the Lord might be telling me something. Actually, He gave all of us this message long ago: "I love you." We read in John 19 that He allowed people to put a crown of thorns on His head, mock Him, strike Him, strip Him, and crucify Him (vv.1–6). He had the power to stop them, but He said very little (v. 11). He did it all for love's sake to pay for our sins and to rescue us from punishment.

How much does God love us? Jesus spread out His arms and was nailed to the cross. He died for us then rose again. That's a precious fact for young and old.

ANNE CETAS

The truest measure of God's love is that He loves without measure!
—Bernard of Clairvaux

The Cross and the Crown

JOHN 19:21–30

*Jesus said to [Martha], "I am the resurrection and the life.
He who believes in Me, though he may die, he shall live."*
JOHN 11:25 (NKJV)

Westminster Abbey in London has a rich historical background. In the tenth century, Benedictine monks began a tradition of daily worship there that still continues today. The Abbey is also the burial place of many famous people, and every English monarch since AD 1066 has been crowned at the Abbey. In fact, seventeen of those monarchs are also buried there—their rule ending where it began.

No matter how grandiose their burial, their end is the same: world rulers rise and fall; they live and die. But another king, Jesus, though once dead, is no longer buried. In His first coming, Jesus was crowned with thorns and crucified as the "king of the Jews" (John 19:3, 19). Because Jesus rose from the dead in victory, we who are believers in Christ have hope beyond the grave and the assurance that we will live with Him forever. Jesus said, "I am the resurrection and the life. The one who believes in me will live, even though they die; and whoever lives by believing in me will never die" (11:25–26).

We serve a risen King! May we gladly yield to His rule in our lives now as we look forward to the day when the "Lord God Almighty" will reign for all eternity (Revelation 19:6).

BILL CROWDER

Jesus's resurrection spelled the death of death.

Take the High Road

JOHN 19:38–42

Act with courage, and may the LORD be with those who do well.
2 CHRONICLES 19:11

When he was a teenager, a driver tried to pass another vehicle on a hill, causing an oncoming car to careen into the ditch. He saw the cloud of dust in his rearview mirror and knew he should stop. But he let his fear overcome his conscience. Fifty years later, it still bothers him: "I should have returned to face the music, but I didn't." The internal struggle that accompanies his memory of this event still haunts him at age sixty-five. How he wishes he had obeyed his higher instincts!

Joseph of Arimathea and Nicodemus, secret disciples of Jesus, must have also experienced inner conflict as they watched Jesus dying on the cross. They loved Him, and they knew they should give Him a decent burial. They also realized that asking for the body could get them into trouble. But they obeyed the impulse to do what was right. They lovingly cared for the body of Jesus and placed it in Joseph's tomb. While both of these men fade out of the biblical record after this, they are revered for making the right choice.

It takes courage to do the right thing, but taking the "high road" leads to peace and fulfillment.

HERB VANDER LUGT

**When a conviction strikes deep enough,
courage will rise to sustain it.**

Dead or Alive

JOHN 20:1–8

When they entered, they did not find the body of the Lord.
LUKE 24:3

Long lines of visitors from all over the world wait patiently day after day to visit the tomb of former Russian leader Vladimir Lenin in Moscow and view his embalmed body. Although he died in 1924, the corpse of that Communist leader has seemingly suffered no decomposition. It looks deceptively lifelike. And its appearance is indeed deceptive. Skillful artists monitor the preserved corpse, artificially coloring its face and using wax to fill in any lines or the smallest spot of decay.

People also regularly visit Jerusalem to see the place where Jesus died and was buried. But there's a striking contrast—there is no body of the crucified Christ anywhere. Oh, there is one rock-hewn tomb, where according to tradition the nail-scarred, spear-driven, thorn-crowned corpse of Christ was laid. But resurrected by the power of God His Father, the Savior left His graveclothes behind when He emerged from the tomb, like a butterfly abandoning its cocoon.

Jesus is alive and you can know His presence today. Because of His atoning death and the empty tomb, you can have eternal life (1 Corinthians 15:20–22). You need only to admit that you are a sinner and seek His salvation. He'll give you new life now, and one day you'll see Him and be with Him forever (1 Peter 1:3–5).

VERNON GROUNDS

Christ's empty tomb guarantees our full salvation.

Known in Heaven

JOHN 20:11–18

"My sheep hear My voice, and I know them, and they follow Me."
JOHN 10:27 (NKJV)

Mary stood by the entrance to the empty tomb and wept in misery that her Lord had died. She longed for "the touch of the vanished hand," as Tennyson lyrically described death's cold finality, "the sound of the voice that was still."

Then Jesus appeared. In her grief, Mary's eyes deceived her, for she thought He was the gardener. But when He called her name, she knew Him immediately. She cried, "Rabboni!" which means *Teacher* (John 20:16).

People ask me if we'll know one another in heaven. I believe that we will know and be known there. When Jesus received His glorified body, His followers recognized Him (John 20:19–20). And someday we too will have a glorified body (1 Corinthians 15:42–49; 1 John 3:2).

"Rejoice," said Jesus to His disciples, "that your names are written in heaven" (Luke 10:20). Someday we'll hear again the voices of loved ones whose names are written in heaven—voices now still. We will hear the father who spoke our name with rough affection, the mother who called us in from play.

There's one voice, however, that I long to hear above all others—my Lord Jesus, calling my name: "David." And, like Mary, I will know Him at once. My Savior!

DAVID ROPER

Goodbyes are the law of earth—reunions are the law of heaven.

The Limits of Sight

JOHN 20:19–31

Then Jesus told him, "Because you have seen me, you have believed;
blessed are those who have not seen and yet believed."

JOHN 20:29

"Seeing is believing," according to the old saying. But if we believe only what we can see, we will never know God or experience His presence.

I traveled to England during the height of an outbreak of foot-and-mouth disease epidemic in 2001. Before I left for the UK, I had read newspaper stories of the tragic effects on farmers. I had watched television reports of slaughtered animals being burned and buried to try to stop the spread of the disease. But as I traveled by train from London to Devon, I saw many flocks of healthy sheep and herds of cattle in the fields. Nowhere did I see a sign warning of foot-and-mouth disease. Should I believe my eyes or the reports of reliable sources?

After Jesus was raised from the dead, Thomas refused to believe the reports that He was alive. He said that unless he touched the nail marks in Jesus's hands and the wound in His side, he would not believe (John 20:24–25). When the Lord appeared to the disciples eight days later, Jesus said to Thomas, "Because you have seen me, you have believed; blessed are those who have not seen and yet have believed" (v. 29).

Even though we have not seen Jesus, we accept by faith the word of reliable witnesses, we embrace the living Lord, and we believe.

DAVID MCCASLAND

Faith sees what the eyes cannot.

Fresh Faith

JOHN 20:24–29

*Let us hold unswervingly to the hope we profess,
for he who promised is faithful.*

HEBREWS 10:23

When our son was struggling with heroin addiction, if you had told me God would one day use our experience to encourage other families who face these kinds of battles, I would have had trouble believing it. God has a way of bringing good out of difficult circumstances that isn't always easy to see when you are going through them.

The apostle Thomas also didn't expect God to bring good out of the greatest challenge of his faith—Jesus's crucifixion. Thomas wasn't with the other disciples when Jesus came to them after the resurrection, and in his deep grief he insisted, "Unless I see the nail marks in his hands and put my finger where the nails were . . . I will not believe" (John 20:25). But later, when Jesus appeared to all the disciples together, out of the dust of Thomas's doubts God's Spirit would inspire a striking statement of faith. When Thomas exclaimed, "My Lord and my God!" (v. 28), he was grasping the truth that Jesus was actually God in the flesh, standing right in front of him. It was a bold confession of faith that would encourage and inspire believers in every century that followed.

Our God is able to inspire fresh faith in our hearts, even in moments when we least expect it. We can always look forward to His faithfulness. Nothing is too hard for Him!

JAMES BANKS

God can change our doubts into bold statements of faith.

I Spy!

JOHN 21:1–7

Then the disciple whom Jesus loved said to Peter, "It is the Lord!"
As soon as Simon Peter heard him say, "It is the Lord," he wrapped his outer
garment around him (for he had taken it off) and jumped into the water.
JOHN 21:7

My wife and I have some friends who used to play a game with their children called "I Spy." If a family member saw what appeared to be God at work in their surroundings, he or she would call out, "I spy!" It might be a beautiful sunset or some special blessing. These experiences reminded them of God's presence in the world and in their lives.

That game reminds me of Jesus's disciples and their futile fishing endeavor recorded in John 21:1–7. Early in the morning they saw through the mist a man standing on the shore, but they didn't know it was Jesus. "Friends, haven't you any fish?" He asked. "No," they replied. "Cast the net on the right side of the boat," He said, "and you will find some." The disciples obeyed and their net was filled with so many fish they couldn't draw it in. "It is the Lord!" exclaimed John. It was an "I spy" moment, and it was John, "the disciple whom Jesus loved," who was the first to recognize Him.

Ask God to give you eyes to "see" Jesus, whether in the extraordinary events or the everyday affairs of your life. If you pay attention, you will see His hand at work where others see nothing. Try playing "I spy" today and let the Lord's presence reassure you of His love and care.

DAVID ROPER

Eyes of faith can see God at work.

Failures Anonymous

JOHN 21:3–17

*When they landed, they saw a fire of burning coals
there with fish on it, and some bread.*
JOHN 21:9

It's my duty to grill the burgers, brats, steaks, or whatever else my wife has on the menu. And while I'm not the greatest chef when it comes to outdoor cooking, I love the unforgettable aroma of grilling over a charcoal fire. So the mention of a "fire of coals" in John 21:9 catches my attention. And I find myself wondering why John would include this detail in the story about Jesus calling a failing Peter back to serve and follow Him.

In verses 1–3, it's apparent that Peter had reopened his fishing business. Just a few days before, Peter was warming his hands over a charcoal fire when he denied Jesus to save his own skin (John 18:17–18 ESV). So why not go back to fishing?

While Peter and his cohorts were casting nets, Jesus built a fire on the beach. Coincidence? I doubt it! And as Peter approached Jesus, I wonder if the pungent aroma of the burning charcoal brought back memories of that other fire where he had failed Christ. Yet Jesus in His mercy took the initiative to call Peter back into His service.

Think of it! Jesus is willing to forgive our failures and call us into His service.

JOE STOWELL

If only perfect people qualified to serve Him,
He wouldn't have anyone to choose from!

What Is That to You?

JOHN 21:15–22

Jesus answered, "If I want him to remain alive until I return, what is that to you? You must follow me."
JOHN 21:22

Social media is useful for many things, but contentment is not one of them. At least not for me. Even when my goals are good, I can become discouraged by continual reminders that others are accomplishing them with greater results. Prone to this kind of discouragement, I frequently remind myself that God has not short-changed me. He has given me everything I need to accomplish the work He wants me to do.

This means I don't need a better work environment or a different job. I don't need good health or more time. God may give me some of those things, but everything I need I already have, for when He assigns work He provides the resources. My assignment is to use the time and talents He has given in a way that blesses others and gives God the glory.

Jesus and Peter had a conversation that got around to this subject. After making breakfast on the shore of Galilee, Jesus told Peter what would happen at the end of his life. Pointing at another disciple, Peter asked, "What about him?" Jesus responded, "What is that to you?"

Like Peter, my business is to follow Jesus and be faithful with the gifts and opportunities He gives to me.

JULIE ACKERMAN LINK

Resentment comes from looking at others;
contentment comes from looking at God.

OUR DAILY BREAD WRITERS

JAMES BANKS
Pastor of Peace Church in Durham, North Carolina, Dr. James Banks has written several books for Discovery House, including *Praying Together* and *Prayers for Prodigals*. He and his wife, Cari, have two adult children.

MONICA BRANDS
Monica is from Edgerton, Minnesota, where she grew up on a farm with seven siblings. She has a master of theological studies degree from Calvin Seminary in Grand Rapids. She treasures time with friends, family, and her awesome nieces and nephews.

DAVE BRANON
An editor with Discovery House, Dave has been involved with *Our Daily Bread* since the 1980s. He has written several books, including *Beyond the Valley* and *Stand Firm*, both DH publications.

ANNE CETAS
After becoming a Christian in her late teens, Anne was introduced to *Our Daily Bread* right away and began reading it. Now she reads it for a living as senior content editor of *Our Daily Bread*.

POH FANG CHIA
Like Anne Cetas, Poh Fang trusted Jesus Christ as Savior as a teenager. She is an editor and a part of the Chinese editorial review committee serving in the Our Daily Bread Ministries Singapore office.

BILL CROWDER
A former pastor who is now vice president of ministry content for Our Daily Bread Ministries, Bill travels extensively as a Bible conference teacher, sharing God's truths with fellow believers in Malaysia and Singapore and other places where ODB Ministries has international offices. His published books include *Windows on Easter* and *Let's Talk*.

LAWRENCE DARMANI

A noted novelist and publisher in Ghana, Lawrence is editor of *Step* magazine and CEO of Step Publishers. He and his family live in Accra, Ghana. His book *Grief Child* earned him the Commonwealth Writers' Prize as best first book by a writer in Africa.

DENNIS DEHAAN (1932–2014)

When *Our Daily Bread's* original editor Henry Bosch retired, Dennis became the second managing editor of the publication. A former pastor, he loved preaching and teaching the Word of God. Dennis went to be with the Lord in 2014.

MART DEHAAN

The former president of Our Daily Bread Ministries, Mart followed in the footsteps of his grandfather M. R. and his dad Richard in that capacity. Mart, who was associated with *Day of Discovery* as host of the program from Israel for many years, is now senior content advisor for Our Daily Bread Ministries. He can be heard daily on the radio program *Discover the Word*.

M. R. DEHAAN (1891–1965)

Dr. M. R. DeHaan founded this ministry in 1938 when his radio program went out over the air in Detroit, Michigan, and eventually Radio Bible Class was begun. He was president of the ministry in 1956 when *Our Daily Bread* was first published.

RICHARD DEHAAN (1923–2002)

Son of the founder of Our Daily Bread Ministries, Dr. M. R. DeHaan, Richard was responsible for the ministry's entrance into television. Under his leadership, *Day of Discovery* television made its debut in 1968. The program was on the air continuously until 2016.

XOCHITL DIXON

Xochitl (soh-cheel) equips and encourages readers to embrace God's grace and grow deeper in their personal relationships with Christ and others. Serving as an author, speaker, and blogger at xedixon.com, she enjoys singing, reading, motherhood, and being married to her best friend Dr. W. Alan Dixon Sr.

DAVID EGNER

A retired Our Daily Bread Ministries editor and longtime *Our Daily Bread* writer, David was also a college professor during his working career. In fact, he was a writing instructor for both Anne Cetas and Julie Ackerman Link at Cornerstone University.

DENNIS FISHER

For many years, Dennis was senior research editor at Our Daily Bread Ministries—using his theological training to guarantee biblical accuracy. He is also an expert in C. S. Lewis studies. He and his wife, Janet, a former university professor, have retired to Northern California.

VERNON GROUNDS (1914–2010)

A longtime college president (Denver Seminary) and board member for Our Daily Bread Ministries, Vernon's life story was told in the Discovery House book *Transformed by Love.* Dr. Grounds died in 2010 at the age of 96.

TIM GUSTAFSON

Tim writes for *Our Daily Bread* and *Our Daily Journey* and serves as an editor for Discovery Series. As the son of missionaries to Ghana, Tim has an unusual perspective on life in the West. He and his wife, Leisa, have one daughter and seven sons.

C. P. HIA

Hia Chek Phang and his wife, Lin Choo, reside in the island nation of Singapore. C. P. came to faith in Jesus Christ at the age of thirteen. During his early years as a believer, he was privileged to learn from excellent Bible teachers who instilled in him a love for God's Word. He is special assistant to the president of Our Daily Bread Ministries, and he helps with translating resources for the ministry. He and his wife have a son, daughter-in-law, grandson, and granddaughter.

KIRSTEN HOLMBERG

Kirsten Holmberg surrendered her life to Jesus at age 22. Kirsten married Mike in 1995 in Boulder, Colorado. Together, they're raising their three children near Boise, Idaho. Her first *Our Daily Bread* articles appeared in early 2017. When she has the time, she enjoys reading, running, and photography.

CINDY HESS KASPER

An editor for the Our Daily Bread Ministries publication *Our Daily Journey*, Cindy began writing for *Our Daily Bread* in 2006. She and her husband, Tom, have three children and seven grandchildren.

ALYSON KIEDA

Alyson has been an editor for Our Daily Bread Ministries for over a decade—and has over thirty-five years of editing experience. Alyson has loved writing since she was a child and is thrilled to be writing for *Our Daily Bread*. She is married with three adult children and a growing number of grandchildren.

RANDY KILGORE

Randy spent most of his 20-plus years in business as a senior human resource manager before returning to seminary. Since finishing his master of divinity in 2000, he has served as a writer and workplace chaplain. A collection of those devotionals appears in the Discovery House book *Made to Matter: Devotions for Working Christians*. Randy and his wife, Cheryl, and their two children live in Massachusetts.

LESLIE KOH

Born and raised in Singapore, Leslie spent more than fifteen years as a journalist in the busy newsroom of local newspaper *The Straits Times* before joining Our Daily Bread Ministries. He's found moving from bad news to good news most rewarding, and he still believes that nothing reaches out to people better than a good, compelling story. He likes traveling, running, editing, and writing.

ALBERT LEE

Albert Lee was director of international ministries for Our Daily Bread Ministries for many years, and he lives in Singapore. Albert's passion, vision, and energy expanded the work of the ministry around the world. Albert grew up in Singapore and took a variety of courses from Singapore Bible College. He also served with Singapore Youth for Christ from 1971 to 1999. Albert appreciates art and collects paintings. He and his wife, Catherine, have two children.

JULIE ACKERMAN LINK (1950–2015)

A book editor by profession, Julie began writing for *Our Daily Bread* in 2000. Her books *Above All, Love, 100 Prayers Inspired by the Psalms*, and

Hope for All Seasons are available through Discovery House. Julie lost her long battle with cancer in April 2015.

DAVID MCCASLAND
Living in Colorado, David enjoys the beauty of God's grandeur as displayed in the Rocky Mountains. An accomplished biographer, David has written several books, including the award-winning *Oswald Chambers: Abandoned to God* and *Eric Liddell: Pure Gold.*

KEILA OCHOA
Keila, who teaches in an international school, also assists with Media Associates International, a group that trains writers around the world to write about faith. She and her husband have two young children.

AMY PETERSON
Amy Peterson has a B.A. in English literature from Texas A&M and an M.A. in intercultural studies from Wheaton College. Amy taught ESL for two years in Southeast Asia before returning stateside to teach. She is the author of *Dangerous Territory: My Misguided Quest to Save the World.*

AMY BOUCHER PYE
Amy is a writer, editor, and speaker. The author of *Finding Myself in Britain: Our Search for Faith, Home, and True Identity*, she runs the Woman Alive book club in the UK and enjoys life with her family in their English vicarage.

HADDON ROBINSON (1931–2017)
Haddon, a renowned expert on preaching, served many years as a seminary professor. He wrote numerous books and hundreds of magazine articles. For a number of years he was a panelist on Our Daily Bread Ministries' radio program *Discover the Word.* Dr. Robinson went home to his eternal reward on July 22, 2017.

DAVID ROPER
David Roper lives in Idaho, where he takes advantage of the natural beauty of his state. He has been writing for *Our Daily Bread* since 2000, and he has published several books with Discovery House, including *Out of the Ordinary* and *Teach Us to Number Our Days.*

JENNIFER BENSON SCHULDT

Chicagoan Jennifer Schuldt writes from the perspective of a mom of a growing family. She has written for *Our Daily Bread* since 2010, and she also pens articles for another Our Daily Bread Ministries publication, *Our Daily Journey*.

JOE STOWELL

As president of Cornerstone University, Joe stays connected to today's young adults in a leadership role. A popular speaker and a former pastor, Joe has written a number of books over the years, including *Strength for the Journey* and *Jesus Nation*.

MARION STROUD (1940–2015)

After a battle with cancer, Marion went to be with her Savior in August 2015. Marion began writing devotional articles for *Our Daily Bread* in 2014. Two of her popular books of prayers, *Dear God, It's Me and It's Urgent* and *It's Just You and Me, Lord* were published by Discovery House.

HERB VANDER LUGT (1920–2006)

For many years, Herb was senior research editor at Our Daily Bread Ministries, responsible for checking the biblical accuracy of the literature published by ODB Ministries. A World War II veteran, Herb spent several years as a pastor before his ODB tenure began. Herb went to be with his Lord and Savior in 2006.

PAUL VAN GORDER (1921–2009)

A writer for *Our Daily Bread* in the 1980s and 1990s, Paul was a noted pastor and Bible teacher—both in the Atlanta area where he lived and through the *Day of Discovery* TV program. Paul's earthly journey ended in 2009.

SHERIDAN VOYSEY

Sheridan Voysey is a writer, speaker, and broadcaster based in Oxford, England. Sheridan has authored several books, including *Resurrection Year: Turning Broken Dreams into New Beginnings* and *Resilient: Your Invitation to a Jesus-Shaped Life*. For many years Sheridan was the host of *Open House*, a live talk show heard in Australia every Sunday night, exploring life, faith, and culture.

JOANIE YODER (1934–2004)

For ten years, until her death in 2004, Joanie wrote for *Our Daily Bread*. In addition, she published the book *God Alone* with Discovery House.

MARVIN WILLIAMS

Marvin's first foray into Our Daily Bread Ministries came as a writer for *Our Daily Journey*. In 2007, he penned his first *Our Daily Bread* article. Marvin is senior teaching pastor at a church in Lansing, Michigan.

Note to the Reader

The publisher invites you to share your response to the message of this book by writing Discovery House, PO Box 3566, Grand Rapids, MI 49501, USA. For information about other Discovery House books, music, or DVDs, contact us at the same address or call 1-800-653-8333. Find us online at dhp.org or send email to books@dhp.org.

Enjoy this book? Help us get the word out!

Share a link to the book or
mention it on social media

Write a review on your blog, on a retailer site,
or on our website (dhp.org)

Pick up another copy to share with someone

Recommend this book for your
church, book club, or small group

Follow Discovery House on
social media and join the discussion

Contact us to share your thoughts:

 @discoveryhouse    @DiscoveryHouse

Discovery House
P.O. Box 3566
Grand Rapids, MI 49501 USA

Phone: 1-800-653-8333
Email: books@dhp.org
Web: dhp.org